KW-050-977

International Socialism 125

Winter 2010

Analysis: Shifting sands of the crisis   3

Snapshots of struggle
Ireland: From shock therapy to resistance   *Kieran Allen*   15
France: From economic to political struggles   *Denis Godard*   19
Opposition and opportunity in Germany   *Stefan Bornost*   22
Greece: The eye of the storm?   *Panos Garganas*   25
Sketches of Spain   *Mike Eaude*   29

Obama's first year   *Megan Trudell*   33

Honduras is not just another banana republic   *Mike Gonzalez*   43

Chris Harman 1942–2009
A life in the struggle   *Ian Birchall*   55
Althusser: the emperor has no clothes   *Chris Harman*   71
Another side of Chris Harman   *Joseph Choonara*   85
Not all Marxism is dogmatism   *Chris Harman*   95
Zombie Capitalism and the origin of crises   *Guglielmo Carchedi*   113
A whiff of tear gas   *Andy Durgan*   127

Marxism and anarchism   *Paul Blackledge*   131

The sex work debate   *Jane Pritchard*   161

Jewish intellectuals and Palestinian liberation   *John Rose*   183

Struggle, continuity and contradiction in Bolivia   *Jeffery R Webber*   193

Reviews   205
Film noir, matchwomen, red Barcelona, Communist authors in India,
Ecological revolution, revolt today, sex between men, historical time, class in China
Mike Wayne, Andrew Stone, Andy Durgan, Barry Pavier, Martin Empson,
Jonathan Maunder, Colin Wilson, Mark Bergfeld, Charlie Hore

Pick of the quarter   .   223

Contributors

Kieran Allen is the author of *The Celtic Tiger?: The Myth of Social Partnership in Ireland*.

Mark Bergfeld is a postgraduate student at the University of Essex.

Ian Birchall is working on a biography of Tony Cliff which is due to appear this year.

Paul Blackledge is the author of *Reflections on the Marxist Theory of History*.

Stefan Bornost is the editor of *marx21*.

Guglielmo Carchedi is the author of the forthcoming work *Behind the Crisis*.

Joseph Choonara is the author of *Unravelling Capitalism: A Guide to Marxist Political Economy*.

Andy Durgan is the author of *The Spanish Civil War*.

Mike Eaude is the author of *Barcelona: The City that Reinvented Itself*.

Martin Empson is the author of the new pamphlet *Marxism and Ecology*.

Panos Garganas is the editor of the Greek newspaper *Workers Solidarity*.

Denis Godard is a member of the National Political Council of France's New Anticapitalist Party.

Mike Gonzalez is the author of *Che Guevara and the Cuban Revolution*.

Charlie Hore has written several articles for *International Socialism* on China.

Jonathan Maunder works at Bookmarks, the socialist bookshop, in London.

Barry Pavier teaches history and politics at Bradford College.

Jane Pritchard is a longstanding member of the Socialist Workers Party.

John Rose is the author of *Myths of Zionism*.

Andrew Stone is a history teacher and NUT rep in east London.

Megan Trudell is currently researching Italy in the wake of the First World War.

Mike Wayne is the co-director of the film *Listen to Venezuela*.

Jeffery R Webber is the author of the forthcoming books *Red October: Left-Indigenous Struggle in Modern Bolivia* and *Rebellion to Reform in Bolivia: Indigenous Liberation, Class Struggle and the Politics of Evo Morales*.

Colin Wilson is researching for a book on sexuality and imperialism.

Shifting sands of the crisis

Despite the euphoria that gripped the financial markets in the second half of 2009, the world economy continues to be hit by severe shocks. Another hit it in late November. The most surprising thing about the announcement that Dubai World had defaulted on $26 billion of its total $59 billion debt was that it had taken more than two years for the Gulf city state to become a casualty of the global economic and financial crisis. For if there was any single symbol of the overblown financial bubbles that have driven global capitalism for the past 15 years, it was Dubai.

In a brilliant portrait published just over three years ago, Mike Davis wrote:

> The coastal desert has become a huge circuit board upon which the elite of transnational engineering firms and retail developers are invited to plug in high-tech clusters, entertainment zones, artificial islands, glass-domed "snow mountains", Truman Show suburbs, cities within cities—whatever is big enough to be seen from space and bursting with architectural steroids... Although compared variously to Las Vegas, Manhattan, Orlando, Monaco and Singapore, the sheikhdom is more like their collective summation and mythologisation: a hallucinatory pastiche of the big, the bad and the ugly.[1]

Dubai's ascension during the credit boom of the mid-2000s

1: Davis, Mike, 2006, "Fear and Money in Dubai", *New Left Review 41*.

depended on the strategic positioning pursued by its autocratic ruler, Sheikh Mohammed al-Maktoum—and on the super-exploited labour of the emirate's predominantly South Asian migrant workforce. To quote Davis again:

> With a tiny hinterland lacking the geological wealth of Kuwait or Abu Dhabi, Dubai has escaped poverty by a Singaporean strategy of becoming the key commercial, financial and recreational hub of the Gulf. It is a postmodern "city of nets"—as Brecht called "Mahagonny"—where the super-profits of the international oil trade are intercepted and then reinvested in Arabia's one truly inexhaustible natural resource: sand.[2]

Symbolic of Dubai's ascension was the 2006 takeover by Dubai Port World—a subsidiary of the state-owned Dubai World—of P&O, once one of the greatest of British imperial companies (the takeover provoked a huge row in the US Congress over an Arab firm running six American ports). But—like the boom itself—the Dubai bubble floated on a vast pool of cheap credit. As the *Financial Times* put it, the sheikhdom became "something resembling a highly-leveraged private equity firm sinking money into fanciful real estate projects and questionably valued assets abroad".[3] It is this frenzied borrowing spree that has now brought Dubai World to its knees under a debt burden estimated at $100 billion and forced al-Maktoum to turn to his oil-rich neighbour and rival Abu Dhabi for help.

Contradictions of the bailouts

Abu Dhabi has twisted the knife in the wound by refusing to bail out Dubai World. But more important than the fate of the bloated sheikhdom is what its collapse signifies for the broader economic crisis. After the very sharp slump that hit the world economy in the winter of 2008-9, a degree of stability returned in the summer and autumn of last year. Driving this have been the massive state rescues of the banks and the government fiscal stimuli that have been pumped into national economies.

A recent Bank of England study estimates that "intervention to support the banks in the UK, US and the euro area during the current crisis...totals over $14 trillion or almost a quarter of global GDP. It dwarfs any previous state support of the banking system".[4] China has also played

---

2:    Davis, Mike, 2006, "Fear and Money in Dubai", *New Left Review* 41.

3:    *Financial Times*, 1 December 2009.

4:    From a Bank of England presentation by Piergiorgio Alessandri and Andrew Haldane, available online at www.bankofengland.co.uk/publications/speeches/2009/speech409.pdf

a major role in the state-directed efforts to stave off global depression. On government instructions, the Chinese banks have behaved very differently from their Western counterparts, lending a mammoth $1,080 billion in the first half of 2009.[5]

State intervention has thus brought the sharp contraction of output and international trade to a halt, for the time being at least. China's return to the high growth rates of the past few decades has also revived the economies that supply it with complex manufactures and raw materials (notably Japan, Germany, South Korea, Taiwan and Brazil). In the US and Britain, the most striking result of this stabilisation has been the renaissance enjoyed by those banks that survived the financial crash in the autumn of 2008. As the *New York Times* explains, the boosted profits—and hence bigger bonus pools—announced by the strongest American banks last autumn are a direct result of state support:

> Titans like Goldman Sachs and JPMorgan Chase are making fortunes in hot areas like trading stocks and bonds, rather than in the ho-hum business of lending people money. They also are profiting by taking risks that weaker rivals are unable or unwilling to shoulder—a benefit of less competition after the failure of some investment firms last year.
>
> So even as big banks fight efforts in Congress to subject their industry to greater regulation—and to impose some restrictions on executive pay—Wall Street has Washington to thank in part for its latest bonanza... the decline of certain institutions, along with the outright collapse of once-vigorous competitors like Lehman Brothers, has consolidated the nation's financial power in fewer hands. The strong are now able to wring more profits from the financial markets and charge higher fees for a wide range of banking services...
>
> A year after the crisis struck, many of the industry's behemoths—those institutions deemed too big to fail—are, in fact, getting bigger, not smaller. For many of them, it is business as usual. Over the last decade the financial sector was the fastest-growing part of the economy, with two-thirds of growth in gross domestic product attributable to incomes of workers in finance.
>
> Now, the industry has new tools at its disposal, courtesy of the government... With interest rates so low, banks can borrow money cheaply and put those funds to work in lucrative ways, whether using the money to make loans

---

5:    *Financial Times*, 10 August 2009.

to companies at higher rates, or to speculate in the markets. Fixed-income trading—an area that includes bonds and currencies—has been particularly profitable... To prevent a catastrophic financial collapse that would have sent shock waves through the economy, the government injected billions of dollars into banks. Some large institutions, like Goldman and Morgan, have since repaid their bailout money. But most of the industry still enjoys other forms of government support, which is helping to stoke profits.

Goldman Sachs and its perennial rival Morgan Stanley were allowed to transform themselves into old-fashioned bank holding companies. That switch gave them access to cheap funding from the Federal Reserve, which had been unavailable to them.

Those two banks and others like JPMorgan were also allowed to issue tens of billions of dollars of bonds that are guaranteed by the Federal Deposit Insurance Corporation, which insures bank deposits. With the FDIC standing behind them, the banks could borrow the money on highly advantageous terms. While some have since issued bonds on their own, they nonetheless enjoy the benefits of their cheap financing.[6]

No wonder that George Soros described the banks' profits as "gifts... from the government".[7] The problem of how to deal with financial institutions that, because they are deemed "too big to fail", are effectively being allowed to gamble with very cheap government money, confident in the knowledge that they will be rescued by the state if their bets go bad, has caused much agonising in ruling class circles. From the free-market right Niall Ferguson has denounced the rise of "State Monopoly Capitalism".[8]

The problem (often described by bourgeois economists as one of "moral hazard") illustrates one of the main themes of Chris Harman's political economy, which is explored elsewhere in this issue by Joseph Choonara and Guglielmo Carchedi. As capitalism ages, the size of individual units rises thanks to the growing concentration and centralisation of capital. This means that the impact of the bankruptcy of particular firms can be very severe. Thus the collapse of Lehman Brothers in September 2008 precipitated the worst global financial crash since October 1929 and helped to

---

6: *New York Times*, 17 October 2009.
7: *Financial Times*, 23 October 2009.
8: Niall Fergusson, 2009, *Too Big to Live* (Centre for Policy Studies), available from www.cps.org.uk

pitch the world economy into the sharp slump of last winter. But when, as they have, states step in to prevent such catastrophic bankruptcies, they let the overaccumulation of unprofitable capital continue, imposing a heavy burden on any economic recovery.[9]

In trying to negotiate this deep contradiction, the leading capitalist classes must confront a number of specific problems. The first is simply how broken the global financial system remains despite the bailouts. The Dubai default detonated an exploded bomb left behind by the wild borrowing that both firms and states undertook during the credit boom. But how many other unexploded bombs are there? "After Dubai, will Greece be next?" asked *Financial Times* columnist Wolfgang Munchau following Dubai World's default.[10]

According to Deutsche Bank, the Greek state has run up debt equivalent to 135 percent of national income. Financial markets reacted to the Dubai crisis by pushing up the interest rate on Greek government bonds and the price of Credit Default Swops (CDSs) insuring against Greece defaulting on its debt. Complicating matters is the fact that Greece is a member of the euro-zone. But neoliberals in Brussels and the main European capitals may decide to make an example of Greece, whose recently ousted Tory government had concealed the scale of the debt crisis. According to Daniel Gros of the Centre for European Policy Studies, "It is one thing if you are in the middle of a systemic crisis. Then you can't allow anyone to fail and don't worry about moral hazard. Now we are out of the woods and it may be a good time to reduce moral hazard".[11]

This kind of reasoning begs the question of whether or not the world economy really is "out of the woods". Letting Greece go bust is a dangerous game. It might further undermine confidence in the European Union, whose response to the crisis has been shambolic. Other member states that enthusiastically helped blow up the housing bubble—from Britain and southern Ireland to Hungary and Latvia—are also struggling with huge debt burdens. Gillian Tett, the *Financial Times* journalist who was one of the first to blow the whistle on the dangerous levels of debt (or leverage) the banks were building up through credit derivatives during the bubble years, argues:

The events in Dubai—and the Greek CDS price...[are] a welcome wake-up call. In recent months, a sense of stabilisation has returned to the financial

9:   Alongside Chris's work, see Alex Callinicos's *Bonfire of Illusions*, forthcoming from Polity.
10: *Financial Times*, 29 November 2009.
11: Quoted in *Financial Times*, 2 December 2009.

system as a whole, as central banks have poured in vast quantities of support. A striking liquidity-fuelled asset price rally has also got under way.

But the grim truth is that many of the fundamental imbalances that created the crisis in the first place—such as excess leverage—have not yet disappeared. Beneath any aura of stability huge potential vulnerabilities remain.[12]

Secondly, as Tett points out, the state rescue of the banking system has been followed by marked rises in the price of shares and corporate bonds, especially in the big "emergent market" economies of the Global South. For apologists and boosters, who have now recovered their nerve after the terrible fright they suffered during the crash in autumn 2008, this is a sign of the intrinsic strength of global capitalism and especially of the much-feted BRICs (Brazil, Russia, India and China).

But Nouriel Roubini, another of the handful of establishment commentators who warned against the dangers of the last financial bubble, argues that a new one is emerging, fuelled by "the mother of all carry trades". A carry trade is when someone borrows in one currency, where interest rates are low, to invest in another, where interest rates are higher, thereby making a profit. In this case, the US Federal Reserve Board's policy of flooding the financial system with ultra-cheap money and letting the dollar fall against other currencies to cheapen American exports is encouraging investors to borrow in dollars to buy shares and bonds, particularly in those Asian and Latin American economies where the recovery is strongest. The resulting bubble, Roubini argues, is creating the conditions for the next crash:

This unravelling may not occur for a while, as easy money and excessive global liquidity can push asset prices higher for a while. But the longer and bigger the carry trades and the larger the asset bubble, the bigger will be the ensuing asset bubble crash. The Fed and other policymakers seem unaware of the monster bubble they are creating. The longer they remain blind, the harder the markets will fall.[13]

The response by an ex-governor of the Fed, Frederic Mishkin, that

---

12: *Financial Times*, 27 November 2009. Another unexploded bomb is commercial property, where borrowers have effectively defaulted on much of their debt—$3,000 billion property debt is outstanding the in US and Europe—but are being kept afloat by the banks in the hope of better times—*Financial Times*, 6 December 2009 .

13: *Financial Times*, 1 November 2009.

the new bubble was a benign one was greeted with widespread derision.[14] Washington's easy money policy is also a source of tension with China, whose status as America's most important economic partner and rival has been confirmed by the crisis. The conflict is partly because the Chinese state continues to use many of the dollars earned by its exports of manufactured goods to buy US Treasury bonds, thereby lending Washington the money it needs to continue spending.

But the decline of the dollar that is being tacitly encouraged by both the Fed and Barrack Obama's administration to boost American competitiveness reduces the value of Chinese investments in the US. When Tim Geithner, Obama's Treasury Secretary, told an audience of students at Beijing University that these investments were safe, they roared with laughter. But the Chinese government's policy of pegging its currency, the renminbi, against the dollar is also a source of tension. Western manufacturing firms complain that this policy keeps China's exports artificially cheap. But when both Obama and an EU delegation pleaded for a revaluation of the renminbi on recent visits to Beijing, they were given the brush-off by President Hu Jintao.

China's economic trajectory is another area of uncertainty. It has become a platitude among global elites that the world economy must be "rebalanced", crucially by the US saving more and consuming less and by China consuming more and exporting less. But the nexus that binds the two economies together, with China supplying both the cheap exports and the capital that the US requires for its current accumulation path, fits the interests of both ruling classes, despite the tensions outlined above.

The giant state rescue of the Chinese economy has concentrated on building up yet more productive capacity in export industries. According to Hung Ho-fung:

> Nearly 90 percent of GDP growth in the first seven months of 2009 was driven solely by fixed-asset investments fuelled by a loan explosion and increased government spending. Many of these investments are inefficient and generally unprofitable... If the turnaround of the export market does not come in time, the fiscal deficit, non-performing loans and the exacerbation of overcapacity will generate a deeper downturn in the medium term. In the words of a prominent Chinese economist, this mega-stimulus programme is like "drinking poison to quench a thirst".[15]

14: *Financial Times*, 10 November 2009. See the letters page in subsequent days.
15: Hung Ho-fung, 2009, "America's Head Servant?", *New Left Review* 60, p23. Despite the silly title, this is a useful analysis of some main features of China's political economy.

Against this background, it's hardly surprised that policy-makers are divided over how to deal with yet another problem, namely when to end the government stimuli that, in the form of extra spending, have been holding up the world economy. All are agreed that the state interventions are temporary measures that must, sooner or later, be ended to allow a return to neoliberal normality. But when? If the stimulus is withdrawn too soon, this might push the world back into slump, producing a "double-dip" recession. But if state support remains in place for too long, then the new asset bubble may become unmanageable and another bout of higher inflation may be ignited.

Representing one horn of this dilemma, International Monetary Fund Managing Director Dominique Strauss-Kahn said last November, "It is too early for a general exit. We recommend erring on the side of caution, as exiting too early is costlier than exiting too late." He was countered by Jean-Claude Trichet, President of the European Central Bank, embodying the other horn: "There is an increasingly pressing need for ambitious and realistic fiscal exit strategies and for fiscal consolidation".[16] In early December Trichet announced that the ECB would soon start withdrawing the emergency measures providing extra liquidity to banks.

Accordingly, what Chris Harman wrote in our previous issue still stands:

> There are two conclusions to draw from all this. First, the crisis, in the sense of the global economy being in a mess, is far from over. Second, the attempts by governments to find an "exit strategy" will lead to continued tensions within and between states and to a concomitant weakening of the ideological messages that capital as a whole would like to convey.[17]

Obama's war

Everyone agrees that one of the major questions posed by the crisis is its impact on the position of the US as the dominant capitalist power. Many have concluded, much too quickly, that the era of American hegemony is over. Obama's administration has been marked, as Megan Trudell shows in her article in this issue, by extreme caution, not to say conservatism, disappointing his supporters and giving the initiative to the Republican right. But Obama's aim externally is not to abandon US primacy, but to maintain

---

16: *Financial Times*, 23 November 2009.

17: Chris Harman, "Wishful Thinking", *International Socialism* 124 (autumn 2009), www.isj.org.uk/ ?id=576

it, in particular by distancing himself from George Bush's unilateralism. His strategy is well explained by Zaki Laïdi:

> The US does understand that it can no longer dominate the world as it pleases, and that the gap that separates it from the rest has shrunk. As a result, the US needs the rest of the world to maintain its pre-eminence, not to dissolve it. The objective is to select privileged partners for international action, to better maintain leadership in all domains.[18]

One of the biggest problems that Obama faces in pursuing this objective lies in the wars in southern and western Asia he inherited from his predecessor. While seeking withdrawal from one, in Iraq, he is escalating the other, in Afghanistan. His announcement on 1 December that he is sending another 30,000 troops to Afghanistan will bring the total US force in Afghanistan to over 100,000, more than double the number when he took the oath of office at the start of 2009. The *Washington Post* website now headlines its coverage of Afghanistan "Obama's War".

Obama hasn't just caved in to the public campaign mounted by General Stanley McChrystal, American commander of the Nato forces in Afghanistan, for 40,000 extra troops. The prolonged debate within the administration over Afghan strategy produced a compromise reflecting pressure from opponents to a military surge, such as Vice-President Joe Biden, as well as Obama's own demands for a rapid build-up.[19] The reinforcements are to be sent in mostly in the next six months, more quickly than McChrystal had planned, and a deadline has been set for July 2011, when US troops will begin to be withdrawn. Moreover, the objective, reaffirmed as recently as March, of defeating the Taliban has been dropped in favour of the more modest goals of containing and splitting them and achieving a degree of political stability. These changes reflect both worries about the unpopularity of the war (especially in Obama's own Democratic Party and among its supporters) and the desire not to give a blank cheque to the corrupt and ineffectual regime of Hamid Karzai (elements of which General David Petraeus, Chief of US Central Command, compared to "a crime syndicate").[20]

The shortfall between the US reinforcements and McChrystal's request for 40,000 extra troops is supposed to be made up by Nato and other American allies. But, as Edward Luce pointed out in the *Financial Times*:

18: *Financial Times*, 3 December 2009.
19: *Washington Post*, 3 December 2009.
20: *Washington Post*, 6 December 2009; *New York Times*, 5 December 2009.

Nato foreign ministers have cobbled together another 5,000 troops to add to the 37,000 already in place... Mr Obama's new troops will be standing shoulder-to-shoulder with their comrades from Finland (165), Bosnia and Herzegovina (460) and Iceland (2). All told the coalition amounts to 43 countries, of which only two, the US and the UK, have more than 5,000. And even the UK, where the war is even more unpopular than it is in the US, could only muster another 500 troops to supplement Mr Obama's undeclared "surge".

Mr Obama's troop escalation will thus catapult the US into an overwhelmingly dominant presence in Afghanistan with almost three-quarters of the boots on the ground by the time it is complete next summer. So much for the "Obama dividend" that supporters were hoping to reap from the rest of the world when the president took his oath of office nine long months ago.

All of which provides Mr Obama another sobering tutorial in the much-diminished status in which the US finds itself. Since taking office, Mr Obama has been feted and cheered around the world. But he has precious little to show for it other than vague sentiments of goodwill.[21]

One state whose cooperation is indispensable to the Obama admin-istration is Pakistan. A senior American official told the *Washington Post* that without "changing the nature of US-Pakistan relations in a new direc-tion, you're not going to win in Afghanistan. And if you don't win in Afghanistan, then Pakistan will automatically be imperilled, and that will make Afghanistan look like child's play". During visits to Islamabad in advance of the troop announcement, secretary of state Hillary Clinton and General James E Jones, Obama's national security adviser, offered President Asif Ali Zardari a new strategic partnership with the US, backed up by economic and military aid, in exchange for a clampdown on jihadi groups. Jones hinted that if Pakistan didn't cooperate, US troops might mount cross-border raids against Taliban bases in Pakistan.[22]

This pressure may, however, backfire. Obama's announcement of a July 2011 deadline for US troop withdrawal from Afghanistan to begin "fed longstanding fears that America would abruptly withdraw, leaving Pakistan to fend for itself", the *New York Times* reported. "Many

---

21: *Financial Times*, 3 December 2009.
22: *Washington Post*, 30 November 2009.

in Islamabad…argued that the short timetable diminished any incentive for Pakistan to cut ties to Taliban militants who were its allies in the past, and whom Pakistan might want to use to shape a friendly government in Afghanistan after the American withdrawal".[23] As it is, the Pakistani military offensive against the Taliban in the Swat valley has provoked a wave of devastating terrorist attacks in the main cities.

Obama's timetable in part reflects his awareness that, as he acknowledged in his speech, a country where at least one worker in ten is unemployed can ill-afford the additional $30 billion annual cost of the troop surge. The cost of the Afghanistan war will rise to over $100 billion in the 2010 fiscal year, five times its level five years earlier.[24] But the administration's efforts to avoid sinking into a quagmire like those in Vietnam and Iraq will probably not succeed. No doubt reflecting reservations in the military, defense secretary Robert Gates told a Senate committee that the July 2011 deadline could be adjusted if necessary. In all likelihood, the US will remain bogged down in Asia for years to come.

Varieties of resistance

This conclusion underlines that resisting the projects of US imperialism will remain one of the most important tasks of revolutionary socialists in the years ahead. But the context is very different from that in 2001 or 2003, because of the scale and severity of the economic crisis. The efforts of the different ruling classes to displace the costs of the crisis onto working people by cuts in public spending, jobs and wages, increased pension contributions and the like are set to dominate politics for years to come. The New Labour government in Britain is grappling with an economy that continued to contract in the third quarter of 2009: economic growth in 2010-1 is likely to be 10 percent lower than the Treasury projected in autumn 2007.[25] Alastair Darling's pre-budget report in December laid down devastating real cuts in public spending in most areas of 14 percent in 2011-4 (though they are carefully timed to kick in after the general election, most probably in May).

As we saw in our previous issue, in Britain, despite a sharp rise in unemployment, 2009 was marked by a wave of strikes and occupations representing a significant increase in militancy and thereby producing, as Charlie Kimber puts it, a situation in which "The elements of old and new

---

23: *New York Times*, 3 December 2009.
24: *Financial Times*, 2 December 2009.
25: *Financial Times*, 8 December 2009.

confront one another in the class struggle".[26] The outcome of last November's national postal strike shows how the old can temporarily overwhelm the new, but it also saw the New Labour government backing away from an all-out confrontation with the most militant group of workers in Britain.

The present issue supplements that analysis with a series of snapshots of the struggles provoked by the recession in a number of European countries. The widely varying levels of workers' resistance in different countries are striking. Nor can these variations be read off from differences in the economic situation in the countries in question. It's not surprising, for example, that Greece and southern Ireland should have seen perhaps the largest fight-backs, given the severity of the crisis there, but Spain, also badly hit, has seen comparatively little resistance.

This points to the facilitating (or obstructing) role played by the political configuration of forces. Thus it may be that in Greece the relative strength of the radical left (itself reflecting the most intense social struggles in Europe, almost unbroken since the 1970s) and in southern Ireland the weakness of social democracy and the decline of the old Fianna Fáil machine have helped the anger provoked by the crisis to burst onto the streets. The three European elections that took place in October did not support the fashionable media image of a left in disarray, unable to respond to the crisis. In Greece, the social-democratic party Pasok dissociated itself from the Third Way politics of its previous leader, Costas Simitis, and tacked left, winning a healthy parliamentary majority. Further to the left, Die Linke in Germany and the Left Bloc in Portugal made significant advances.

It is the parties of the mainstream neoliberal centre, whether social-liberal or conservative, that have suffered the greatest setbacks. The situation in Britain is not that different, as moribund New Labour sleepwalks towards defeat, while a lacklustre Tory opposition may not generate enough popular enthusiasm to win a parliamentary majority. But the radical left in Britain has yet to recover from the self-destruction of both the Scottish Socialist Party and Respect. Overcoming these divisions (some pre-dating these splits, others caused by them) sufficiently to offer a united left alternative to New Labour in the general election is now a matter of some urgency. But the decisive test for the revolutionary and radical left, regrouped or divided, will lie in its ability to support and strengthen workers' resistance to the developing bosses' offensive.

26: Michael Bradley and Charlie Kimber, "Will the Sparks Flare Up?", *International Socialism* 124 (autumn 2009), www.isj.org.uk/?id=579

Ireland: From shock therapy to resistance

Kieran Allen

Ireland is undergoing a form of shock therapy and major political changes are in the offing. The government has embarked on pay cuts and reductions in the public sector as its principal strategy for getting out of a recession that will see its economy fall by 8 percent this year. With deflation running at 5 percent it wants to cut the pay of the 300,000 strong public sector workforce in order to unleash a new round of wage cuts throughout the economy. In February the Irish Business and Employers Confederation (IBEC) demanded a 10 percent reduction in pay but could not match its rhetoric with significant action. A recent survey indicated that only 30 percent of all workers experienced a wage cut, and this tended to take place in smaller non-unionised workplaces. By inflicting a major defeat on the public sector, where the vast bulk of unionised workers are concentrated, the state and the employers hope to launch a new and devastating pattern of deep wage cuts.

Simultaneously, the Fianna Fáil-Green coalition government is trying to reduce public spending by €4 billion in its current budget. Support for this strategy is repeated daily by the private media that is controlled by two tax fugitives, Denis O'Brien and Tony O'Reilly.[1] A strident and vindictive

---

1:    The status of tax fugitive is Ireland's unique contribution to neoliberalism. Rich people who are outside Ireland for more than 183 days a year—and few check when their private planes come and go—are allowed to escape all Irish tax simply by claiming residency in Bermuda or some other offshore tax haven

rhetoric that scapegoats a "bloated" public sector workforce has become the main ideological weapon of the wealthy.

The reality is, of course, very different. As a proportion of GDP, Ireland has the third lowest spending on public services among OECD countries. Whereas state spending accounts for an average of 41 percent in these industrialised economies, it accounts for just 31 percent in Ireland. Even at the height of the so-called "Celtic Tiger" economy, before the crash of 2008, this extreme form of neoliberalism had led to run down health and childcare services. Inadequate creche facilities compelled Irish parents to pay the highest childcare costs in the EU, and an underfunded education system forced many of these same parents to collect Tesco tokens just to get an extra computer for their schools.

Now a brutal and incompetent ruling class are signalling even more cuts. They display not the slightest embarrassment when a contrast is drawn between these cuts in basic services and their bailout of the banks. In 2009 about €13 billion of state money was spent propping up Ireland's banking system. This, it so happens, is equivalent to the total amount spent on the health service for a whole year. The major recipient of these funds is the now nationalised Anglo-Irish Bank, which effectively functioned as the financial wing of Fianna Fáil. Its board of directors, full of Fianna Fáil hacks, sanctioned the lending of billions to Fianna Fáil-supporting builders who hyped up the property bubble. A staggering €70 billion was lent out by this bank to Irish property developers who became the second largest purchasers of commercial property in Europe.

In order to rescue its banking and builder friends, the government has devised an extraordinary scheme to turn the Irish state into the largest property owner in the world. Known as the National Assets Management Agency, it transfers all the bad debts of the banks to the state for a staggering €54 billion. The state will gain control of the deflated property assets of those who cease paying for their debts. The theory is that the cleaned out banks will then start lending money and so restart the Irish economy. The state pretends that it will get its money back when the property market revives, which it predicts will happen in ten years time. Yet even this enormous bailout will not be sufficient to breathe life back into the zombie banks and it is predicted that they will need another €14 billion.

This incredible state of affairs has led to extreme anger which is now manifesting itself in two main ways. First, the frozen landscape of Irish politics has finally started to melt as Fianna Fáil loses its political dominance. Fianna Fáil has been in government for the past 18 years and before that enjoyed long periods in office. Each of the last ten major opinion polls has recorded a drop in its vote to a low to mid 20 percent range. Its current tentative hold on office is only possible because of the spineless behaviour of a Green Party which justifies every attack on working people's living standards as a necessary compromise to allow it to be a "party of government" which can effect green policies.

The immediate beneficiary of Fianna Fáil's decline is its right wing rival Fine Gael. This shift has led some on the left to adopt a pessimistic view. The Irish, according to these doom-laden commentators, are a hopelessly conservative bunch who can do no more than switch from Tweedledum to Tweedledee.

This is to misread what is happening: Fianna Fáil is Western Europe's most successful populist right wing party and has long held the allegiance of many workers. It built on a republican tradition and translated this into the language of economic nationalism. Through mechanisms such as social partnership, it successfully submerged all forms of political class consciousness underneath a sea of Irish national progress. A break with this party is therefore highly significant. Moreover, Fine Gail's ascent is highly fragile. It does not have the same roots among workers and is seen by many merely as the quickest way to rid themselves of Fianna Fáil.

At one stage the Labour Party appeared to be about to catch up on Fine Gael's electoral ascent and in the Dublin area it emerged as the largest political party. It did this when it tacked left and challenged the bank bailouts. But the scale of the crisis facing Irish capitalism means that its leadership is terrified about raising expectations. It has therefore systematically discouraged mass protests and has rushed to its historic safe ground, preparing to settle in as a junior partner in a future government dominated by Fine Gail.

The second significant manifestation of anger has been a major public sector strike. Nearly 300,000 workers took action on 24 November 2009, reviving a tradition of militancy among many young workers. New activists began to come to the fore as strike committees organised rotas and in some cases campaigned against the media propaganda with their own leaflets. Even the police are about to vote on taking strike action.

The radical left intervened well around the strike by calling on workers to "take French lessons" by following the example of France's brilliant 1995 strike which combined picket lines with mass demonstrations. Calls for a march on the Irish parliament, the *Dáil*, and an escalation of action met with huge popular approval.

At the time of writing, it is not possible to predict the outcome. The union bureaucracy, which has close ties to the Labour Party leadership, is terrified of the movement that is welling up beneath it. In the midst of the strike it repeatedly issued "instructions" to various groups to cross picket lines and began intensive negotiations with the government on alternative ways of cutting the public sector budget. Under the slogan that they could offer "more for less", it indicated that it was willing to trade up to 15,000 redundancies and new forms of flexibility if pay cuts were withdrawn. The union bureaucracy even offered to give up overtime rates in hospitals by allowing its members to be rostered to work anytime from 8am to 8pm. But despite getting on their knees, the Fianna Fáil-Green government arrogantly brushed the union leaders offer aside, proclaiming "Not enough".

This rebuff has signalled the death of social partnership and means that the union leaders are now under the spotlight as many ask: will they lead a fight? Up to now they are showing extreme reluctance to do so. They appear stunned by the collapse of a cosy 22 year relationship with the Irish state and are desperate to avoid a strategy of national stoppages to drive a deeply unpopular government out of office.

On the other hand, there is a growing anger and militancy emerging in new networks such as the 24/7 alliance which groups together nurses, firefighters, the police and the army. This alliance held open mass meetings which 5,000 workers attended. At one such meeting, a representative of the police told the gathering, "No government in the world has ever cut the pay of the police—they should realise that loyalty is a two way street." An empty chair was kept for a representative of the soldiers, who the government banned from attending.

A weak, unpopular government which has lost the support of its main agents of repression is therefore confronting an organised working class which has woken from the slumbers of social partnership. It may again find that its last line of defence is a union bureaucracy that is more terrified of its own members than it is of the neoliberal revivalists who dominate the state. Yet no matter what the outcome of the present conflict, a dark cloud looms over the Irish capitalism. In order to make an eventual return to the European Union's Growth and Stability Pact, it has to embark on the same scale of cuts for the next three years. Watch out for even bigger confrontations on the edge of Europe.

France: from economic to political struggles

Denis Godard

After last year's huge days of action, demonstrations and the radical conflicts against redundancies in the car industry, has French rebelliousness disappeared over the past few months? Are we witnessing a downturn in struggle as a result of the social movement's inability to remove the obstacles put in its way by trade union leaders?

The most emblematic struggle of this period, that of workers at Continental Tyres, won important concessions from management—but the factory is going to close all the same. Another important conflict, at the Molex factory (producing parts for the car industry), ended in defeat. In contrast to previous years, the trade union leaders did not call even one day of action this autumn. In response, most organisations of the radical left have decided to accept the position of the French Communist Party (PCF) which, in order to hang on to its elected representatives in France's regional assemblies, has issued a call for left unity in forthcoming elections based upon building "majorities to manage" with the Socialist Party (PS) and the Liberal Ecologists led by Daniel Cohn-Bendit.

First of all it needs to be said that "social" France only appears to have gone silent. It seems that the failure to achieve a generalised movement last spring has not translated into a nationwide downturn in struggle but has instead resulted in a series of very localised struggles, less "visible" to the media. A railway worker explained how the call by his union for a day of action on 20 October translated into an unusual level of local calls for strike action. Drivers of trains linking Paris to the *banlieues* took four separate days of strike action in early November—without the backing of the main CGT trade union confederation—against longer working hours, and won. Workers in a small firm subcontracted by the Post Office in the Paris *banlieues* took strike action when the firm was threatened with closure, organising pickets outside postal depots demanding redeployment. In Dreux at the end of September the local CGT section proposed "the creation of a 'workers' council' in firms to advance class struggle in the face of capitalism and these lying thugs of bosses".

But what characterises the present phase of class struggle is the increasing prominence of conflicts of a political nature: marches against "precarious" employment and mobilisations around the Copenhagen summit on climate change and, most significantly, campaigns against the privatisation of the postal service and for the regularisation of *sans-papiers* (immigrants denied residence rights).

For the second time since 2008 the CGT has launched a wave of strikes and workplace occupations in the Paris area in support of the regularisation of workers without residence papers. But this wave is much bigger than the last, and more united, involving more than 40 companies.

The campaign against the privatisation of the Post Office reveals even greater possibilities. A nationwide "citizens' referendum" was arranged for Saturday 3 October by a broad range of organisations including parties of the left (including the PS), associations and trade unions, giving rise to a multitude of local unitary networks. The results went beyond even the most optimistic predictions with 2.3 million signatures collected, for the most part in a single day, outside post offices and certain left wing town halls. In the days that followed Olivier Besancenot, a leading spokespeson for the New Anti-Capitalist Party (*Nouveau Parti Anti-Capitaliste*, NPA) responded to the government's refusal to give way by calling for a demonstration to impose a referendum. In spite of the anxiety of the PS and trade union leadership in the face of rank and file mobilisation, the idea began to take hold. Not only were demonstrations held but the popular support expressed in the citizens' referendum gave postal workers the confidence to take national strike action (alongside teachers' unions) on 24 November.

What links these two struggles is the potential they reveal for a qualitative step forward in the class struggle in France, the possibility of establishing a practical link between social and political struggles. In both cases it is political themes which are mobilising workers as workers, in the workplace, both against their bosses and the state. Conversely, the weapon of strike action is being applied in local mobilsations, giving political struggles a class character.

One ancecdote is illustrative of the potential to go beyond the separation between political and economic struggles. During a demonstration against the repression of activists who destroyed genetically modified crops in Versailles in mid-November, Xavier Matthieu, leader of the Continental strikers and himself faced with prosecution by the state, came to give his support. The demonstration went past a picket of *sans-papiers* workers. They were invited to intervene in the debate which followed the demonstration.

During the process of building the NPA, we argued that a potential alternative leadership has begun to emerge to the traditional leadership of the labour movement, whose role has been to paralyse struggles. This has begun to manifest itself in a limited way through the links forged between striking sections of the car industry. On 17 September they organised a very radical rally outside the Paris stock exchange. On 22 October Bernard Thibault, general secretary of the CGT, was whistled at and insulted by a third of the 20,000 workers the CGT had mobilised "for jobs".

The debates under way over the regroupment of the radical left for the regional elections of March 2010 take on a new significance in this context. Since the summer the NPA has initiated unitary meetings to reach an agreement, proposing that united electoral lists should be based on opposition to those who seek to manage the crisis of capitalism and the need for an alternative to them. The cycle opened up by the strikes of winter 1995 in France continues. What is needed today is to bring into being, through different struggles and elections, forms of working class organisation which provide both the basis for resistance to attacks and the prospect of an alternative to capitalism. This excludes any possibility of co-management at a regional or local level with the PS.

Opposition and opportunity in Germany

Stefan Bornost

Just one month after Angela Merkel's new conservative-liberal government took office in Germany it faces its first difficulties. Franz Josef Jung of Merkel's Christian Democratic Union (CDU) resigned from the government amid allegations of a cover-up relating to the Kunduz massacre in Afghanistan in which up to 142 people lost their lives, including numerous civilians. Also dismissed the previous day for the same reason were general inspector Wolfgang Schneiderhan, the most senior military figure, and state secretary Peter Wichert.

At the same time, protests by students and school pupils including the occupation of parts of the main universities have forced the government to promise better funding of education. Referring to the billions in taxpayer money given to the banks, one student banner read, "€500,000,000,000 and what do we get?" Since the introduction of tuition fees, many students have been forced to find part-time jobs and many other young people think twice about beginning study at all.

The press has attributed the new government's disastrous early days to the incompetence of the cabinet. But there are far deeper contradictions that will plague Angela Merkel in the months ahead.

The election of 27 September brought to power a conservative-liberal government—the most right wing combination possible in German politics. But this does not represent a rightward shift in German society. The conservatives of the CDU and Christian Social Union of Bavaria (CSU) had their worst showing since the Second World War. The conservative-liberal camp actually lost a total of 300,000 votes.

The coalition came to power on the back of a collapsed social democracy. The losses of the centre-left Social Democratic Party (SPD) are dramatic. The support for the SPD has halved since 1998. This is a legacy of the so-called Agenda 2010 reforms—a general attack on the welfare state started by SPD chancellor Gerhard Schröder and furthered by his successors.

The coalition of the CDU and the pro-business Free Democratic Party (FDP) won despite the majority of the population's rejection of their core projects. For example, 77 percent of people are for a legally enshrined minimum wage, which the new government rejects. 61 percent want a shift away from nuclear energy, while the government wants to give nuclear bosses a longer running time for their plants. 55 percent are for an immediate military withdrawal from Afghanistan, but the government wants to send more troops.

The new government is all too aware of the unstable ground on which it stands. It announced that it will correct "social injustices" brought about by the SPD—chancellor Angela Merkel is doing her utmost to give the impression that she will not cut social standards.

But attacks will come. State debt soared after the banks were bailed out. The government pledged to reduce the debt fast, but at the same time they want to start their term with a €20 billion tax break for big business. You don't have to be Sherlock Holmes to work out that they will try to get the money from the working class.

But Germany's party of the radical left, Die Linke, was one of the winners in the election. Results across the entire former West improved, while in the former East 16 candidates were directly elected—13 more than in 2005.

Die Linke's demands were aimed at workers, school and university students, pensioners and job seekers. As a result, 56 percent of voters believe that Die Linke stands up for the socially disadvantaged. 18 percent of workers and 26 percent of all unemployed people voted for Die Linke.

Now the debate begins inside Die Linke about working in the new political environment. A common position is to opt for a double strategy in the fight against the CDU-FDP. First, to build on the ground side by side with trade unions and campaigns against CDU-FDP attacks. Second, to prepare the way for an SPD-Die Linke-Green Party national government after the 2013 general election by engaging in similar state governments.

This strategy has two big problems. For starters, its two prongs do not complement one another, but rather one undermines the other. Resistance against the coming cuts and opposition on the streets are absolutely necessary. Die Linke can play an important role here because it is credible and has earned people's trust. This credibility would suffer massively through any government participation under the current fiscal conditions.

The capitalist crisis has meant a drastic slide in federal budget revenues. If in coalition, Die Linke would be part of sharp attacks. This has already happened in Berlin, where the party rules together with the SPD, resulting in a drastic loss of support. In spite of that experience, Die Linke and the SPD formed a government in the federal state of Brandenburg. The SPD dictated the terms, forcing through a decision to cut the number of workers employed in public services from the current 51,000 to 40,000 over the next few years. Die Linke in Brandenburg is taking part in destroying every fifth job in the public service sector. This is flying in the face of the commitment of Die Linke nationally to expand the seriously understaffed public services and has led to anger among many activists of Die Linke, who feel sabotaged by the Brandenburg comrades.

The second problem with the "double strategy" is that it pins its hopes on a "reformed" SPD that will become a working partner for social policies in government. But past experiences offer the opposite picture. The SPD has often moved to the left in opposition, just as it did under the leadership of Oskar Lafontaine towards the latter part of CDU chancellor Helmut Kohl's term in 1995-8. But this was followed by the Schröder government's Agenda 2010 policies.

The political problems of the SPD lie deeper than a few bad individuals—all factions in the SPD are united in the perspective that excessive profits form the basis of social welfare policies. This leads to the sell-out of all manner of reformist policies. Under the given circumstances it is more likely for pigs to fly than for the SPD to make a sustained shift to the left.

The debates about Die Linke's trajectory will shape the political landscape on the left for years to come.

Greece: the eye of the storm?

Panos Garganas

"The social climate in Greece is charged with the electricity that you find in the air before a tropical storm." That was the description by a leading columnist on Greece's most popular daily newspaper. He is not alone in this view. Costas Karamanlis, the outgoing leader of the conservative New Democracy party, gave his reasons for calling an early parliamentary election in similar terms. His government could not push through the tough measures needed to deal with the economic crisis because of the "bad social climate". The fact that he lost the election by a wide margin confirmed his fears. The prospect of a new uprising, similar to what happened last December when a police officer shot Alexis Gregoropoulos, a 16 year old schoolboy, dead, is hanging over Greek politics. Thousands of young people and many trade unionists took to the streets then and demanded the overthrow of that "government of murderers". The Tory government may have survived the uprising by nine months but in the end it collapsed.

The new government of Pasok, a New Labour type party led by Giorgos Papandreou, is trying to defuse the social tension and at the same time cut the huge public deficit that is running above 12 percent of GDP. It is like trying to square a circle.

In the pre-election period Papandreou promised his government would not freeze wages and would rather provide a stimulus package to boost demand and push the economy out of recession. It was a promise that did not last for even 30 days. The preliminary budget plan for 2010 raises taxes by €3 billion and aims at cuts in public spending of another €4 billion. The government is sacking 40,000 temporary workers immediately under the pretext that they are not proper employees but are employed in training schemes. And there is to be a freeze on new employment in the public sector until a public watchdog can root out "clientelism" and ensure new recruits are employed "on merit".

Even these draconian plans are not deemed sufficient by international bankers and the European Union. The Commission of the EU is viewing Greece as a basket case. According to the *Financial Times*:

> The Commission identifies five countries as at particular risk—Greece, Ireland, Latvia, Spain and the UK—because their public finances will come under strain… This is particularly the case for Greece…its high debt ratio adds to concerns on sustainability… Greece's public debt could hit 135.4 percent of GDP in 2011, a level for which there is no precedent since the euro's creation in 1999.[1]

Both Jean Claude Trichet of the European Central Bank (ECB) and Joakin Almunia of the EU Commission attacked the unreliability of Greece's economic statistics. Papandreou's finance minister responded by rewriting his budget plan to make it tougher and by announcing plans to cut pensions and increase the retirement age.

Experienced parliamentarians are advising Pasok to crowd all the unpopular measures between now and next summer, while the government is still new and will have time to recover before the next election. Government ministers, however, have to look over their shoulders constantly because they are worried that anger might explode again despite the change in government.

They are right to do so. The signs are already there.

Temporary workers were the first to move. They held a very successful national demonstration in Athens on 5 November and are creating their own union network with a national coordinating committee. They plan to stay on the move with national demos every second week and local demos in between. This movement is putting pressure on trade unions to change tack and demand permanent jobs for all. Contract workers were the first group to confront the then newly elected Tory government back in 2004, so there is some experience in Greece of this kind of fight.

The first powerful group of organised workers that clashed with the

---

1:    *Financial Times*, 9 November 2009.

new Pasok government are the dockers of Piraeus. The Karamanlis government had signed and ratified through parliament an agreement handing over large parts of the docks to a Chinese company, Cosco. The dockers' union opposed the privatisation with a series of strikes. Pasok took the position that the deal was "neocolonial" and promised to renegotiate it when it comes into office. On 1 October, when Cosco was meant to take over the docks three days before the election, the dockers walked out and stayed out despite Pasok winning the election. The minister responsible for port authorities had to renew the promise of renegotiation before the dockers agreed to put the strike on hold after ten days. But instead of putting pressure on Cosco the government did a u-turn, so the strike started again. It took a court decision, ruling that the strike was illegal, plus a new promise to negotiate, for the strike action to be suspended again on 10 November. The dock privatisation scheme remains a testing ground for Papandreou's ability to carry out his gyrations.

The most severe test, however, will come over the pension "reform" scheme. These so-called reforms have been attempted twice in the recent past and both times the governments have had to retreat in the face of generalised strike waves. In 2001 a general strike crippled the previous Pasok government of Costas Simitis. And in 2008 a series of strikes formed the background to the December uprising. Now the union of workers in local authorities has already announced a strike for 3 December demanding that plans to raise the age of retirement are dropped.

Any doubts about the radical mood prevailing particularly among young people were dispelled by the size and militancy of the demonstration on 17 November to commemorate the 36th anniversary of the polytechnic uprising against the military dictatorship. The turnout was bigger than anyone can remember for many years. And the march was led by contingents of the anti-capitalist left that constituted roughly one third of the total.

Two developments accelerated events in Greece in early December. The fiscal crisis became more acute after economic worries in Dubai, with credit rating agencies downgrading Greek debt. Papandreou has rushed to reassure the ECB that his government will restore credibility by slashing the budget deficit with "state of emergency" measures. The new government has effectively handed economic policy over to the bankers. According to press reports Papandreou had a secret meeting with the deputy governor of the ECB Loucas Papademos—who ran the Greek central bank ten years ago—to hammer out an agreement for wage cuts and sweeping privatisations.

But it remains to be seen whether the government can implement these attacks on living standards. The second development has been the anniversary of last December's uprising, which was greeted by mass demonstrations on 6 and 7 December: not just in Athens but in most major cities. A huge police operation with two thousand preventive arrests failed to stop tens of thousands of students, school students and teachers from taking to the streets. Many faculties were occupied in response to police harassment. And despite the General Confederation of Greek Workers holding back, many trade unions were preparing for strike action on 17 December when the budget is debated in parliament. A rank and file revolt is unfolding and the bankers may not have it all their way after all.

To sum up, it is eyes to the left in Greece. Pasok was carried into office by a wave of radicalisation. New Democracy, the Tory opposition, is in tatters. The latest opinion polls put it at 22 percent. People expect the opposition to come from the left.

The leaderships of the parliamentary left, however, are inward looking at the moment. Syriza, the coalition of the old "eurocommunist" left with small groups coming from the far left, is embroiled in an internal fight over its constitution and there is tension between those who are open to consensus with Pasok and left wingers. The Communist KKE was shocked to discover that its vote dropped in the last election. Members are asking why this should be the case when there are so many opportunities for the left.

It will be up to the anti-capitalist left to take the initiative and lead the left into taking these opportunities. Antarsya, the anti-capitalist front, has made a promising start in that direction.

Sketches of Spain
Mike Eaude

"We are coming out of the tunnel," affirmed finance minister Elena Salgado creatively, when the third quarter unemployment figures came out in late October. 4,137,500 people were jobless, 17.93 percent of the population available for work. The Spanish state's official unemployment rate is higher than in any other European country except Latvia (19.7 percent). These official government figures exclude a large number of women and immigrants who want to work but don't register.

The last 12 months have seen over a million and a half jobs lost. Over one million families have two adults out of work. Some areas, such as Andalusia, have unemployment at nearly 30 percent. Salgado and the PSOE (Socialist Party) government base their optimism on the fact that unemployment "only" rose by 0.5 percent in the third quarter. This is in comparison to a leap from 13.9 percent to 17.4 percent in the first quarter that had panicked the Spanish ruling class.

The recession in the Spanish state began in the second quarter of 2008 and GDP has fallen by 4 percent in the six quarters since. Most analysts think that Spain will recover more slowly than the rest of the EU, despite being Europe's fifth largest economy. There are structural reasons for this: the Spanish state depends heavily on foreign investment and is not a large exporter. It took longer to recover from the 1970s recession than the rest of the continent, and its unemployment rates have always been higher than in the rest of Western Europe, even in times of boom.

Ever since the dictator Franco opened Spain up to foreign investment in 1959, the country's economy has been excessively dependent on construction and tourism. The collapse of the 50-year construction bubble in 2007-8, the first manifestation of the crisis in the Spanish state, has left countless blocks of flats half finished and one million new homes unsold, all this in a sector which just two years ago accounted for 9 percent of GDP.

The Spanish state's biggest export industry is cars, but the factories developed by multinationals such as Ford, Renault, Fiat, General Motors or Volkswagen several decades ago are no longer viable. Although Spain is still a low-wage economy in Western European terms, many capitalists are now relocating to lower-wage countries in Eastern Europe.

Socialist government: workers' friend?

Prime minister Zapatero was elected in 2004 on the back of the mass demonstrations against the Iraq war and a general rejection of the conservative Partido Popular (PP), and he was re-elected in 2008. After the financial crash Zapatero insisted that the Spanish model was the way forward for capitalism. He argued that the greater regulation of banks Spain meant it was protected against the kind of bank collapses seen in Britain and the US. It is true that Spanish banks have not needed such enormous bailouts, but there are deeper problems within the economy. The level of household debt tripled in the decade to 2008, and major banks have sustained huge losses with the bad debt of construction firms. Surreptitious government support and accounting manoeuvres may keep banks afloat for now, but in a semi-catatonic state, without the ability to invest and so kick-start the economy.

Zapatero has claimed repeatedly that "we will never make the workers pay for the crisis". His government has used subsidies to employ 400,000 construction workers on public projects and has been paying benefit of €421 a month to the approximately 25 percent of unemployed people with no social security entitlement. The employers and the PP have helped Zapatero appear left wing with their rabid attacks on the "socialist" government. They call for reforms to make labour more "flexible", arguing that if sacking workers is easier, then companies will take on employees. In a country where labour law reforms over the past 20 years have left workers increasingly unprotected and levels of precariousness extremely high (over 80 percent of the under-30s employed have no fixed contracts), it has been easy for Zapatero to pose as the "workers' friend".

In 2003-4 Spain had the biggest anti-war movement in Europe and in June 2002 a one-day general strike defeated the PP's plans to cut unemployment benefit. The gap between a militant recent history and the low levels of struggle today needs to be explained.

Union response

The measures taken by Zapatero have been sufficient to keep the two major union federations, *Comisiones Obreras* (Workers' Commissions) and the UGT (General Workers' Union), on board. They wield the fear and hatred of the right to keep workers in line. Zapatero and the PSOE are the government that the Spanish ruling class needs at present: resistance would almost certainly be much more widespread if the PP were in power.

Although Zapatero has not had to resort to massive bailouts, the government has made billions of euros available to entities "with problems". It is not clear exactly how much money has been pumped into the big construction firms to stop major bankruptcies which could ripple through the economy. But these hand-outs will have to be paid for and it is clear that huge cuts in social expenditure, already the lowest in percentage terms of the EU15[1] in education and health, will be needed. Zapatero's balancing act of "protecting" workers while administering the capitalist crisis is coming to an end. Just this October, the government announced measures to pay for the crisis that include a rise in VAT.

The subservience of the union bureaucracies and the weakness of Spain's trade unions (only around 15 percent of workers are unionised) mean that the union left, partly at the base of *Comisiones* and UGT, but mainly in a multitude of small unions, has a big fight on its hands to unite and mobilise. The biggest of these small unions is the sectarian but militant CGT, of anarchist origins. Others have developed through expulsions from *Comisiones*. Still others have their origins in the 1970s transition from dictatorship to democracy, such as STE (a teachers' union). There are radical nationalist unions, such as LAB in the Basque Country, now being repressed. It is notable that the anti-capitalist movement in the Spanish state, capable of mobilising hundreds of thousands of mainly young people, has not spilled over into union activism. Many anti-capitalist militants, prepared to face down the police in the big mobilisations of recent years, do not yet see the need to fight in the workplaces.

The lack of a strong *political* voice to the left of Zapatero is a major weakness. Millions of people in the Spanish state are part of a "social left", many of them influenced by anarchist or autonomist ideas, but the organised political left is very weak. *Izquierda Unida* (Left Unity), the coalition led by the Communist Party, is in long-term decline and has only two parliamentary seats. Unlike neighbouring Portugal or France, no new party

---

1:    The name given to the group of 15 member states of the EU before the accession of the Eastern European states in 2004.

has emerged from the anti–capitalist movement. At present, the small forces of *En Lucha*[2] are pressing for unity with the Fourth International group, organised as *Izquierda Anticapitalista*.

Buses and oranges

None of this gloomy summary means that the working class has been defeated. It is more a question of caution and political perspective. Time and again workers faced with the sack come out and demonstrate, but union leaders seek to divert every struggle to defend jobs into the "realist" option of negotiating greater financial compensation for job losses. Nevertheless, there have been a number of struggles this year, and a clear victory in an important sector could transform the situation.

The most talismanic struggle recently was that of the Barcelona bus drivers. In 2008 they won the right to two days off a week after a long series of strikes. They based their fight on mass assemblies of up to 1,500 drivers and the involvement of anyone who wanted to be involved, whatever their union affiliation. Despite this victory, the bosses have manoeuvred to cut wages and staff in exchange for the two days a week off. At the time of writing the drivers have scheduled an all-out strike from 10 January to defend their conditions. It will be a key test of strength.

A more recent victory was recorded by orange pickers and packers in the Guadalquivir valley in the province of Córdoba. On 5 November these seasonal workers, mainly women and immigrants working in highly precarious conditions, won a nine-day strike. They demanded that the bosses respect the collective agreement to pay €6.42 an hour instead of the common €5 and not force workers to do overtime. The implementation of the agreement will lead to 1,400 more workers being taken on. The orange strike was led by a small militant union, the SAT (Andalucian Workers' Union). As in the case of the Barcelona bus drivers, the presence of a leadership insisting on workers' democracy, with daily assemblies of up to 2,000 workers and flying pickets, and confidence that the struggle could be won was key to victory.

We hear a lot about green shoots these days. It is a pleasure to quote one of the SAT's leaders, Lola, on the new militant unionism: "The tree's growing and every day it has more branches."

2: *En Lucha* is the International Socialist Tendency group in the Spanish state.

From a bang to a whimper: Obama's first year

Megan Trudell

The Obama presidency is in a quagmire. The tremendous promise encapsulated in the campaign slogan "Change we can believe in" and the enormous expectations of reform after the Bush years have not been realised. Energy has given way to hesitancy and the Obama government's first year has seen it become increasingly entangled in the contradictions of profound crisis in the US. The conjuncture of recession and the deepening morass of war in Afghanistan have intensified divisions in the US political establishment. Government responses to the crisis have produced the twin, mutually reinforcing, effects of failure to deliver change for its most enthusiastic supporters and stoking political opposition to its right.

Obama's visit to China highlighted some of the economic difficulties the US is experiencing. The combination of the vast costs of the stimulus package ($780 billion) and rising military spending is weakening its international economic position. In March 2009 the Chinese central bank called for a new global reserve currency to replace the dollar due to concerns about falling dollar values which threaten its investment in the US. When treasury secretary Timothy Geithner did not rule this out, the dollar plunged. Its value in November was 15 percent lower than its peak earlier in the year. The US trade deficit with China remains vast—$165.8 billion for the first nine months of 2009. Obama's hopes for a more flexible exchange rate with China to boost US exports were predictably disappointed. China's commerce ministry attacked the US for hypocrisy: "We've always known the

US and the West as free-market economies. But now we're seeing a pro-tectionist side," said a spokesman, citing several trade actions taken against China this year.[1] On the day Obama arrived, the chair of China's bank reg-ulators also criticised US monetary policy, arguing that depreciation of the dollar combined with a refusal to raise interest rates was creating "new, real and insurmountable risks to the recovery of the global economy, especially emerging-market economies".[2] The two economies are so intertwined—an "uneasy co-dependency" according to the *Washington Post*—that the crisis is being mutually reinforced.

The Obama government's stimulus package has staved off eco-nomic meltdown, but begs the question of what happens when it is withdrawn. With the US economy's relative decline, its role as global military superpower becomes ever more important. Yet high and rising arms spending is increasing the pressure on the economy. The financial cost of the Afghanistan war has risen year on year. The figure in 2009 was $60.2 billion—up from $36.9 billion in 2007, $20 billion in 2005 and $14.7 billion in 2003.[3] Overall US defence spending is $680 billion for 2009.[4] These costs are set to rise further as Obama commits yet more troops to its disastrous Af-Pak strategy; troop levels are currently around 62,000 and Obama announced an increase of 30,000 in 2010—all this for a war which is more likely to profoundly destabilise US imperialism than to lift the country out of the economic doldrums.

In August, General Stanley McChrystal, commander of the Nato forces in Afghanistan, warned the US government that "failure to gain the initiative and reverse insurgent momentum in the near-term (next 12 months)…risks an outcome where defeating the insurgency is no longer possible".[5] Over 900 US soldiers have been killed in the war so far, nearly 300 in 2009—the highest by far of any year since the war began, and higher than any year between 1956 and 1964 during the Vietnam War.[6] The larger the US presence, the higher the number of casualties, the more routine (and accurate) the comparisons with Vietnam in the media, the greater public opposition becomes. Polls in November show that a majority of the US population—58 percent—opposes the war in Afghanistan for the first time since it began in the wake of 11 September 2001.

1:   *Wall Street Journal*, 16 November 2009.
2:   *Business Week*, 17 November 2009.
3:   Figures from nationalpriorities.org
4:   Figures from globalissues.org
5:   COMISAF Initial Assessment published in the *Washington Post*, 21 September 2009.
6:   Figures from icasualties.org

The crisis bites

Approval ratings for Obama are down to 49 percent, with 44 percent disapproving of his performance. Behind these figures remain the pronounced class differences in support for Obama that were evident during the election. So while Obama's approval rating has fallen among Americans of all income brackets, it remains highest among those on the lowest incomes: 59 percent of those who earn less than $2,000 a month compared with 48 percent among those on the highest (over $7,500) and 44 percent among those who earn between $5,000 and $7,500. Among black and Hispanic voters support for Obama is still stubbornly high—91 percent and 70 percent respectively.

Obama's continued popularity with poor and working class Americans, and among black and Hispanic voters, who are more likely to be in the lower income categories, reflects the extent to which the exigencies of the economic crisis are wrecking people's lives. As Gary Younge put it recently, "The impatience to see concrete results is not driven solely by unrealistic expectations but also by the fact that people are broke and desperate. For a growing number, change is not a slogan—it's an urgent human need".[7]

Despite US treasury secretary Timothy Geithner's declarations of an imminent end to recession in the summer, the recovery seems unreal for millions of Americans. A common term among US economists is the "jobless recovery". In a masterpiece of understatement, Geithner in October referred to the recovery as likely to be "a little choppy". The real situation for vast and growing numbers of Americans is increased unemployment, foreclosures and the loss of health benefits. 558,000 people lost their jobs in October, bringing the total to 15.7 million unemployed—8.2 million of them out of work since the recession began in December 2007.[8] The unemployment rate has broken the 10 percent barrier—hitting 10.2 percent in October, the highest for 26 years—and is projected to remain there for much of 2010.

One US economist recently stated, "The bottom line is that although labour market deterioration is clearly not occurring at the pace suffered late in 2008 and early this year, conditions remain brutal." Moreover, there is no apparent end in sight. "We continue to believe that the healing process will be a slow one, and that households will be contending with weak income growth and balance sheet issues for some time".[9]

7:   *Guardian*, 8 November 2009.
8:   Bureau of Labor Statistics.
9:   Quoted in the *Financial Times*, 6 November 2009.

A breakdown of the unemployment figures shows just how disastrous the situation is. Over one third of young black men are now out of work: "Joblessness for 16 to 24 year old black men has reached Great Depression proportions—34.5 percent in October, more than three times the rate for the general US population".[10]

Even among those who are not in such dire need, increasing numbers polled state that their financial position is precarious: 65 percent of Americans say their personal finances are in fair or poor shape, a figure that has steadily increased over the course of the year.[11]

The "jobless recovery" would be an oxymoron were it not for the fact that US profits have recovered. Productivity increased by an annual rate of 9.5 percent during the third quarter of 2009—the largest gain since 2003.[12] At the same time labour costs fell at a rate of 5.2 percent. Those workers who have kept their jobs are, in other words, being squeezed harder. Companies that have not made significant job cuts are cutting costs through shorter working weeks, unpaid holidays, wage cuts and shutdowns. These tactics are being pursued by large firms like Dell, Cisco and Motorola in the new technology sector that has boomed over the last three decades, but are also being used by smaller businesses. Profits exceeded expectations for 81 percent of Standard & Poor's 500 companies—widely regarded as the best measure of the US economy—between July and September 2009.[13]

Banks are also benefiting from the recovery and are profiting directly from the government bailout. As Dean Baker of the Centre for Economic Policy Research (CEPR) wrote in the *Guardian*:

As we are constantly reminded, the financial crisis is behind us and the banks are back on their feet. In fact, they are more than just back on their feet. In many ways they are doing better than ever. The most recent data from the commerce department shows that the financial industry profits now account for more than 31.5 percent of all corporate profits. This is a higher share than at any point during the housing bubble years. Of course, it is not that hard to make profits when you get to borrow money from the Fed at almost no interest and then lend it back to the government at 3.5 percent interest.[14]

10: *Washington Post*, 24 November 2009.
11: Pew Research Centre, http://people-press.org/report/561/anti-incumbent-sentiment
12: Bureau of Labor Statistics. Labour productivity figures exclude the farming sector.
13: Data from *Bloomberg*, 5 November 2009.
14: *Guardian*, 5 October 2009.

Restructuring and recession

Beneath the surface of the "jobless recovery" is the pressure US capitalism is under to offset the costs of the crisis.

For 30 years US capitalism's answer to falling rates of profitability has been to restructure industry, often with the support of the unions, to the detriment of workers. The subsequent pattern of concessions, give-backs and "shared sacrifices" has enabled US business to transform productive operations leading to disorientation in the US labour movement.

The methods, and the suppression of resistance that was the union side of the bargain, have been part of a process, described by David Harvey as the "restoration of class power", that has dramatically increased inequality in the US. A 2009 CEPR report concludes:

> Taken together, these policies—a low and falling minimum wage; the de- or re-regulation of major industries; the corporate-directed liberalisation of international capital, product, and labour markets; the privatisation of many government services; the decline in unionisation; and other closely related policies—are the proximate cause of the rise in inequality. Of course, the underlying cause is a shift at the end of the 1970s in the balance of economic and political power following almost five decades of ascendancy of labour and other social movements.[15]

More workers had been driven into poverty by this process even before the current crisis hit. Between 2002 and 2006 (a period of economic growth) there was an increase of 350,000 families living on low incomes. In 2008, early in the recession, there were 42 million adults and children living in low income families. These workers typically pay more for housing, lack health insurance, but work harder, often in dead-end, non-union jobs.[16] Their numbers can only have risen over the last year.

As Kim Moody explained in his recent book, *US Labor in Trouble and Transition*, US capital's restructuring has been a remarkably successful process. Between 1990 and 2003 output per hour went up by two thirds and production rose 72 percent, meaning productivity increases accounted for 90 percent of manufacturing growth in this 13-year period. This was achieved at the same time as jobs were cut and wages were held down—in

---

15: Schmitt, 2009.
16: "Working Hard, Still Falling Short", report on the working poor. Low incomes are defined as 200 percent of the poverty threshold (around $41,000 a year in 2006—roughly £25,000 for a family of four), www.workingpoorfamilies.org

other words, the rate of exploitation was forced up through technological developments in transport and communication, and the importation of "lean production" or "constant improvement" (*Kaizen*) techniques from Japan. By 2003 "a workforce with almost three million fewer workers was producing much more with only modest gains in wages and almost no additional cost to capital".[17]

Economic crisis has accelerated this restructuring process. The car industry is a good example: from the late 1970s assembly and parts plants began to relocate. There were several incentives for choosing the Southern states: cheaper labour, energy and land, state subsidies and lower taxes and—crucially—low to non-existent levels of unionisation.

Between September 2008 and 2009 average wages in the manufacturing section of the car industry fell by $1.42 an hour, while workers on average work an extra half an hour a week than they did a year ago.[18] The South has largely escaped the plant closures that are devastating Michigan and Ohio after the GM and Chrysler bankruptcies. While jobs have been lost throughout the industry, the traditional "rust-belt" states have borne the brunt. In Michigan, which has the highest unemployment rate in the US—15.1 percent—the number of car workers has been cut from 47,800 to 31,100 in the last year, a fall of 14.2 percent. In Ohio 7,800 car jobs have gone. In the same period 800 workers have been sacked in Alabama, bringing the total to 11,000, and in Texas 200 jobs have been lost, leaving 9,300 car workers. The dramatic losses of GM, Chrysler and Ford have provided increased market opportunities for non-US car companies which have expanded into the South. Toyota, Nissan, Mercedes, BMW, Hyundai and others have benefited from Southern states' "right to work" (anti-union) status and from large financial incentives from individual state coffers since the 1990s; the South Korean firm Kia, part of the Hyundai company, began production at its new plant in Georgia in November 2009.

The crisis in the industry as a whole is also facilitating continual developments in the intensification of work practices. At the Toyota plant in Huntsville, Alabama, which employs 900 people, "continuous improvement" measures have been voluntarily undertaken by workers in an ideological atmosphere of "shared sacrifices". A woman assembly line worker describes how it works: "I came up with a couple of *Kaizens* for my work. I found that there was a fair amount of motion muda [waste] at my work station." She suggested that the location of her tools and parts be

---

17:   Moody, 2007, pp25-26.
18:   Bureau of Labor Statistics.

rearranged, shaving three seconds off her work per engine. During a three month period employees came up with ideas that cut annual plant expenses by $1.2 million.[19]

Political tensions

The inequality of the recovery, with workers being forced to pay while banks and corporations have returned to profit and are justifying new bonuses, has generated real anger. As the *Financial Times* put it:

> Over the next few months, the miseries on Main Street are likely to continue to diverge from the taxpayer-enabled profit taking on Wall Street. And the electorate's sullenness could easily spill over again into raw anger—as it did in January and February amid revelations of the extraordinary bonus culture at AIG, Merrill Lynch and others.[20]

There is a significant problem for the left in relating to this anger, however, and the problem is Obama. Obama has presided over the continuation and extension of inequality, escalated the Afghanistan war, forced concessions in the car industry and given way to the private insurance companies over healthcare. The weight of the crisis is being felt particularly sharply by those—especially poor, working class and black voters—at the core of Obama's electoral support and his support, though still real, is eroding as disappointment sinks in. The impressive movement that the Obama campaign mobilised to deliver the election a year ago has not been marshalled to fight for a public option in healthcare, to fight for jobs or for the Employee Free Choice Act (EFCA) which would make it easier for workers to organise and join unions, and is opposed by much of US business, including Citigroup which was bailed out to the tune of $50 billion.

In the absence of a strong movement for reform from the left or pressure from a resistant working class, the louder voices are once more those of a minority of conservative politicians and radio presenters opposed to "big government". The weakness of the Obama government in the face of deepening economic gloom is stoking that opposition, encapsulating as it does a degree of class anger among "ordinary" Americans which has no other obvious outlet.[21]

19:   *Reuters*, http://blogs.reuters.com/route-to-recovery/2009/11/16/toyota-plant-workers-sheltered-from-the-downturn/
20:   *Financial Times*, 29 October 2009.
21:   See Trudell, 2006.

As a result, the Republicans made gains in the recent elections for state governor in Virginia—a state won by the Democrats for the first time since 1964 in the Obama election—and New Jersey. The results suggest, in addition to local factors, that those—mainly white—workers who came late to the Obama campaign have found little in the government's priorities to alleviate their economic predicament.

The re-emergence of visible manifestations of conservative populism, however, are indicative of the weakness of the Republican Party as a political force; instead the likes of Sarah Palin and "shock-jock" Rush Limbaugh are increasingly vocal and are backing conservative candidates against those chosen by the party machine. The mobilisations of the right, such as those in opposition to healthcare reform, have been small but nonetheless illustrate the potential for anger over economic pain to be channelled by conservative forces if progressive forces sit on their hands.

Gary Younge makes this point about the healthcare protests: "The problem is not that the right were organised but that—with a few exceptions—the left has not been. At the very moment when he needed the 'movement' that got him elected most, it appears to have largely stopped moving".[22] It has stopped moving largely because Obama has refused to mobilise it and there is not sufficient confidence and pressure for independent action on a mass scale. It is not a surprise that the US president prefers not to revive a movement that may escape the control of the Democratic Party apparatus. But his equivocation risks alienating his own constituency and those who were pulled into his orbit by the tremendous power of his campaign for change, as well as reigniting cynicism of the "liberal" Democratic establishment that could well benefit the right.

The lesson from the Great Depression of the 1930s in the US is that reform and resistance to the effects of the crisis will ultimately depend on a significant movement from below pushing for them. At the moment that movement is absent. There are, however, other social and political processes taking place that suggest possibilities. The intensification of work, job cuts, falling wages and demands for concessions prevent, but can also cause, struggle; capital's drive to save itself also forces more groups of working class people to resist. As Kim Moody argues, "The very barriers thrown up by capital and its worldwide reorganisation of production and work are the consequence of the same forces that propel these different groups of workers to fight in the first place".[23]

22: *Guardian*, 30 August 2009.
23: Moody, 2007, p6.

One telling example in the current climate is the substantial vote of car workers in October against accepting an agreement from Ford and the United Auo Workers Union for the next four-year contract due to be negotiated in 2011. The proposals included a "no-strike" provision on wages and benefits and the reclassification of skilled jobs in order to reduce Ford's costs. Seven out of ten assembly plants voted down the contract. In Kansas City workers voted 92 percent against the deal and in one Kentucky union branch representing two assembly plants the vote was 84 percent against.[24]

The car votes are important because they indicate a fracture in the acceptance of a key tenet of US capitalist ideology, more prevalent than ever during economic crisis: that all classes are "in it together" and that the American dream—the equal entitlement of all Americans to shares in prosperity—rests on an equal contribution to productivity. The adherence of US unions to the belief that raising productivity delivers benefits for their members has been deeply damaging. As US business has forced through continual concessions and weakened collective bargaining, the idea has been a profound hindrance to building an alternative to capitalism.

The harsh realities of devastated and abandoned industrial areas, job cuts and inadequate or non-existent social assistance has put workers under pressure to accept the logic of "shared sacrifice" in times of trouble. But the same conditions can also provoke the bitter realisation that the American dream is a fiction for the great majority, and that governments—including Democratic ones—will always take the side of bankers and corporations unless forced otherwise. This is a key ideological aspect of the shift leftward in the US; working class consciousness, the realisation that workers are not "middle class" at all, but are engaged in a battle with US capitalism, is being forged through the painful experience of the realities of class division during the crisis.

Obama's election reflected this, as large numbers of workers, white as well as black, broke from the Republicans to vote against the erosion of their living standards and for the possibility of change. The potential exists for these workers to be mobilised to protect their livelihoods. Kim Moody makes the point that if the union membership was mobilised to defend workers and build the unions, it could organise recruitment campaigns that could in turn fight for the EFCA, healthcare, to organise the South, and fight for a "stimulus" for workers rather than bankers. With imaginative, grassroots campaigning it could be harnessed to fight for these things and could also conduct the ideological argument that Americans are not "all in it together".

24: Reuters, 1 November 2009.

The deep desire for change that got Obama elected has not gone away. The potential for organisation of immigrant workers has not disappeared. The occupation at Republic Windows and Doors in Chicago, like Visteon in Britain, was a glimpse of struggle producing new tactics to fit a changing world. The potential for real change in the US is there. As ever in the history of US working class politics, it is leadership that is the 64 thousand dollar question.

References

Moody, Kim, 2007, *US Labor in Trouble and Transition* (Verso).

Schmitt, John, 2009, *Inequality as Policy*, Centre for Economic Policy Research report, www.cepr.net/documents/publications/inequality-policy-2009-10.pdf

Trudell, Megan, 2006, "The Hidden History of US Radicalism", *International Socialism 111* (summer 2006), www.isj.org.uk/?id=216

Honduras is not just another banana republic

Mike Gonzalez

The tone of media reports of the events in Honduras has been generally tongue in cheek, as if this were simply another episode in the ongoing tale of banana republics and their regular coups. On 29 October, for example, Sophie Nicholson reported from Tegucigalpa, the country's capital, on the difficulties that journalists have in sleeping on hard floors.[1] For some weeks journalists were locked inside the Brazilian embassy in Honduras together with President Manuel Zelaya, deposed on 28 June in a military-civilian coup. Outside the embassy demonstrators and protesters have been attacked, shot at, tear-gassed and in some cases killed by riot police and soldiers. Opponents of the new regime (the "de facto" government, as everyone now calls it) have been arrested, their bank accounts frozen, their relatives persecuted. The peasant movement, which mobilised as soon as the coup happened and has remained on a war footing ever since, has faced weapons in the capital and gunmen on the estates of the landowners who vigorously supported the coup. In Honduras's universities student resistance has met with a similar level of repression.

This is not comic opera.

In fact it is a deeply serious and significant moment in the history of Latin America. In the first months of a post-Bush foreign policy Honduras offers two conundrums for solution. The first is how a coup of this ferocity

---

1: Available online at http://bit.ly/hondurascoup

was not only permitted by a new US administration ostensibly committed to diplomatic solutions in the region; the coup makers were actively encouraged and protected from universal criticism by Washington. The second is how it was that in a society as unequal as Honduras, and with a recent history of such oppression, its people have sustained a level of mass popular resistance unprecedented in its determination and its level of organisation.

A kidnapping
When the president of Honduras, Manuel Zelaya, was kidnapped in his pyjamas and dumped on the tarmac of an airfield in Costa Rica, the immediate response was a massive protest movement in the city and the countryside. Huge demonstrations demanding the return of Zelaya were violently suppressed, and demonstrators killed and injured. TV and radio were censored and two popular radio stations (Globo and Progreso) immediately shut down. A curfew was imposed and the government later announced it would appropriate the bank accounts of anyone involved in demonstrations, particularly the highway blockades organised by trade unions and mass organisations.

At first sight, Manuel Zelaya was not an obvious candidate for this level of mass support. A conservative and Liberal Party member, he was elected in 2005. He had put forward no radical programmes or policies at that time. His removal from power in June 2009 was the response of Honduras's ruling class to specific recent policy changes, especially on the question of the minimum wage, and to Zelaya's decision to hold a consultative referendum on 28 June to call a constituent assembly to change the constitution. This decision was bitterly opposed by Honduras's ruling class, parliament, army and Supreme Court—and there were dark hints that he was trying to imitate Hugo Chávez's recent referendum proposals on extending the number of presidential terms. That was, of course, a pretext—though Venezuela was a significant element, for Zelaya had taken Honduras into the Latin American Bolivarian Alternative (ALBA), the Latin American regional organisation set up by Chávez. As a consequence Honduras became eligible for cheap oil from Venezuela as well as loans and other benefits. Zelaya's newly emerging enthusiasm for the Bolivarian project was never very convincing, at least for this writer; but as in the case of his equivalent in Nicaragua, Daniel Ortega, there was much to be gained from the relationship with a powerful and generous Venezuela, especially by small Central American and Caribbean countries with no access to oil.

Latin America's decade of resistance

Zelaya's association with Chávez was certainly an important factor in explaining the coup. Yet Bush's administration, already embroiled militarily in Iraq and Afghanistan, had generally moved away from supporting direct military intervention in Latin America. This is not to say that the strategy of political control and economic domination had changed in any way—only the tactics for achieving it. US policy had centred on Colombia in particular, as the bridgehead for its military oversight of the region. Plan Colombia, drafted under Bill Clinton's regime, was ostensibly about social and economic development—but something like 90 percent of its $1.3 billion allocation was actually spent on military operations disguised under headings like "the war on drugs" and later "the war on terror", resources administered by an increasingly militarised Colombian state.[2] In Venezuela the US has openly supported a sustained right wing assault on the Chávez government. It was clearly directly implicated in the failed coup against Chávez in April 2002 and equally in the savage bosses' lockout of December 2002 to February 2003 which was intended to destroy Venezuela's oil production and create an economic crisis so profound that the population would turn against the Bolivarian revolution. In fact the effect was the reverse, as the masses mobilised to challenge and eventually defeat the bosses' strike.

In Bolivia the election of Evo Morales in 2005 marked the high point of a six-year wave of mass popular resistance. Here again, the response of Washington was to support the right wing opposition—in this case the powerful forces of the Media Luna, the six non-Andean provinces where much of Bolivia's oil, gas and agricultural wealth lies. Under the wing of Philip Goldberg, the US ambassador (until 2008) whose particular expertise had been gained in Belgrade, where he oversaw the break-up of Yugoslavia, the political campaign for the "self-determination" of the Media Luna laid the basis for a sustained, vicious and openly racist assault on the Morales government. Even in Ecuador, where the government of Rafael Correa was elected on a progressive and independent programme (he has since closed down the US base at Manta, whose construction was legitimised by Plan Colombia), the wealthy landed interests around Guayaquil have begun to echo the demands of their Bolivian class allies. In Venezuela, the municipal and gubernatorial elections of 2008 provided a context in which similar demands began to be insistently heard in the

---

2:   See Gonzalez, 2003.

states that bordered on Colombia.[3] The strategy of fragmentation and the encouragement of internal conflict became more intense after the flat rejection in 2007 of the Free Trade Area of the Americas (FTAA) proposals put forward by Bush, and Chávez's claim that ALBA represented the only viable independent regional alternative.[4]

Honduras could not claim to have the same strategic, economic or political significance as Venezuela (60 percent of whose oil still goes to the US and whose anti-imperialist discourse stung the Bush regime so deeply) or Colombia (the US's wealthy and powerful ally and its key weapon in "the war on terror", if not its war against the drugs barons!), or Ecuador or Bolivia with their major untapped gas and oil resources. In economic terms, Honduras has not advanced very far from its dependence on and subordination to the interests of the US banana companies which led the great American short story writer O Henry to coin the term "banana republic" at the beginning of the 20th century. Its seven and half million inhabitants still depend on export agriculture, two thirds of which goes directly to the US. Some 50 percent of its people live below poverty levels. It sits at number 149 in the world for per capita income, and one third of its GDP comes from the remittances sent by Hondurans working, mostly illegally, in the US; 40 percent of its population work in agriculture (which produces just 13 percent of the national income) and 30 percent in the maquiladoras, or assembly plants, owned by multinational companies which have transferred their operations to Honduras because of its cheap labour. In the words of the CIA's *World Factbook*, "Honduras, the second poorest country in Central America, has an extraordinarily unequal distribution of income and high unemployment".[5]

There are specific issues that might explain the timing of the coup. Zelaya had resisted attempts to privatise Honduras's mass media, which would have delivered its main television channels into the hands of a consortium whose leaders included John McCain, Obama's failed Republican presidential opponent. The deeper explanation, however, goes back to the early 1980s and the war mounted by the US against the Sandinista Revolution in Nicaragua. The Contra War was organised by the US; its "advisers" armed and trained 15,000 anti-Sandinista fighters who operated from Honduras across the long and poorly defended

---

3:   See Gonzalez, 2009.
4:   In fact ALBA is still far from offering any kind of alternative to the pre-existing regional economic block, Mercosur, which Venezuela has also joined.
5:   Ironically enough, the best source of these and other data is the CIA's *World Factbook*. Available online at www.cia.gov/library/publications/the-world-factbook/geos/ho.html

frontier with Nicaragua. The war cost 50,000 Nicaraguan lives and effectively destroyed its economy, bringing down the Sandinista government in February 1990. It was a war waged with exemplary savagery. Victims of the contras were tortured before death, and many of their corpses were left to terrorise the communities from which they had come to defend the revolution. Back-up and logistical support came from the massive US base near San Pedro Sula.

The person who oversaw Honduras's transformation into a US military base was a sinister individual called John Negroponte, ambassador to the Honduran capital Tegucigalpa for four years, during which the US military aid budget to the country rose from $4 million to $78 million annually. Negroponte would go on to distinguish himself as a high representative of imperialism at the UN and later in Baghdad before becoming national security adviser to Bush and later an adviser to current secretary of state Hillary Clinton. It should be noted that Honduras's current constitution, which Zelaya contemplated changing, was drafted under Negroponte's watchful eye. His right hand man, Otto Reich, is notorious in Latin America as the head of the State Department's Latin America desk for much of the last 25 years and a ruthless cold warrior, as well as ambassador to Venezuela for several years. Like McCain, he also speaks for the interests of media corporation AT&T.

Honduras in a wider world

The 28 June coup was not entirely unexpected within Honduras. Zelaya had dismissed the army high command three days earlier, before the parliament and the Supreme Court restored them to their former posts. Business leaders, among them Micheletti who later became "de facto" president, had made their hostility very clear, as had the Supreme Court and the judiciary. They argued that the consultative referendum proposed by Zelaya was unconstitutional, a claim with no basis in fact or in the document itself.

Given Honduras's history, and its absolute dependence on the US economically, militarily and politically, the coup would have been inconceivable without support from inside the US, including close advisers to Clinton. The coup was immediately denounced by the Organisation of American States and every Latin American president. President Obama's response was oddly ambiguous, however, calling for a "resolution through dialogue and negotiation". The UN even added its voice of condemnation 24 hours later. While Obama hesitated, Clinton's response was to tacitly recognise the government installed by force as a legitimate interlocutor. Within days a delegation from the Honduran regime arrived in Washington and met with McCain and Clinton. The meeting was organised by her close associate Lanny Davis, who represents the Honduran chamber of commerce, and Venezuelan lawyer Carmona Borjas, now resident in the US, who was a key player in the attempted coup against Chávez.

Had Washington whispered, the coup makers of Tegucigalpa would have had no choice but to fall to their knees. Instead, while Zelaya waited in Costa Rica, there was a resounding silence from Obama and Clinton. The new regime acted quickly and violently against the mass protests that exploded as soon as news of Zelaya's abduction began to spread. The National Resistance Front against the coup was formed and drew together every section of Honduran society.

Yet no decisions were taken in those first few days. The diplomatic silence was broken only four days later, when the delegation from the new "de facto" Honduran government was received with full pomp in Washington. Empty phrases abounded, but this was clearly going to be Clinton's (and Negroponte's and Reich's) province and Obama was left disarmed. Much time and print has been spent wondering whether he knew the coup was coming. My sense is that he did not, but, more importantly, he had no resources to change the situation, withdraw US economic support or otherwise demonstrate his democratic credentials or his independence from the Honduras lobby.

Those who were vocally arguing the case for Honduras's new rulers in Congress represented a continuity of policy from Bill Clinton through Bush. While Obama's policy towards Latin America at this early stage was as yet unclear, there was no evidence that this would be a new dawn for the Americas. The discourse of hostility towards Hugo Chávez was unabated, plans were announced for the building of three new US bases in Colombia, and the thawing of relations with Cuba seemed slow and reluctant. Furthermore, there was Obama's election campaign comment that "we seem to be losing Latin America". Against that background, the Honduras coup and the response to it from the administration and particularly from Hillary Clinton strongly suggest that this was a pre-emptive move from a hard right Latin America lobby to hold back any softening of relations with the more radical Latin American governments. There are still troops in Haiti, for example, swollen by a Brazilian contingent, and the Colombian government's role in the region remains as before and is being actively reinforced.

It seems clear that Washington's strategy was to prolong matters as much as possible, and undermine Zelaya's credibility and his popular support through interminable negotiations. Elections in November would thus take place but Zelaya would not be able to stand again. It was with this in mind that Clinton called in President Oscar Arias of Costa Rica, who has considerable experience of sabotaging revolutionary movements. The Contadora process in the early 1980s functioned in that way, drawing the revolutionary Sandinista government of Nicaragua into negotiations which isolated it from the revolutionary movements of Central America and sapped its will in endless negotiations which continued even as the US fuelled $77 million of military aid to fund the contra war mounted from Honduras. Arias's new intervention served exactly the same purpose, keeping Zelaya waiting in Costa Rica while the "de facto" government won "de facto" legitimacy in negotiations in which it was regarded, at US insistence, as a legitimate partner. Somehow, by sleight of hand, Zelaya and Micheletti had become equals in this sponsored dialogue.

The persistence of the people's movement

No one had reckoned, however, with the absolute determination of the resistance. Despite ferocious repression, peasant organisations moved quickly to occupy lands and to block highways, before marching to the capital to join the protests. There were violent confrontations on the university campus in the capital. The teachers' unions were active from the beginning and two of their leading members were killed at an early stage. Yet when Zelaya announced on 6 July that he was returning to Honduras there were up to 50,000 people gathered at Toncontin airport to welcome him back. His plane, needless to say, was never allowed to land. One month later only Israel had recognised Micheletti's regime! His finance minister had declared that the economy would not be able to survive six months when the World Bank and the Interamerican Development Bank announced a freeze on loans. Yet what was most striking was the confidence of Micheletti and his cronies. They were cocksure and unmoved by the hostility of Latin American governments. They clearly knew that, whatever cautious criticism might be advanced in public, Washington—and the State Department in particular—would protect them.

But the mass movement of resistance had put a new piece on the board and complicated matters. The return of Zelaya under "negotiated" conditions was a real possibility at this stage—though he would be unlikely to be allowed to see out the remaining six months of his presidential term. But he might be allowed to return on condition that the proposals for a constituent assembly and constitutional reform were abandoned. Now, however, Washington (and indeed the OAS) was faced with a different problem. Zelaya's return would inevitably be seen as a victory for the resistance movement, and the political repercussions of that could be very serious.

The coup always had to be located in the context of a Central America that seemed to be slipping out of Washington's control. Daniel Ortega's return to the presidency of Nicaragua could be seen as a radical shift, although Ortega's willingness to negotiate with his Sandinismo organisation's bitterest enemies to get himself into power, accepting Latin America's most reactionary abortion laws as the price to be paid, suggests a different interpretation. In fact Ortega is a living caricature of the Sandinismo that overthrew the 30-year Somoza dictatorship in 1979 in the name of popular revolution. His Sandinismo is a corrupt political apparatus entirely concerned with maintaining him in power. Yet he has identified himself with Venezuela (for similar reasons to Zelaya). In El Salvador an ex guerrilla leader was recently elected to the presidency, albeit with an economic programme that seemed very close to neoliberalism. And Mexico, while currently "safe" in the hands of neoliberal Fernando Calderon, has witnessed extraordinary levels of mass mobilisation—first around the alternative candidacy of Lopez Obradors and later in the profound challenges set out by the struggles in Oaxaca.

Against that background the resistance could not be seen to win, especially if the whole Honduran process was seen as an opportunity to place the US at the centre of Latin American politics once again. The key was Zelaya himself. He returned to Honduras in early October in odd circumstances and took up residence in the Brazilian embassy. Despite threats by the regime to burn him out, and the cutting off of electricity and water supplies briefly to the embassy, Zelaya remained inside the embassy and it became increasingly clear that he was negotiating from there.

The agreement of 30 October, supervised by the former US assistant secretary of state Thomas Shannon, who was also in Honduras in the days before the coup, was in every sense a defeat for Zelaya. It allowed him back subject to a vote by the parliament and the Supreme Court, who backed and organised the coup, on whether he could legitimately return as president for the 29 November elections. He was blocked and the elections went ahead under the supervision of a committee that included right wing ex-president of Chile Ricardo Lagos and the ex secretary of labour of the US. In effect Zelaya accepted the conditions imposed by the US, including the abandonment of any plan to reform the constitution.

The election: an end or a beginning?

On 29 November Zelaya was still trapped inside the Brazilian embassy from where he issued often contradictory calls to those who for so long had defended his right to resume his presidency. But the reality was that the battle had moved on to a different terrain. Symbolically, Zelaya remained a focus for the resistance movement; but the ex-president had made too many compromises to continue to claim leadership of the protests. He had participated in the dialogues promoted by the US government, despite the obvious contempt of Micheletti and his people. As the elections drew nearer, repression intensified and the attacks on demonstrators and protesters multiplied, and it did their cause no good at all that from his enclosure in the embassy Zelaya set aside his promise to reform the constitution, only to find that his compromises carried no weight with those who had thrown him out of power.

The attitude of the United States also changed a number of times. But while what had happened in Honduras was a matter of concern to all Latin American governments, beyond the denunciations of Hugo Chávez there was little in the way of concerted action against the regime. And it is quite clear that Clinton has achieved her objectives—placing herself centrally in the political negotiations and raising her profile in Washington. It was obvious that Obama's administration would recognise whatever new government was elected, so long as it restored the relationship with Washington that had existed before.

Voting is compulsory in Honduras—though abstention is always quite high. On this occasion, faced with an election with no external observers and polling places supervised by the army and the police, who had conducted the June coup, the National Front for Resistance called on the people to observe a voluntary curfew and remain in their homes—a poignant reference to the curfew imposed across Honduras after 28 June. An unprecedented number of Hondurans—at least 50 percent and probably close to 70 percent—answered the call. Those who voted elected Lobo, a wealthy conservative who will faithfully represent the political class and its intimate relationship with the US.

Zelaya is no longer an actor in the Honduran process. But what of the movement that sustained the flame of resistance, that now mourns its many victims who died in the course of their extraordinary struggle? The movement has vowed to continue. If Honduras has shown that imperialism's objectives have not changed, the lesson of these months is that Honduras's working population have become the protagonists of their own history. Their resistance has been extraordinary, heroic, and their level of organisation and coordination impressive. Those organisations will be needed in the months to come, to fight the high levels of unemployment and the inequality that the coup makers resolved to defend. The important thing now is that the National Resistance Front neither forgives nor forgets what it has learned since 28 June—that the independent organisations of the masses can take on the ruling class.

References

Gonzalez, Mike, 2003, "Colombia", in Farah Reza (ed), *Anti-Imperialism: A Guide for the Movement* (Bookmarks).

Gonzalez, Mike, 2009, "Chávez Ten Years On", *International Socialism 121* (winter 2009), www.isj.org.uk/?id=507

A tribute to
Chris Harman
1942–2009

This issue of International Socialism *appears soon after the sudden and tragic death of its editor for the past five years, Chris Harman. He died of a heart attack on 6 November in Cairo where he was speaking at a socialist conference.*

In this collection we devote several articles to his life and work. Ian Birchall offers a political and intellectual biography, Andy Durgan a personal memoir and Joseph Choonara an assessment of his distinctive approach to understanding capitalism.

Guglielmo Carchedi responds to Harman's last book, Zombie Capitalism, *as the starting point of a discussion of the capacity of Marxist political economy to explain the present crisis. Harman's final contribution to debates among Marxist economists, a review of the evidence for a long-term crisis of profitability, appears alongside an incisive and characteristic critique of the thought of the French Communist philosopher Louis Althusser.*

Chris Harman: a life in the struggle
Ian Birchall

I first met Chris Harman in the spring of 1963, in Peter Sedgwick's attic.[1] We had gone to Liverpool for a meeting of the Young Socialist paper *Young Guard*. There had been a danger that control of the paper would pass from the International Socialists (IS) to various orthodox Trotskyists, but we won the vote. Long-forgotten froth of far-left factionalism. But not entirely so. *Young Guard* had real influence in the Labour Party Young Socialists, and through it what had been the tiny Socialist Review Group, with less than 40 members, grew by 1964 to a couple of hundred comrades, the people who went on to take advantage of the industrial upturn of the mid-60s and then the upheavals of 1968.

Chris had become politically active in Watford while still at school.[2] He was involved in an independent left youth group formed after the 1959 election by people with a range of left wing views, but distrustful

1: In order to prevent this article drowning in footnotes I have given sources in the text; *SW* indicates *Socialist Worker* and *IS1:* and *IS2:* the two series of *International Socialism*. A collection of Chris's writings, which will be expanded, is on the Marxist Internet Archive at www.marxists.org/archive/harman/index.htm. Other pieces, at the time of writing not on the MIA, can be found on Chris's own website http://chrisharman.blogspot.com/ There are also items on the two *International Socialism* and *Socialist Review* websites, www.isj.org.uk/ and www.socialistreviewindex.org.uk/. Since most readers are probably more adept than I am at navigating the internet, I shall leave it to them to locate the material.

2: Some of this account is based on a two-hour interview I did with Chris in April 2009.

of the Labour Party.[3] There were contacts with the New Left; on an Aldermaston CND March he bought a copy of *International Socialism* and assumed that such a well-produced journal must be the product of a large organisation. Subsequently Tony Cliff was invited to speak. Chris's ideas were still in flux—he thought Russia was state capitalist, but that Poland and Cuba were socialist.

In autumn 1961 he went to Leeds University where he teamed up with Mike Heym. He joined the Socialist Review Group, which became IS the following year. Building a branch was not easy in Leeds, where the Communist Party was still strong, and the Socialist Labour League (forerunner of the Workers Revolutionary Party) was also influential. They sold *Young Guard*, *International Socialism* and *Socialist Review*. Cliff came to Leeds about twice a year to speak.

In 1964 Chris came to do a PhD at the London School of Economics (LSE). Here he began to develop as a significant student leader. He played a major part in the LSE occupation of 1967 when disciplinary action was taken against students protesting at the appointment of a collaborator with the Rhodesian racist regime as LSE director. This marked the beginning of the student movement in Britain.

At the same time Chris was active on the editorial board of *Labour Worker*, forerunner of *Socialist Worker*. There were not many of us and there could be no question of specialising. We all had to turn our hand to whatever was required. Chris began to acquire his enormous breadth of knowledge and interests. In the first few months of 1965 he wrote on the witch-hunt of Communists in the engineering union, on incomes policy and on the United Nations.[4] He later wrote, as "our mining correspondent", a sharp critique of a Communist Party pamphlet on the future of the mining industry.[5] He refused to use his name "in case I ever meet a miner". The following year he wrote a major piece on the tenth anniversary of the Hungarian Revolution. The next month the paper carried a letter from a Hungarian émigré stating that "even a Hungarian who witnessed those days could not have given a more detailed and better informed account of the uprising".[6]

It was not all writing. In July 1966 a demonstration against the Vietnam War was attacked by police. A number of those arrested were charged with assaulting the police and "possessing an offensive weapon", that is, a placard

---

3: Loosely connected with the similar group in Newcastle described in Charlton, 2009.
4: *Labour Worker*, Mid-January 1965, 1 April 1965, Mid-April 1965.
5: *Labour Worker*, September 1965.
6: *Labour Worker*, November, December 1966.

on a stick! Some were jailed. However, Chris managed to turn the tables. "With a well-briefed lawyer and able witnesses he received merely a fine. On the basis of previous case law the offensive weapon charge was dropped".[7] He thus helped to establish that a placard was not an offensive weapon.

It was partly as a result of Chris's intervention at a meeting of the Vietnam Solidarity Campaign in the summer of 1967 that the first big Grosvenor Square demonstration in October 1967 was organised.[8]

Then came 1968. This was a crucial turning-point for the International Socialists.[9] Chris, still only 25 years old, established himself as an indispensable part of the leadership. From 1964 to his death he was always a member of the leading body of the organisation under the various names of Working Committee, Executive Committee and Central Committee.

There is a wonderful description of Chris at the LSE in 1968:

> "We have to be absolutely clear about this," said Chris Harman from the platform of the LSE Old Theatre, as he always said when starting a speech. A groan went round the theatre and Harman brandished his moped crash helmet. "We must be quite clear what's happening. 1968 is a year of international revolution no less than 1793, 1830, 1848, 1917 and 1936. We are experiencing the re-birth of the international Marxist movement after over 30 years of defeat and hibernation." The audience of prematurely hard-bitten student lefties gathered to inaugurate the Revolutionary Socialist Students Federation looked impressed. Harman, although fairly widely disliked, was also widely respected as a Marxist intransigent. When he started evoking the Paris Commune, the Russian Revolution, the Barcelona uprising, he meant it. Militants were to be seen conferring about what did actually happen in 1830.[10]

In 2008 I chaired a meeting where Chris spoke on the legacy of 1968. In private conversation he commented sourly—but alas prophetically—that the reason why the fortieth anniversary was being commemorated was that most of us would be dead by the fiftieth. But in speaking he defended the spirit of 1968 as passionately as he had done four decades earlier. His book *The Fire Last Time* is a powerful record of

---

7:   *Labour Worker*, 5 August 1966.
8:   Harman, 1988, p149.
9:   See my article "Seizing the Time: Tony Cliff and 1968" (IS2: 118).
10: Widgery, 1976, p341. Widgery notes that he is quoting contemporary personal diaries, including his own, so it is not clear whether this was observed by Widgery himself or one of his friends.

the origins and impact of that legendary year.[11] It's now fashionable for bright young journalists to sneer at 1968. Chris centred his account on class struggle and separated the serious issues of human liberation from the trivia of lifestyle. "May 1968" was not about "student riots", as is often ignorantly repeated, but the biggest general strike in human history. Yet he never forgot the cultural dimension, above all with references to his beloved Bob Dylan, who provided a couple of chapter titles.

As the euphoria of 1968 began to subside, new arguments emerged. Chris, with his concern for clarity, sometimes lost friends. A notorious example was the memorial meeting for Vietnamese leader Ho Chi Minh, who died in September 1969. An eyewitness describes Chris's contribution:

> He addressed the meeting with a certain lack of style but no more than one would expect and proceeded in fairly forthright terms. He dealt first with Ho Chi Minh's contribution to the world revolutionary movement...
>
> After a while Harman proceeded to get on to the question of Ho Chi Minh's contribution to killing off the Trotskyist movement in North and South Vietnam. He expanded on various themes and pointed out that from the International Socialists' point of view, though they supported fully the Vietnamese people's struggle against American imperialism and had done a great deal practically in Britain on this theme, it was crucial to realise that Ho Chi Minh and the regime he had headed were not the answer to North Vietnam or Vietnam as a whole and what was eventually necessary was a workers' republic which would have to get rid of the present set-up. This went almost unnoticed by the audience... Anyway, Harman finished his speech and a lady aged about 55 to 60 got up and marched to the front and said that it was absolutely outrageous that people should just sit there and vegetate when somebody had just made a totally slanderous attack on the leader of the Vietnamese Revolution who had just died. Whereupon there was thunderous applause from the 60 percent of the audience who weren't in IS. Harman looked slightly surprised and slightly grieved and slightly pleased by the reaction to his address. Tariq Ali looked very unhappy indeed because he could see his meeting falling apart in front of him. At the back of the hall a Maoist shouted "Washington spy!" at Chris Harman, which seemed to please him further. The audience now became somewhat heated.[12]

11:   Harman, 1988.
12:   Widgery, 1976, p414. Again it is not clear who was actually the author of this account.

Chris had not quite finished with the academic world. In 1968-69 he was employed teaching social science at Enfield College of Technology (one of the forerunner colleges of Middlesex University). His contract was not renewed. He told me recently that he had been contacted by Eric Robinson, the head of department responsible for his dismissal, who had read Chris's *A People's History of the World* and now regretted his decision. Chris replied thanking him for liberating him from the academic world.

Chris had no patience with the division of labour which characterises the academic profession. Was he an economist, a sociologist, a historian, a political scientist or a philosopher? His work spread cheerfully over a range of disciplines. Ask an academic historian a question, and often you will be told, "It's not my period." To the author of *A People's History of the World*, such professional demarcations were an utter irrelevance.

Chris was an "organic intellectual" in Gramsci's sense of the term.[13] It should be remembered that when Chris wrote his review of John M Cammett's book on Gramsci in 1968 (*IS1: 32*) the Italian Marxist was little known in Britain, other than through the dubious interpretations of Stalinists or the New Left Review team. Chris was one of the first British writers to point to Gramsci's importance; later he would vigorously defend the revolutionary content of Gramsci's work as against the Eurocommunist misrepresentation that it pointed to the abandonment of class politics (*IS1: 98/99*).

1968 unleashed new waves of struggle around the globe, and a new internationalism was born. Chris embarked on one of the activities that would continue for the rest of his life—travelling abroad to meet socialist activists, to discuss with them and to learn from them. At Easter 1969 he attended an international seminar on socialism and revolution organised by students at Prague University while Czechoslovakia was still under Russian occupation (*SW* 26/4/1969). There is a memorable description of Chris's intervention by the writer John Berger:

> A political activist from London described the daily struggle in British factories to resist anti-trade-unionist legislation and his group's long-term aim of creating workers' councils to act as soviets. Could some of the lessons they had learned apply to the Czech situation? His was the longest and most passionate speech, which remained uninterrupted. After it a Czech student

---

13: Gramsci distinguished "traditional" intellectuals—such as academics who claim to be autonomous of the class struggle—from "organic" intellectuals who act directly on behalf of one of the contending classes.

remarked, "Do you know what most of us would reply to all that you have just said? We'd ask you whether you had read Dostoyevsky's *The Possessed*." The activist, who had held the floor with such force, shook his head—not to answer "No": he had surely read it—but as though to free his face from a mesh of cobwebs into which he had mysteriously and inadvertently walked.[14]

In September 1970 he was in Jordan when the government attacked Palestinian organisations and began to drive them out of the country. *Socialist Worker* carried a front-page lead by "Chris Harman just returned from Amman" which described how "the shells have been tearing apart the corrugated iron huts, tents and crude concrete dwellings where the refugees somehow eke out an existence. Whole blocks of flats have been blown apart in order to 'flush out' a single sniper" (*SW* 26/9/1970).

By now he had become a full-time worker for the party; he remained one for the rest of his life. Although his main work was on publications, he also took a close interest in day to day activity. George Paizis, an old comrade from the LSE, joined IS in 1970 and rapidly became North London District Secretary. He recalls: "Chris helped me a lot. He was on the end of the phone every day, whenever I needed him. He would listen to all my questions and suggestions and come up with ideas".[15]

At the end of 1968 Chris took over as editor of *International Socialism*. Under Mike Kidron and Nigel Harris the journal had played a vital role in developing the IS analysis of the world. Now, with the rapid recruitment in 1968 and the turn to industrial struggle that followed, the journal had to be more directly oriented to party building. Chris's article on "Party and Class" (*IS1: 35*) was an important contribution to the debate on democratic centralism that took place in the organisation during 1968; it has been frequently reproduced since.[16] A special issue devoted to Trotsky's writings on fascism and the united front provided the foundation on which IS anti-fascist work was developed during the 1970s (*IS1: 38/39*). Three articles by

---

14: Berger, 1972, p241. Chris is not named, but the description is unmistakable to anyone who knew him at that time.

15: Interview with George Paizis, October 2008.

16: Since Chris is sometimes seen as merely a disciple of Cliff it is worth noting that this article contained criticisms of Cliff's views on both Lenin and Luxemburg. In particular Chris dissented from Cliff's formulation in *Rosa Luxemburg* that "for Marxists in the advanced industrial countries, Lenin's original position can much less serve as a guide than Rosa Luxemburg's", a formulation which Cliff changed in the edition of *Rosa Luxemburg* issued shortly after Chris's article. (See Cliff 2001, p113 for the text of the changes.) Influence was not all one way.

Jim Higgins laid out the foundations of revolutionary tactics and strategy in the trade union movement (*IS1:* 45/46/47). Chris also saw the importance of the journal in developing a broader socialist culture. He published Peter Sedgwick's remarkable article on Orwell (*IS1:* 37). I personally had several arguments with Chris in which he sharply attacked my enthusiasm for Sartre, arguing that Sartre was an apologist for Stalinism. Then, rather paradoxically, he urged me to write a defence of Sartre (*IS1:* 45/46). He was thus of enormous encouragement to me, as he must have been to many other comrades, in developing as a writer.

Chris relinquished the editorship at the end of 1971, but resumed it in September 1973. Again the journal, now a monthly, had to steer the organisation through a difficult period which saw the Chilean coup, the Middle East war, the end of the post-war boom and the intense industrial struggle culminating in the defeat of the Heath government. Chris's contribution went far beyond what appeared under his own signature. The piece "April Dream in Portugal" published under my name was substantially rewritten by Chris with a number of additional passages (*IS1:* 69). I believe "Towards a Rank and File Movement" by Andreas Nagliatti (*IS1:* 66), which laid down the IS position on this important question, actually had a substantial input from Chris.

Chris also worked on *Socialist Worker*, then edited by Roger Protz. Roger had developed the weekly paper from a rather scruffy four-pager launched in 1968 to a well-designed 16-page paper. The Heath government of 1970-4 saw the biggest upturn in class struggle in Britain since the 1920s. In 1972 the Saltley Gates picket mobilised thousands of engineering workers in support of the miners; a few months later the threat of a general strike ensured the release of five dockers imprisoned under Heath's anti-union laws. In 1974 a second miners' strike led to the fall of the Heath government. Analysing the Communist Party's role in recent industrial struggles (*IS1:* 63) Chris concluded that "in an increasing number of struggles, the CP as a party refuses to give a lead of any sort... The short term aim of a revolutionary socialist organisation like IS must be to replace the CP as the main focus to which militants in industry look for a lead."

At the same time came the overthrow of the dictatorship in Portugal and the start of a wave of mass workers' struggle. Chris reacted to this from the very beginning, insisting that there was a pre-revolutionary situation in Portugal; often he seemed to be nagging comrades to urge us to do all we could to intervene. The next tumultuous 18 months proved him right. He visited Portugal more than once, to see things for himself, and to discuss with members of the Portuguese revolutionary left. However, Chris shared with Cliff the belief that the choice ahead was between socialist revolution and the return of the far right. In autumn 1975 he wrote in "Portugal: The Latest Phase" (*IS1:* 83), "There is no possibility of evading for more than a few months (at most) sharp, armed clashes between the classes." He and Cliff both underestimated reformism, which in the shape of Mario Soares's Socialist Party saved the system.

The 1970s were also stormy years inside the party. In 1974 Cliff made a number of demands for changes in *Socialist Worker*, which led to the removal of Roger Protz. Paul Foot took over, and then in 1975 Chris became editor. There were new challenges for the paper—the way in which the trade union bureaucracy had gone along with Labour's "Social Contract", the shift from major national strikes to smaller struggles like that by Asian women at Grunwicks for union rights, the rise of unemployment and the launch of the Right to Work Campaign, and the threat of racism and the far right. Chris supported Cliff's policy of developing a paper not written for workers but substantially written by workers.

The argument over *Socialist Worker* led to a more general internal dispute, which at the end of 1975 led to the departure of not only Roger Protz, but other veteran leaders from the 60s like Jim Higgins and John Palmer, as well as a number of trade union activists, notably in Birmingham. Chris sided with Cliff throughout this dispute.[17]

So it must have been a shock to Chris when he in turn came into conflict with Cliff. In early 1978, with Cliff's support, Chris was removed from the editorship and *Socialist Worker* was "relaunched". The result came to be known as the "punk paper". The aim, to relate to the new audience around the rapidly growing Anti Nazi League, was laudable. The means employed, a paper with more coverage of sport and music, and even a soap opera style serial, but with diluted politics, and less coverage of the—admittedly quiescent—industrial struggle, were more questionable. That summer a conference of the Socialist Workers Party (SWP), as the organisation was now known, voted to reject the new orientation of the paper. The four journalists primarily responsible—Paul Foot, Jim Nichol, Laurie Flynn and Pete Marsden—resigned. Chris was restored to the editorship, but within days Cliff manoeuvred to ensure that he was forced to stand down again.[18] Cliff himself then assumed the editorship.

17:   In Jim Higgins's account Chris is depicted as the archetypal Cliff loyalist, whose role was to produce "the justification for Cliff's latest wheeze"—Higgins, 1997, p116. Jim felt somewhat threatened by the younger generation, and though he was only twelve years older than Chris he used to refer to him as "the boy".

18:   For a detailed account by a participant see Steve Jefferys, "The politics behind the row

Not surprisingly, Chris found this "disturbing", but he viewed the situation positively. He could now do what he felt necessary to build the organisation without having to consult with Cliff twice a week. He had to think for himself.[19]

Chris was effectively marginalised within his own organisation. He was still under 40 and had an impressive record of publications. He could easily have returned to the academic world, and achieved much greater comfort and prosperity for the last 30 years of his life. I don't think the possibility even crossed his mind. He was totally devoted to the party and to socialist principles.

At the beginning of 1979 he wrote a remarkable article entitled "The Crisis of the European Revolutionary Left" (*IS2: 4*). This analysed the problems faced by revolutionaries in various parts of Europe and was an important complement to ideas Cliff was developing about the downturn, raising major questions about how the party should reorient to a changing situation. Looking back on the early 1970s Chris noted that "the expectations of the revolutionary left look absurd in retrospect", and argued that "In a downturn in the class struggle, it is the duty of revolutionary organisations to relate to all sorts of movements that develop outside the workplaces among oppressed and exploited groups. But it has to do this while never forgetting that the agent of revolutionary change lies elsewhere...the link with the working class movement has to be an active one, not merely a rhetorical one."

At the end of 1979 he became editor of *Socialist Review*, a position he described as a "consolation prize". *Socialist Review* had been launched the previous year, also to relate to the ANL milieu. Its first issues had been lively but somewhat chaotic. Chris transformed the magazine into an important educational tool for the party as the ascent of Thatcherism made life a lot more difficult for revolutionaries.

Throughout this period Chris had been turning out not only a flood of journalistic writing, but some much more substantial contributions to Marxist understanding.[20] Cliff's work on state capitalism had been at the

on the paper", in the Steve Jefferys Archive, Modern Records Centre, University of Warwick, MSS.244/2/1/2

19: Interview with Chris, April 2009. Chris gave his own account of the dispute in his article "The Revolutionary Press" (*IS2: 24*).

20: I've only mentioned a small part of Chris's enormous output. Many readers will be indignant that I have omitted their favourite article or pamphlet. To cover everything would require an article four times as long which would have read like a bibliography rather than an appreciation.

centre of Chris's intellectual work since the early 60s,[21] but he did not simply parrot Cliff's conclusions. Rather he produced a number of important pieces which complemented Cliff's work.

In 1967, for the fiftieth anniversary of the Russian Revolution, Chris had written "How the Revolution Was Lost" (*IS1:* 30), frequently reproduced as a pamphlet. Cliff in his book on Russia had given an account of the structures of Russian state capitalism. What was missing was an account of the origins of the system. This was an important question since Cliff—unlike other theorists of state capitalism—had always defended Bolshevism and denied that Leninism led to Stalinism. Chris's carefully argued account showed how the revolution had been defeated.

In 1974 came his first book, *Bureaucracy and Revolution in Eastern Europe*.[22] This was in a sense the sequel to Cliff's 1952 book *Stalin's Satellites in Europe*. Cliff had shown how the Eastern European Stalinist states had come into existence. Chris's account showed the internal contradictions that became ever more visible. Cliff had argued that Stalinism produced its own gravedigger, the working class. Chris gave a vivid narrative account of how workers had fought back, in East Germany in 1953, Hungary in 1956 and Czechoslovakia in 1968. The revised edition under the title *Class Struggle in Eastern Europe* took the story forward to Poland in 1980 and the rise of Solidarity.[23] The epilogue came in 1990 with Chris's article "The Storm Breaks" (*IS2:* 46), where he argued that the collapse of "Communism" was "neither a step forward nor a step backwards, but a step sideways [sic]".

Asked if the failure of the Russian Revolution had been inevitable, IS members would reply that the revolution failed because it did not spread, that if the German Revolution had succeeded things would have been different. But most of us had only the haziest idea of what actually happened in Germany in 1918-23. Chris's *The Lost Revolution* (1982) provided a readable and concrete account of the process. He drew on Pierre Broué's monumental study[24] (only available in English in 2004) and on a range of German-language sources.[25]

The German Revolution raised many questions of strategy and

21: Chris's major contributions in the field of political economy are dealt with in Joseph Choonara's piece in this issue.

22: Harman, 1974.

23: Harman, 1983.

24: Broué, 2004.

25: Chris had a remarkable capacity for reading foreign languages. At speaking he was not so successful. Though he had read Althusser in the original, when I visited France with him I had to ask where the toilet was on his behalf.

tactics—ultra-leftism, the united front, the call for a "workers' government", etc. It is doubtful if an academic with no practical experience of revolutionary organisation could have written the book. Take, for example, Chris's account of the crisis in the first year of the German Communist Party. A large section of the membership held wildly ultra-left positions, such as refusal to participate in elections and to work in the trade unions. Such positions were a serious problem for the party, limiting its capacity to intervene and to recruit widely in the working class. The party leadership forced confrontation and lost half the membership. As Chris wrote:

> The party leadership would have done better to have pushed through its own policies at the congress and then taken on and removed the most irreconcilable opposition figures in the localities one at a time—especially since in the months that followed it became clear that different forms of impatience were driving the different oppositionists in completely different directions.[26]

Chris was doubtless thinking of his own experience at the LSE and of the rapid recruitment of revolutionary students into IS in the aftermath of 1968.[27]

In spring 1982 Chris returned to the editorship of *Socialist Worker*, a post he would keep for the next 22 years. It was a bleak time. Thatcher was on the attack, and the level of resistance was low. The SWP had decided to wind up its rank and file trade union groups and the Right to Work Campaign. Tony Benn's attempt to rally the Labour left had passed its peak. Now Thatcher was fanning the flames of nationalism with the Falklands war, which gave Chris what he later called a "golden opportunity" to reorient the paper. There were organisational problems too, and initially Chris was spending 60 to 80 hours a week on editing.

Through two decades Chris steered the paper through a long downturn punctuated with occasional sharp rises in the level of struggle, trying to neither miss opportunities nor arouse false hopes. Again he was a central figure in the leadership; his quarrel with Cliff was made up. He was a regular speaker at meetings around the country. Though never as impressive an orator as Cliff or Paul Foot, he was a lucid speaker whose talks had a powerful intellectual content.

Throughout the 12 months of the miners' strike it was the central

---

26: Harman, 1982, p153.
27: Broué's account of this episode is far more sympathetic to the manoeuvres of the KPD leadership—Broué, 2004, pp317-321.

question in *Socialist Worker*. From 10 March 1984 to 9 March 1985 every issue of *Socialist Worker* but one had a front-page lead on the strike. In the early months the paper concentrated on proposing strategies which could enable the strike to achieve victory. As it became a long war of attrition, *Socialist Worker* focused more on the need to build solidarity with a defensive struggle. Even in the last week of the strike *Socialist Worker* headlined "Fight On", and argued that "staying out remains the only way to ensure a settlement which will keep the union intact...and ready to fight off future attacks" (*SW* 2/3/1985). The paper never admitted that defeat was inevitable until the hard core of militant miners themselves accepted the reality.

Chris was a theoretician as well as a journalist, and this helped him to guide the paper through difficult situations. After the poll tax riot in 1990 there was a virulent press witch-hunt against "anarchists" alleged to be responsible for the violence. *Socialist Worker* responded with an editorial headed "No Wonder They Fight Back", seeing the riot as a response to unemployment, student poverty and police harassment. "Of course no socialist believes rioting will beat the poll tax, but neither should any socialist condemn the howl of rage which filled the fashionable West End last Saturday." Doubtless Chris remembered what he himself had written about the March Action in Germany in 1921.[28] There was a constant interaction between theory and practice.

In autumn 1992, when the Tories announced a programme of pit closures, *Socialist Worker* headlined "General Strike Now!" (*SW* 24/10/1992). This was not a rush of blood to Chris's head, but resulted from the fact that the paper had a network of organisers and supporters throughout the country, and was able to respond to the mood of anger within the working class movement.

The revolutionary hopes which we had shared in the aftermath of 1968 had evaporated, but Chris continued to use the paper as an organiser and an educator, preparing the new cadres who would respond to whatever opportunities the years ahead might bring. Chris gave particular attention to developing a team of journalists. Among many tributes that appeared after his death, there were several from journalists who had worked with him.

Kevin Ovenden recalled that:

Chris had a rare gift for crystallising a nuanced political position or difficult concept into a few, vivid words of plain English... The effort he expended, and made those of us working on the paper sweat over too, to make even

---

28: Harman, 1982, pp192-220.

a single headline accurately capture a complex reality and cut through it, was an indication of how seriously he took the task of communicating our tradition to a mass audience.

Hazel Croft remembered him "bringing editorial meetings down to earth by insisting that the paper covered the hardships and concerns of its working class readers".[29]

In the 1978 dispute Chris and Paul Foot had been bitterly opposed, but Chris never let personal grudges interfere with his political judgment. In 1984 he persuaded Paul to write a weekly column for *Socialist Worker*, saying, "We'll like it, but that's not the point. It will do you good".[30]

In 1994 Chris wrote an important article on Islamic fundamentalism, "The Prophet and the Proletariat" (*IS2:* 64). Beginning with the Marxist analysis of religion, Chris set out to give a detailed account of the social context which produced Islamism, with extensive examples from Egypt, Algeria, Iran and Sudan. He also made a creative application of Tony Cliff's theory of deflected permanent revolution. Stressing the contradictory nature of Islamism, he concluded:

> The left has made two mistakes in relation to the Islamists in the past. The first has been to write them off as fascists, with whom we have nothing in common. The second has been to see them as "progressives" who must not be criticised.

He urged socialists to aim to "win some of the young people who support it [Islamism] to a very different, independent, revolutionary socialist perspective".[31]

Chris's most substantial work came in 1999 with his massive *A People's History of the World*.[32] It contained a vast amount of information on different periods and topics, but was given its focus by the consistent attempt to apply the Marxist method to the whole of human history. Chris drew on a lifetime's breadth of reading, but he also needed to fill the gaps with intense labour. Though carrying on with his editing and general political duties, he managed to get to the British Library a couple of times a week, where, as he once told me during a hurried lunch, he read four books in a day.

29: See http://tinyurl.com/yazcyc6
30: Foot, 1990, p xv.
31: The journalist Nick Cohen quite disgracefully added the word "secretly" to this sentence in order to give it a meaning diametrically opposed to Chris's intention—Cohen 2007.
32: Harman, 1999.

With its attention to detail it was a valuable educational resource, which helped to give revolutionary activists, constantly caught up in the short-term preoccupation with the next paper sale, a sense of their place in the long sweep of human history. Despite its title, this was not the "history from below" much promoted in the late 20th century. Certainly Chris opened his account with some lines from Brecht:

Who built Thebes of the seven gates?
In the books you will find the names of kings.
Did the kings haul up the lumps of rock?

Human history could not have happened without the labour of nameless millions. But for Chris it was equally important to grasp history from above, to understand how our rulers have ruled us, so that we can learn how to overthrow them. Academic specialists may find errors in the treatment of particular periods and countries, but few academics would have dared to take on such an ambitious venture.

The new century brought enormous new opportunities with the post-Seattle anti-capitalist movement and then the anti-war movement. As Chris wrote in "Anti-Capitalism: Theory and Practice" (*IS2*: 88):

Hundreds of thousands, perhaps millions of people are beginning, for the first time, to challenge the global system... No one can dictate what they think and how their ideas develop. But that does not mean there are not arguments over ideas, or that any of us should abstain from those arguments... It is up to all of us to help build the new movement—and to help it to learn to deal with these issues.

In 2004 he retired from *Socialist Worker* and again became editor of *International Socialism*, which he had first edited 35 years earlier. The new period also produced problems, and with the Respect debacle the party went through a difficult patch, which Chris analysed in his article "The Crisis in Respect" (*IS2*: 117).

Just after his remarkable appearance before a committee of the US Senate in 2005, George Galloway addressed a packed rally in the Friends Meeting House in London where he was, quite justifiably, greeted with enormous enthusiasm. In the course of his account Galloway mentioned that while waiting to appear he had smoked a Cuban cigar. This produced a spontaneous wave of applause. I felt no obligation to endorse Fidel Castro's export trade; glancing around the hall I saw that Chris too was sitting with his hands calmly folded. A principled gesture or a reversion to the sectarian habits of our 1960s youth?

Revolutionaries have a double duty: to encourage the maximum possible unity in struggle and to seek the greatest possible clarity in understanding the situation. Did Chris always achieve the correct balance? Perhaps not. But he had absolutely nothing in common with those whose only response to new initiatives is to stand back and predict failure—the ultimate soft option. Right up to his death Chris remained an indispensable figure in the SWP leadership.

Chris had a broad range of cultural interests, and one reason among so many for lamenting his untimely death is that he was never able to develop these in writing. As John Rose reminds us (*SW* 10/11/2009), he had a great admiration for Flaubert's novel *Sentimental Education*, which depicted the 1848 revolution in France. A critical study by Chris would have been enthralling.

He also had a surprisingly wide knowledge of popular culture. I remember him intervening in a discussion on Walter Benjamin with a reference to the Honeycombs.[33] Only sport eluded him. Last year at a book launch for Dave Renton's *CLR. James: Cricket's Philosopher King* he appalled many of his own comrades by arguing that James's writings on cricket were no more significant than a Labour MP professing to be an Arsenal supporter.

The last discussion I had with Chris was during the lunch break at an SWP day school on Lenin, just five days before he died. Referring to Althusser's claim that Marxism is not about human happiness but about "a change in the mode of production",[34] I asked him if he thought socialism was about happiness. He frowned at me, clearly feeling the question was too complex for my simplistic formulation, and said, "It depends what you mean by happiness." We had no time to pursue the question, and now I shall never know what he thought. I do know that few people compare to Chris in the way he devoted his life and his powerful intellect to the struggle for a fairer and happier world.

33: The first band with a female drummer to reach Number One (August 1964).
34: Sartre, Gavi and Victor, 1974, p197.

References

Berger, John, 1972, *Selected Essays and Articles* (Penguin).

Broué, Pierre, 2004, *The German Revolution, 1917-1923* (Brill).

Charlton, John, 2009, *Don't You Hear the H-bombs Thunder?* (North East Labour History/Merlin).

Cliff, Tony, 2001, *Selected Writings: Volume One* (Bookmarks), www.marxists.org/archive/cliff/ works/1959/rosalux/note.htm

Cohen, Nick, 2007, *What's Left?: How Liberals Lost Their Way* (Fourth Estate).

Foot, Paul, 1990, *Words as Weapons* (Verso).

Harman, Chris, 1974, *Bureaucracy and Revolution in Eastern Europe* (Pluto).

Harman, Chris, 1982, *The Lost Revolution* (Bookmarks).

Harman, Chris, 1983, *Class Struggles in Eastern Europe, 1945-1983* (Pluto).

Harman, Chris, 1988, *The Fire Last Time: 1968 and After* (Bookmarks).

Harman, Chris, 1999, *A People's History of the World* (Bookmarks).

Higgins, Jim, 1997, *More Years for the Locust* (IS Group), www.marxists.org/archive/higgins/1997/ locust/index.htm

Sartre, Jean-Paul, Philippe Gavi and Pierre Victor, 1974, *On a Raison de se Révolter* (Gallimard).

Widgery, David, 1976, *The Left in Britain 1956-1968* (Penguin).

The emperor has no clothes

Chris Harman

*A review of Gregory Elliott, **Althusser: The Detour of Theory** (Haymarket Books, 2009), £19.99*

The economic crisis of the last two years has provided an extra impetus to the revival of interest in Marxism. A new generation is beginning to reach out to ideas that we were told were finished once and for all in the aftermath of 1989.

But no generation develops its conceptions without borrowing from what went before. So some of the best names associated with Marxism are still ones that made their first impact more than three decades ago, and young would-be Marxists can find themselves confronting debates from a previous era. One of the names re-emerging is that of the French Communist philosopher Louis Althusser, who died in 1990. There is barely an issue of *Historical Materialism* that does not carry some article on him; his influence pervades the North American journal *Rethinking Marxism*; and long-established academics will refer to his ideas as if they can be taken for granted.

Yet from the moment Althusser began to put his ideas forward in the mid-1960s they were met with a very strong challenge from many of us who regarded ourselves as revolutionary Marxists. We saw his approach as not merely problematic but pernicious. The republication after more than 20 years of Gregory Elliott's critical, even if half-admiring, account of his ideas provides an opportunity to explain why.

Althusser's most influential books, *For Marx* and *Reading Capital*,[1] first appeared when Western capitalism was still going through its longest ever boom, while the state capitalist countries of the supposedly "Communist" bloc seemed to have recovered their stability after the 1956 traumas of Khrushchev's denunciation of Stalin and the Hungarian Revolution.

The rival belief systems on both sides in the Cold War had one great thing in common: they denied the possibility of the mass of people changing society. This was true of the "consensus" ideologies in the West preached by theorists like Talcott Parsons, Robert Merton and Daniel Bell. It was also true of the caricature of Marxism which prevailed in the East, where Marx's vision of the working class emancipating itself had been replaced by identification with accumulation of the means of production in one country. The Marxist tradition in the West suffered not merely from its marginalisation by anti-Communism but even more by its creative impulses continually being undermined by edicts from Moscow on everything from philosophy to genetics.

The first big break in this wall of intellectual conservatism had come with the events of 1956. A significant number of Communist workers and intellectuals broke with Stalinism without swinging into the Western camp and what was known as the "New Left" was born.[2]

The New Left did not manage to sustain itself as a living movement for long—this was, after all, a time in which capitalism was expanding and providing real reforms. Nor did the current have a homogenous conception of social change: its leading figures fudged the issue of reform and revolution. But it did begin to create a new tradition of Marxism that challenged the orthodoxies of East and West by stressing the role of the mass of people in making history. Hence the impact of Jean-Paul Sartre, courageously opposing France's Algerian War as well as trying to find room within Marxism for his existentialist emphasis on individual human choice. Against the dehumanised Stalinist caricature of Marxism, the New Left raised the banner of "Marxist humanism".

Much of the inspiration came from the works of the young Marx—they had been published in German just 25 years before and were

---

1:   They both appeared in French in 1965 as *Pour Marx* and *Lire le Capital*, which included essays by his disciples as well as by Althusser himself; the English translation of *Pour Marx* as *For Marx* appeared in 1969; an English translation of *Lire le Capital* as *Reading Capital* was published in 1970, excluding essays in the original by Roger Establet, Jacques Rancière, and Pierre Macherey. I quote from both the English and French editions of *Pour Marx*, and from the French edition of *Lire le capital*.

2:   Blackledge, 2006.

only then becoming available in other languages.[3] They also reached back to the writings from the great movement of revolutionary action that followed the Russian Revolution. For some that meant the discovery of Trotsky's writings—pure manna to those brought up on the dry crusts of Stalinism. For others the image of Rosa Luxemburg was very important.[4] And for those delving into the Marxist method there were the philosophical writings of Karl Korsch, Antonio Gramsci and, above all, George Lukács.

Lukács had begun his major work, *History and Class Consciousness*, as a member of the Hungarian workers' council government of 1919. It not only gave full expression to the revolutionary hopes of those years, but also provided an account of society very similar to that later to be found in Marx's as yet unpublished early writings. The central concept was "reification"—literally "turning into a thing". For Lukács capitalism was a system under which human activity took on the character of a system of things that oppressed human beings. He provided an account of the history of philosophy, which reached its pinnacle in Hegel's writings in the aftermath of the French Revolution, as a history of philosophers' attempts to decipher this reality. Lukács argued success in this task was only possible by identification with the struggles of the class whose crystallised labour constituted the edifice of capitalist society, the working class. The revolutionary action of that class could overcome reification both in practice and in theory.

Lukács' account was highly abstract, with little about how class struggle actually develops and how workers concretely move to class consciousness—on these questions it was less interesting than, for instance, what Gramsci had to say in those passages of his prison notebooks concerned with contradictory consciousness, let alone Trotsky's writings on strategy and tactics. Nevertheless, it was immensely important in reasserting the central thesis of Marxism—that the working class produced by capitalism could be its gravedigger.

Marxist humanism, like the New Left of which it was part, could move in two directions. It could lead back towards a version of reformism that used talk of humanism to blunt any stress on class struggle—a tempting approach for Stalinist parties making their own reformism more explicit. But it could also lead towards a thoroughgoing revolutionary socialism from below, which is why *International Socialism* was born from it just as much as *New Left Review*, printing articles on Korsch and translating

---

3:    The first English edition of Marx's 1844 manuscripts, translated by the blind Scottish Communist philosopher Martin Milligan, did not appear until 1959.

4:    This was when Tony Cliff's political biography *Rosa Luxemburg* first appeared—Cliff, 1959.

articles by Lukács and his disciple Lucien Goldman. It meant that when new movements of opposition to capitalism and imperialism began to arise from 1967 onwards there were at least the embryos of organisations trying to draw them in the direction of "socialism from below".

It was then that someone who seems not be have been stirred at all by the great ferment of 1956 arrived on the scene—Louis Althusser. *For Marx* and *Reading Capital* set out to demolish the central tenets of the sort of Marxism we had been reconstructing. These works insisted:[5]

(1) Marxism is not "humanism" in the sense of a theory about how human beings can take control of their own lives.

(2) Marxism is not a theory developed by the workers' movement as it became conscious of the society in which it struggled, but a "science" evolving in the same way as Althusser saw the physical sciences emerging—as the work of a specialist group of scientists guided only by a concern for knowledge. The mass of people could never escape from the grip of ideology—pre-scientific notions and beliefs—even when they are engaged in struggles that shake society to its foundations. The scientific elite can recognise that "ideologies" are necessary to the masses, but will themselves see through such primitive notions.

(3) The truth of theory is not tested by the practice of the masses, but purely by the degree to which it agrees with criteria for truth arrived at by science itself.

(4) The unity of theory and practice in fact means a particular form of practice ("theoretical practice"), with its own means and methods of production.

(5) Friedrich Engels's words about turning Hegel upside down are misleading. The Marxist dialectic is quite different to the Hegelian dialectic. The key to understanding society does not lie in seeing it as a "totality", bound together by a single unitary force, but rather in seeing it as the articulation of different structures—the economic, ideological, political, etc—all developing at different speeds.

(6) "Historical materialism" is the specialist study of the way in which different structures combine in any particular "social formation" at any point in time. "Dialectical materialism" is simply the name given to the scientific method which underlies other studies as disparate as physics or psychoanalysis. Once this is grasped, you have to throw out of the window

---

5:    The list of major points is based on one I drew up when writing a critique of Althusserian ideas many years ago, elements of which appeared in my article of 1983, "Philosophy and Revolution"—Harman, 1983. All the points are born out in Elliott's text.

all the dialectical terminology of Hegel—"the unity of opposites", "the transformation of quantity into quality", "the negation of the negation", "freedom and necessity". Much more useful is Mao Zedong's distinction between "principal" and "secondary" contradictions, each with its "principal" and "secondary" aspect.

(7) Modes of production are combinations of different elements, with a different determining element for every distinct mode. The development of the forces of production—of human beings' interaction with nature to obtain a livelihood—does not play a determining role in producing a shift from one mode of production to another. Rather, the "relations of production" determined "the forces of production".

(8) "Revolutionary crises" are not the expression of some single, fundamental contradiction in society, rooted in economic relations, but of a particular "conjuncture" when the crisis in any one structure is "over-determined" by the simultaneous occurrence of crises in other structures.

(9) There was a clear breaking point ("coupure") in the development of Marx's ideas which is revealed by a "symptomatic reading" of his texts. In his youth, influenced by Hegel and Feuerbach, Marx spoke of "human alienation", of history as the domination of human beings by the products of their own activity. But as he matured he came to see this was all nonsense. History was not the expression of an "alienated human subject", but "a process without a subject". The "works of the break" in the mid-1840s and those that followed represented a complete change in Marx's approach, or "problematic".

Althusser's Marx and the actual Marx

Althusser's approach was not merely slightly different to that developed by those of us inspired by the revolutionary insurgency of 1956. It was in many respects the complete opposite, since Marxism was no longer seen as a theory connected to the struggle for human emancipation from the alienated structures of capitalism, in which self-conscious self-activity of workers plays the pivotal role.

Althusser did at points suggest that the Stalinist version of Marxism got some things wrong. But he shared with the Stalinist caricature the rejection of the notion that workers, from being the objects of history, could become its subjects—that they could supersede their own alienation (or, in Hegelian terminology, "negate the negation"). His hardest polemics were precisely on this point. Stalin's "expulsion of the 'negation of the negation' from the domain of the Marxist dialectic", he wrote, "might be evidence of theoretical perspicacity".[6] As Elliott puts it, "while noting that 'Stalinist dogmatism'" had "as yet not been buried by history", the "butt of his criticism" was "focused on the return to Hegel associated with Lukács, Korsch and to a lesser extent Gramsci".[7]

Althusser's "symptomatic reading" of Marx ignored the actual content of Marx's own writings. The key Althusserian text on Marx's method was the unpublished "Introduction" to the *Contribution to the Critique of Political Economy* (not to be confused with the famous "Preface"). This was written at the same time as the manuscript that constitutes the *Grundrisse*. The *Grundrisse* is marked by many of the "Hegelian" formulations that Althusser claimed Marx had broken with, and, as Elliott recognises, "is a protracted challenge to Althusser's periodisation of historical materialism".[8] Yet the text is ignored in Althusser's account of Marx—"an astonishing lacuna".[9]

Theoretical holes

The fact that Althusser diverged from Marx's own position did not, of course, prove that his theory was mistaken. It failed because it contained theoretical problems he could not resolve.

First, there was the question of how we validate claims to truth—that is, how we test what we believe against the reality of the world around us. Althusser argues that we can only know the external world through our conceptions of it. However hard we try, we cannot escape from this conceptual prison house. Despite his attacks on Hegel, Althusser was in this repeating arguments made very well by Hegel in his *Phenomenology of Mind*[10] to the effect that we cannot give any fixity to the fleeting impressions of the world that pass before our eyes without the use of concepts. This then raises the problem of how we know these concepts are correct. Hegel gave two answers. The first was that reason can eventually arrive at a total view of the world which provides proof of the truthfulness of the concepts that determine how we perceive things. This answer was inadequate because it assumed that thought alone could prove its own objectivity and provide

---

6:    Quoted in Elliott, 1987, p86. All my quotes are from the 1987 edition; the main text of the new edition is identical, but the pagination is slightly different.

7:    Elliott, 1987, p89.

8:    Elliott, 1987, p132.

9:    Elliott 1987, p132.

10: See Hegel, 1964, pp131-227.

a justification for the particular concepts we use.[11] Hegel's second answer, never fully developed, was to argue at various points in his writings that we can test the objectivity of our concepts not simply by "contemplative reason" but by "practical reason"—that is by action which, by attempting to mould the world around us, shows the reality or otherwise of the ideas we hold. We can grasp reality truthfully because we make and remake it.[12] It is this notion of the role of human practical activity that Marx uses to go beyond the Hegelian approach, "putting it on its feet", as he put it:

> The question whether objective truth can be attributed to human thinking is not a question of theory but is a practical question. Man must prove the truth, ie, the reality and power, the this-sidedness of his thinking, in practice. The dispute over the reality or non-reality of thinking which is isolated from practice is a purely scholastic question... All mysteries which lead theory to mysticism find their rational solution in human practice and in the comprehension of this practice.[13]

Althusser, by turning his back on practice as a test of theory, ends up with a schema very much like that put across by the conservative interpretation of Hegel, in which truth is arrived at simply by the application of reason to concepts—baptised "theoretical practice" by Althusser.[14]

11: For Hegel it was not the thought of the individual, but of what he called the "Absolute Spirit"—variously interpreted as meaning the mind of god which humanity came to understand though history, or the collective knowledge humanity arrived at in the course of its history. Hegel's view is usually described as an "objective idealism"—ideas determine the world, but not the random ideas of individuals.

12: There is an important ambiguity in Hegel's writings on this. The social world, that is human history, has been made by human action; it is the crystallisation of human action going back to the moment our ancestors descended from the trees. Because of this we can endeavour to "get inside" historical events by grasping the interaction between people's motives and the world around them. But this is not true of the natural world; we did not make it. This is something which Hegel seems to recognise at certain points. But his system seems to imply that "spirit" or "objective mind" makes the natural world and that human thought, as part of "spirit", can understand the natural world also from the inside. For an important discussion on such ambiguities in Hegel, see Lukács, 1978.

13: Marx, 1845.

14: In Althusser's rather obtuse formulation, Generality ll, Theory, operates on Generality l, Concepts, to produce Generality lll, Truth. The similarities are marked with the crude "trinity" version of Hegelianism in which the purely conceptual interaction of thesis and antithesis produces synthesis. For such a static, purely conceptualist reading of Hegel, see Stace, 1955. In fact, Althusser's position involves a backsliding from Hegel—something he himself admitted when he confessed to his preference for Spinoza over Hegel.

Associated with this static philosophic approach was a static analysis of society. The account of modes of production in *For Marx* and *Reading Capital* provided no room for one mode of production to give way to another, since any particular society is dominated by a single, unchanging, structure of structures. As Elliott puts it, his method "endows social formations with such consistency (modes of production generate their own 'conditions of existence') that their reproduction as unities is ensured, their transformations theoretically unthinkable".[15] Althusser's collaborator, Jacques Rancière, later admitted that "it superimposed 'a Comtean or Durkheimian type of sociology' concerned with maintaining the social order upon historical materialism".[16] Its attempt to overcome the crudities of Stalinist Marxism in fact involved incorporating into it notions from the "structuralism" of the anthropologist Claude Lévi-Strauss,[17] whose notion that human behaviour in all societies as determined by unchanging structures was the fashionable equivalent in mainstream French intellectual life of the structural functionalism reigning in American sociology.[18]

Missing is precisely what is central in Marx and Engels—the changing processes by which human beings carve out a living from nature. These are seen in *The German Ideology*, *The Poverty of Philosophy*, the Preface to *A Contribution to the Critique of Political Economy* and *The Role of Labour in the Transition from Ape to Man* as continually disturbing old "fixed fast" social relations—and the ideologies that sustain them. For Althusser, as Elliott puts it, "the productive forces were deprived of their status as an independent variable and conceived of as a variety—or a subset—of the relations of production".[19]

The Althusserians denounced Marx's own proclaimed position as "technological determinism". Such a critique was doubly wrong. It assumed that technological development is an impersonal process, not an aspect of conscious human labour in action. It also assumed that to see new ways of getting a livelihood as giving rise to new social relations that challenge old ones is somehow to fall into a mechanical view of history whereby the new social relations automatically overthrew the old ones. This was the view implied by some of the writings of the generation of Marxists after Marx

---

15: Elliott, 1987, p179.
16: Elliott, 1987, p177.
17: Althusser argued in 1964 "that Lévi-Strauss was more an immediate ally of historical materialism than Sartre"—Elliott, 1987, p62.
18: For an account of the influence of structuralism, see Bradbury, 1988.
19: Elliott, 1987, p163.

and Engels—what is often called "Second International" Marxism[20]— and was the view articulated explicitly by the Stalinist caricature of Marxism. But for Marx and Engels it led to a very different conclusion. The clash between new forces of production and established relations of production heralded the beginning of an "epoch of social revolution", the outcome of which depended on the organisation of the different classes—and the subjective factors of the revolutionary and counter-revolutionary leadership played an important role. As they put in the *Communist Manifesto*, one outcome could be a revolutionary reorganisation of society, but the other could be "the mutual destruction of the contending classes".

Althusserianism, by erasing this element from Marxism, could not avoid going around in circles when it came to trying to explain how one mode of production could give way to another.

This was a problem never resolved by Althusser. But it did lead him into an often-ignored turn away from much of the argument of *For Marx* and *Reading Capital*. As Elliott says, from "1967 to 1974" Althusser "retracted" his "theory of theoretical practice", "acknowledging an erstwhile 'theoreticism' and a failure to appreciate the 'organic relationship' between philosophy and politics... The novelty of 'dialectical materialism' was no longer thought to reside in its scientificity as a theory of science, but in its 'partisan', 'materialist' practice of philosophy".[21] It was now "the continuation of revolutionary politics by theoretical means",[22] the view "from the proletarian standpoint".[23]

Effectively, Althusser was turning his back on the very interpretation of Marxism that he had insisted on a decade earlier—and just as it was being accepted by many academics as the correct Marxist approach.

This "turn towards politics" did leave unchanged two important features of his old approach. Marxism might be philosophy "from the proletarian viewpoint", but Althusser still saw ideology as always completely

---

20: It followed from the period in which Marxists found themselves between the crushing of the Paris Commune and the outbreak of World War One. Capitalist states generally were too strong to be overthrown by the insurrectionary methods of the past, but the growth and spread of capitalist industry was producing an enlarged and potentially more powerful working class. But until this growth had gone a good deal further, it was not possible to overthrow the system and it was necessary to have patience, knowing things would change. This understanding could be expressed through mechanical formulae, but it contained an important element of truth until 1905, when near-revolution in Russia presaged a new stage with insurrectionary potential, although incorporating a method, the mass strike, hardly known in the past.

21: Elliott, 1987, p198, see also pp204-205.

22: Elliott, 1987, p205.

23: Althusser, quoted in Elliott, 1987, p214.

clouding the minds of the workers themselves. It was still wrong to inform "workers that men make history",[24] since "history" was still "a process without a subject".[25] The validity of the "proletarian viewpoint" came not from the practice of workers in struggle, but from the efforts of those who carry out "the class struggle in theory". What is more, classes were defined not just by relations in production but also by "their members' positions in political and ideological relations".[26]

As Elliott rightly puts it, "In the name of anti-economism and anti-evolutionism, Althusser abandoned the classic tenet of historical materialism, substituting such theses as the dominance of the ideological level".[27] History was a process without a subject, but somehow those who waged the ideological struggle could move it forward as they arrogated to themselves the decisions as to who the workers actually were and what the class struggle was. Voluntarism was a necessary correlative of an idealist theory of knowledge.

Althusser's u-turn had political as well as intellectual roots. His original formulations were in part inspired by increasingly open criticisms directed at Khrushchev's post-Stalin regime in the USSR by Mao's regime in China asserting its different strategic goals. The Chinese regime was just as Stalinist as the Russian, and so its criticisms were within the matrix of orthodox Stalinism, with its view of history as only decipherable by the party elite. The structure of Althusser's thought in these years reflected this.

This posture appealed to a layer of young French Communists worried by the habit of the French Communist Party of pursuing a social democratic strategy in practice. They saw Althusser's writings as providing a "left critique" of the party's "revisionism" and proclaimed it as the genuine Marxism—even though Althusser himself was careful not to break with the party.

After the publication of *For Marx* and *Reading Capital* in 1965, Althusser enjoyed an enormous influence over young left wing intellectuals in France. This spilt over internationally, with the editors of *New Left Review* in Britain moving overnight from a version of Marxism inspired by Sartre to an intense, although short lived, love affair with Althusserianism. As a result many of those radicalised elsewhere in Europe and North America by the movements from 1967 onwards saw Althusser as representing the epitome of Marxist thought and accepting uncritically the diatribes directed against

---

24: Elliott, paraphrasing Althusser's argument, 1987, p221.
25: Althusser, quoted in Elliott 1987, p220.
26: Elliott, 1987, p195.
27: Elliott, 1987, p223.

thinkers like Lukács.[28] Those of us trying to build some sort of revolutionary organisation with roots in the working class in 1968-9 were subject to the most vehement attacks by the proponents of *Theoretical Practice*.[29]

But even as the influence of Althusserianism continued to spread, two things happened to upset Althusser's own theoretical balance. The first was the Cultural Revolution in China (1966-9). This started as one section of the Chinese leadership, headed by Mao and the army chief Lin Biao decided that the only way to dislodge a rival section was a carefully orchestrated mobilisation of teenage "Red Guards". To many in the West, this seemed to cast Maoism in a new light. Struggle from below appeared to matter, not the "scientific" elaboration of a party line from above.

The second was the French May of 1968. Althusser, sick at the time of the events, failed to rise to the occasion and remained within the Communist Party, providing a partial justification of its stance of trying to restore France to normality.[30] It was the criticism he faced from the left, as well as the conservative leadership of the Communist Party, that led Althusser to make his u-turn, with its attempt to incorporate agency and change into his theory.

Elliott traces a second great shift in his position a decade later. Those who had identified with Althusserianism from a Maoist standpoint ten years before now began to move away from it in all sorts of directions, under the combined impact of the ebbing of the global radicalisation produced by the events of 1968[31] and the revelations that China was a very unrevolutionary state, with Mao welcoming Nixon to Beijing and the army crushing "red guard" and "red rebel" groups who took Cultural Revolution slogans about the masses seriously. Some, like Poulantzas, moved towards forms of left Eurocommunism of their own.[32] Some, like Britain's Paul Hirst, abandoned Marxism for empiricism and social democracy; some, like André Glucksmann, became fervent supporters of US imperialism. The Althusserian theory that society was built of combinations of different structures articulated somehow by the economic structure was transmuted by "post-structuralists"[33] into theories which saw each structure as operating independently of the others, so that racism, sexism, homophobia and

---

28: Most were ignorant of what Lukács actually argued, since *History and Class Consciousness* did not appear in English until 1971.
29: A short-lived British Althusserian journal as well as a particularly arid caricature of Marxism.
30: See Elliott, 1987, pp197, 235, 238, 266.
31: Harman, 1979.
32: On Poulantzas's ideas and political itinerary, see Barker, 1979.
33: See Bradbury, 1988.

ecological destructiveness all had distinct causes and had to be dealt with separately. Postmodernists added that any attempt to deal with them as part of a totality would, in fact, lead to totalitarianism.

Confronted by the collapse not only of his school but of the political hopes of 30 years, Althusser felt compelled to make one last theoretical stand, identifying a "crisis of Marxism" and trying to come to terms with it. He could not do so without for the first time coming out with a trenchant critique of the theory and practice of Stalinism. He denounced the "massacre and deportation of peasants denounced as Kulaks, the Gulag archipelago, the repression that still goes on 25 years after Stalin's death" and the way "the bourgeois ideology of the omnipotence of ideas triumphed in the monstrous unity of state-party-state ideology", where "the masses had only to submit themselves in the very name of their liberation".[34] The one time theorist of Marxism-Leninism now separated Marxism off from it and contradicted the basic premise of the original Althusserianism by asserting that Marxist theory grows out of the terrain of workers' struggles.[35] Yet the old notion that Stalinism was an heir to Marxism persisted, only now in a negative sense: the faults in Stalinism, he asserted, had their roots in "lacunae" in Marx's own writings

The most influential critique of Althusserianism was from the best known representative of the original New Left, Edward Thompson, who felt compelled once more to defend "the agenda of 1956" in his 1978 collection *The Poverty of Theory*.[36] It was a masterpiece of polemic, devastating in unpicking the holes, the contradictions and the weak points in the original Althusserian facade—and in taking apart the pretentions of some of his British disciples. Its central strength was that it highlighted what the Althusserian system and Stalinism had in common—the disdain for conscious working class actions that characterises all versions of what Hal Draper many years ago baptised "socialism from above". Reading it, I felt many of my own criticisms were brilliantly expressed.[37]

Yet one of the ironies of history was that Thompson's critique appeared in the very year that Althusserianism in France collapsed into

---

34: Quoted in Elliott, 1987, pp307, 319.
35: See Elliott's summary of Althusser's "Il Marxismo Oggi" of 1978, Elliott, 1987, p315.
36: Thompson, 1978, pp333, 382.
37: I had started to write a long critique of Althusser's first system in the early 1970s based on notes I had made when working on an unfinished (and lost) PhD thesis several years before, but decided that trying to build a party with roots in working class struggle was more important. Some of my conclusions appeared subsequently in my article "Philosophy and Revolution"—Harman 1983.

fragments. By that time the actual political positions of Thompson and Althusser were not so far apart. Both stood for radical reformism rather than revolutionary change. Both also rejected Marx's insight that changes in the way humans made a livelihood ("the forces of production") create a dynamic tension with old social relations. Thompson argued that Marx had, in writing *Capital*, fallen into "a trap" of "over-developing" the "formal side" of capitalism as an economic system and that it was necessary to see that there were "other 'circuits'"—"circuits of power, or reproduction of ideology, etc". This was remarkably close to the later Althusserian notion of different structures coexisting without the economic playing a determining role.[38] Both left unresolved the question of agency—of what prompts people in their millions to challenge structures they have accepted in the past. The optimistic voluntarism of 1956 in Thompson's case, and of 1967-74 in Althusser's, could easily give way among their disciples to deep pessimism and a "post-Marxist" retreat from politics.

In my view, the new generation coming to Marxism have a lot more to learn from Thompson than from Althusser and even more from the revolutionary tradition that goes back to the post-1917 thinkers so attacked by the Althusserians. Elliott's book vindicates my view. It constitutes a painstaking attempt to trace the development of Althusser's system by someone who believes it to be of some value, but who in fact shows how flawed it was—proving that the emperor has no clothes, but not daring to admit it. Anyone who feels under pressure to find out what Althusserianism was about should read it.

38: Thompson, 1978, pp250-260. His critique of the early Althusser moved from the correct understanding that humans have the capacity to react against the structures that imprison them to failing to recognise the sheer power of the structures created by alienated labour under capitalism. This even leads him to "go a good part of the way" with the "critique" of Marxist tradition by those like Castoriadis who embraced postmodernism—Thompson, 1978, p360.

References

Althusser, Louis, 1969, *For Marx* (Allen Lane, Penguin Press).

Althusser, Louis, 1965 *Pour Marx* (Maspero).

Althusser, Louis, 1970, *Reading Capital* (New Left Books).

Althusser, Louis, 1965, *Lire le Capital* (Maspero).

Barker, Colin 1979 "A 'New' Reformism?—A Critique of the Political Theory of Nicos Poulantzas", *International Socialism* 4 (spring 1979), www.isj.org.uk/?id=294

Blackledge, Paul, 2006, "The New Left's Renewal of Marxism", *International Socialism* 112 (autumn 2006), www.isj.org.uk/id=251

Bradbury, Richard, 1988, "What is Post-structuralism?", *International Socialism* 41 (winter 1988).

Cliff, Tony 1959, *Rosa Luxemburg* (International Socialism), www.marxists.org/archive/cliff/works/1959/rosalux/index.htm.

Elliott, Gregory, 1987, *Althusser: the Detour of Theory* (Verso).

Harman, Chris, 1979, "The crisis of the European revolutionary left", *International Socialism* 4 (spring 1979), http://chrisharman.blogspot.com/2009/11/crisis-of-european-revolutionary-left.html

Harman, 1983 "Philosophy and Revolution", *International Socialism* 21 (autumn 1983), http://chrisharman.blogspot.com/2009/10/philosophy-and-revolution.html

Hegel, GWF, 1964 [1807], *The Phenomenology of Mind* (Allen and Unwin), www.marxists.org/reference/archive/hegel/phindex.htm

Lukács, Georg, 1971 [1924], *History and Class Consciousness* (Merlin), www.marxists.org/archive/lukacs/works/history/index.htm

Lukács, Georg, 1978, *Ontology of Social Being: Hegel* (Merlin).

Marx, Karl, 1976 [1845], "Theses on Feuerbach" in Marx and Engels, *Collected Works* vol 5 (Lawrence and Wishart), www.marxists.org/archive/marx/works/1845/theses/index.htm

Stace, WT, 1955, *The Philosophy of Hegel* (Dover).

Thompson, E P, 1978, *The Poverty of Theory and Other Essays* (Merlin).

Another side of Chris Harman

Joseph Choonara

For those of us who joined the Socialist Workers Party from the mid-1990s—too late to have worked closely with Tony Cliff, Duncan Hallas, Paul Foot or Mike Kidron—Chris Harman played a special role. For one thing, he seemed more than anyone else to embody what had drawn us towards the International Socialist tradition, not just the theories of state capitalism, deflected permanent revolution and the permanent arms economy, but also the possibility of workers' self-emancipation that these theories helped to maintain.

He was, in addition, an encyclopaedia of Marxist theory and practice. Besides his own enormous output of books and articles, and his relentless schedule of meetings, Chris was indirectly responsible for much of the remainder of the output of the organisation. Personally, I discussed almost everything I wrote with Chris, who would unfailingly suggest a sharper way of framing my main point or some historic example that would clinch the argument. If I was completely wide of the mark, he would pause for a while and say, "Yes, but you have to think it through",[1] before embarking on a detailed elaboration of the topic in question.

For Chris, such discussions often meant puncturing illusions in

---

1:    This was one of his catchphrases and, for a long time, the title of his column in *Socialist Review*. Anyone wanting to understand Chris's impact on younger comrades need only read a few of these columns and imagine contributions of the same clarity and sharpness day after day in the offices of *Socialist Worker* or *International Socialism*.

some new and fashionable theory or theorist. He would show that the emperor was not merely naked, but that he was really the same emperor from many years ago, and that the invisible garments were pretty much identical.[2] But Chris was not simply a defender of a political tradition. He also deepened and extended it. He was able to combine his rich knowledge of Marxism[3] with a rare sense of iconoclasm and disregard for academic specialisation.

I want to emphasise Chris's impact in just one of the areas in which he contributed, that of Marxist political economy.

At those points in his life when he felt the need to engage with this field, often moments of economic crisis when there were pressing political reasons to do so, he read extensively on the subject. His overriding feeling, as he put it in at a meeting he gave in autumn 2007, was that much of what he read fell into one of two errors. Either it was bogged down in interminable debates on value theory that became almost theological in their abstractness ("How many angels can dance on the head of a pin?" was a favourite analogy) or it was based on detailed empirical studies that were not grounded in a serious understanding of *Capital*. The hallmark of great political economy was, for him, that it bridged the gap between theory and the empirical reality of the system as it developed in time. That was definitely the hallmark of Chris's output in this field.[4]

Even the most basic arguments about value, contained in the opening chapters of the first volume of Capital, had to be related to the system as a whole. Capitalism is a system characterised by both a division between capitalists and labourers, and divisions among the capitalists themselves. Chris argued that you could only make sense of Marx's concept of value if you understood the pressure that different units of capital put on each other. It was this competitive pressure that produced the drive to accumulate, forcing capitalists to behave as capitalists, to exploit workers and pump the profits squeezed out of them back

---

2:   See Chris's article on Althusser in this issue of *International Socialism* for an example.

3:   This was partly gleaned during his time studying, but never completing, a PhD under Ralph Miliband (father of the current foreign secretary). Miliband was a "kind but hopeless supervisor. He just signed the paperwork each year so I could carry on with my studies. Meanwhile I read everything published in English at that time by Marx, Engels, Lenin and Gramsci."

4:   Chris was always happy to acknowledge those whose theoretical work he admired and those who conducted the empirical studies he drew on. The latter were particularly essential, as mathematics did not sit well with him. He consoled himself with the fact that Marx managed to botch some of his numerical work in the manuscripts of *Capital*.

into the system.[5] The point was made particularly sharply in a series of critiques of and exchanges with Ernest Mandel, a key theorist of the Fourth International:

> Marx's original starting point was alienated labour, the situation in which the products of man's labour appear as independent forces, constraints on his activity. In its developed form this implies the separation of the worker from control of the means of production, expropriation of the actual producers, the creation of a proletariat... Competition between rival owners of the means of production...forces each to try and resist the inroads of the other by continually expanding the means of production. This establishes a relationship between the different accumulations of alienated labour making up the competing means of production that defines each as capital, and their owners as capitalists.[6]

The centrality of alienated labour and the need to penetrate the mystified surface appearance of capitalism created by commodity exchange to grasp its real relations featured in many of Chris's major writings on economics. This forms a bridge to his more general philosophical commitment to a "humanist Marxism" of the kind that emerged as cracks appeared in the Stalinist monolith from 1956 onwards.

Once capitalism was understood as a system of competing "accumulations of alienated labour" it was possible to get to grips with both the dynamism of the system and its inner contradictions:

> Marx's own approach was...to identify the individual elements of the system through analysis and then to show how they interacted dynamically, changing one another in the process. That is why he insisted his method was dialectical, concerned with interaction and mutual transformation. Once you miss these interconnections, you miss the dynamic of the system... For Marx, the categories he developed were significant because they enabled you to see the system as a self-contradicting totality, which is

---

5:    Towards the end of his life, Chris was delighted to rediscover a section in one of the unpublished manuscripts of *Capital* that clearly expressed the way that value production flows out of the dynamism of the system as a totality. This section, "Results of the Direct Production Process", was published as an appendix in the Penguin edition of *Capital*, volume one, and is available online at www.marxists.org/archive/marx/works/1864/economic/

6:    Harman, 1969, p36.

in a permanent process of transformation—a transformation that must affect the very categories of analysis themselves.[7]

Such an analysis had profound political implications during the Cold War. For if the process of competitive accumulation by rival blocs of capital was placed at the centre of analysis, the Soviet Union after 1928 could be understood as a variant of capitalism:

Every change in production processes in the West will force changes in production processes in Russia, and vice-versa. Accumulation in the West will force accumulation in Russia (and again, vice-versa). In other words, a total system of reified relations is set up in which the anarchic and unplanned interaction of the products of labour determines the labour process, in which dead labour dominates living labour, in which every concrete act of labour is related to abstract labour—on a world scale—in which although there may be many partial negations of the law of value these are on the basis of the law of value.[8]

Or as he summarised his position four decades later:

The organisation of production inside the USSR might involve the putting together of different use values (so much labour, so many physically distinct raw materials, such and such a particular sort of machine) to produce further use values. But what mattered to the ruling bureaucracy was how these use values measured up to the similar conglomerations of use values produced inside the great corporations of the West. And that meant comparing the amounts of labour used in the USSR to the labour used in the Western corporations. Or, to put it in Marx's terms, production within the USSR was subject to the law of value operating on the global scale.[9]

7:   Harman, 1978, pp80-81. Whatever else changed in Chris's analysis over the years, his hatred of scholastic jargon that confused more than it explained was a constant. A footnote to this article snarled, "'Valorisation' is the trendy new translation of Marx's term *Verwertung*." Three decades later he was still annoyed. A footnote to his final book informed readers, "'Valorisation' is the French translation of the German term...*Verwertung*. 'Valorisation' in French means an expansion in the value of something... But the general English meaning of the word is different, meaning simply 'fixing the price or value of a commodity'... All this is confusing for newcomers to Marx's writings—and encourages an academicist tendency to dense, often nearly unintelligible, expositions of Marx's analyses"—Harman, 2009a, p355.
8:   Harman, 1969, p38.
9:   Harman, 2009a, p176.

While Cliff had pioneered this analysis of Russia as a "bureaucratic state capitalism",[10] and Kidron had drawn out some of the wider implications of the approach for the global economic system,[11] it was Chris who produced path-breaking studies of the state capitalist regimes in Eastern Europe and explained both the dynamism that was possible in these economies for a time, and their own particular internal contradictions that led them into crisis.

Behind the illusion of smooth and planned expansion the "relentless drive to accumulate had as a necessary by-product disorganisation, chaos and waste".[12] And in the background was a tendency towards over-accumulation similar to that in the West, as a growing quantity of plant and machinery was required to produce a certain level of output.[13] The Eastern Bloc countries might be particular variants of capitalism, and as such the peculiarities of their dynamic had to be explored, but they were capitalist nonetheless. They had to be understood, and condemned, in those terms.[14]

If Chris was scathing about those who had illusions in Eastern state capitalism, he was just as dismissive of fashionable notions about the Western state. He rejected the idea that the growth of state intervention in the years following the Second World War represented a move towards socialism in the West. He also challenged the view that the world had entered a new phase in which the state's role would diminish in the face of globalisation. The state had become everywhere a key component in the process of capitalist accumulation—training and maintaining the required forms of labour power through the education and health systems,[15] intervening directly in the economy and clashing militarily with its rivals on a global scale.[16] It was this that informed Chris's attitude to "productive" and "unproductive" labour. Marx had written that labour was productive if it produced surplus value, the source of profit, for the

---

10: Cliff, 2003.

11: Kidron, 1970, 1974.

12: Harman, 2009a, p177.

13: Harman, 2009a, p203.

14: His final piece for *Socialist Review* entitled "State Capitalism—The Theory that Fuels the Practice" is a great summary of the theory, written on the anniversary of the fall of the Berlin Wall that vindicated many of his arguments, but aimed at a new audience, unaware of the crucial role the theory played—Harman, 2009b.

15: Harman, 2008, pp103-104, 112-116.

16: Harman, 1996, 2003. These two articles, on globalisation and imperialism, both brilliant summaries, have saved the skin of countless revolutionary socialist undergraduates too busy demonstrating to finish their essays. See also Harman, 2009a, pp255-275.

capitalist. Chris agreed, but also argued that in modern capitalist societies much other labour, including that of many public sector employees, was best regarded as "indirectly productive" because it was a prerequisite for accumulation to take place.

State intervention might alter the dynamic of capitalism in important ways but it could not remove the system's tendency towards crisis. Chris took seriously Marx's description of the law of the tendency of the rate of profit to fall:

> This is in every respect the most important law of modern political economy, and the most essential for understanding the most difficult relations. It is the most important law from the historical standpoint. It is a law which, despite its simplicity, has never before been grasped and, even less, consciously articulated.[17]

Chris elaborated and defended this law in the series of articles, written at the start of the 1980s, "not merely to show that capitalism was crisis prone, but also to grasp the character of the new period of crises the system entered in the mid-1970s".[18] These later formed the basis for the book *Explaining the Crisis*. He returned to the subject in 2007, managing to produce an article on the subject just as signs of the current economic crisis began to emerge.[19] This was the first of many articles written in preparation for his final book, *Zombie Capitalism*, which represents the most rounded and complete presentation of his economic thought.

The enthusiasm with which he engaged with two decades worth of Marxist economic theory since his previous major book on the subject should be evident from his illustrated talk, "Not all Marxism is Dogma", reproduced in this issue of the journal, which must stand as the most comprehensive survey yet of recent studies of the profit rate.

However, to his enormous frustration, Chris found once more a gulf between most empirical studies of profit rates and the "pure" theoretical works that discussed Marx's famous law. In particular, a number of works pointed out an abstract possibility that productivity increases could, over time, cheapen constant capital (plant, equipment, raw material, etc), leading to rising rather than falling profit rates.[20] Chris insisted that in the

---

17: Marx, 1973, p748.
18: Harman, 1999, p11.
19: Harman, 2007.
20: Readers unfamiliar with Marx's basic concepts can consult Harman, 2007, Harman, 2009a, or Choonara, 2009, for details.

real world capitalists had to recoup the cost of the constant capital they had actually invested in at the point they invested, not just the cost of the constant capital they could buy if they were purchasing it in the present: "You can't build the houses of yesterday with the bricks of today." It was during economic crises that constant capital could be driven down in price in a systematic way, through bankruptcies and the dumping of goods, allowing surviving capitalists to obtain their investments more cheaply, boosting profitability and restoring the system to "health".

In other words, the law of the tendency of the rate of profit to fall and the "countervailing tendencies" discussed by Marx in the third volume of *Capital*, do not operate to push profit rates up and down in a smooth, uninterrupted manner. They are tendencies that are worked out explosively, through crises.

But the changes undergone by the system as it aged did lead to changes in the working out of crises. Chris had first explored this in his defence of the theory of the Permanent Arms Economy that had been developed by Mike Kidron. The theory sought to explain the duration of the post-war boom by showing how surplus value that could otherwise have been accumulated, raising the organic composition of capital and thus putting pressure on profit rates, was leaking out of the productive sphere and into arms expenditure and other "waste" areas.[21] While this could postpone the crisis, it could not prevent it altogether. Profit rates did fall, even if they fell more slowly.[22]

By the time he wrote *Zombie Capitalism* there were new elements deferring the crisis. Chris argued that capitalism had never fully resolved the underlying crisis of profitability that had emerged at the end of the post-war boom.[23] But because the units of capital had grown far larger over the course of the 20th century, the ruling class was reluctant to risk the "creative destruction" of a major crisis. The failure of one giant firm, linked to countless others, could bring down healthy as well as unhealthy chunks of the system. Again and again states stepped in to bail out failing companies. The problems persisted and led to further changes to the face of capitalism. Chris grasped that the bloated financial system, which on the surface appeared to be a source of dynamism, was a product of the weakness of profitability in the wider economy.

Financial bubbles formed as capital shifted away from productive

21:   Harman, 1999, pp75-154; Harman, 2009a, pp161-190.
22:   See the review of *Zombie Capitalism*, Kliman, 2009.
23:   Harman, 2007, p150.

areas of the economy. This masked the underlying problems by creating possibilities for capitalists to grab short-term paper profits and by bankrolling a growing level of consumer debt that helped provide the demand needed to keep the system going. Financialisation also led to new forms of instability. Chris's contribution was both to grapple with the altered dynamic of the system[24] and to reassert, crucially, that the crisis that broke out in 2007-8 was a systemic crisis of capitalism rooted in sustained low profitability, not merely a banking or financial crisis. It was for this reason that he quickly realised just how serious the crisis was, and what political possibilities it might throw up, even while explaining that it was not possible to predict in advance how deep or long it would be.[25]

Chris's interventions in political economy, as elsewhere, were not simply original. They were often made against the current and, while he was never personally offensive to his opponents, he was prepared to engage in a sharp polemic. Occasionally it might be suggested that he show a little more restraint towards his fellow leftists. Chris would have none of it: the important debates needed to be had out. The tributes paid to him show just how deeply he was respected as a result—not just by his closest allies, but also by his sometime adversaries.

One final point about Chris's work deserves to be stressed. None of it was undertaken for self-aggrandisement. During the time I knew him he was increasingly concerned with developing and training a new generation of Marxists. From the late 1990s a growing audience for anti-capitalist ideas emerged. Chris recognised how, as the movement began to face new challenges along with old debates in new forms, some of that audience could be won towards Marxist ideas.[26] He loved the rows this produced as the young heretics of yesterday turned into the rounded Marxists of today, and he relished the part he played in that process. The young heretics, in turn, gravitated towards him, because they knew where to look for a good argument.

Chris was unique and entirely irreplaceable. To wait for another like him to emerge would be thoroughly un-Marxist. But the

---

24: Harman, 2009a, pp277-304.

25: As he frequently complained, "If I say it's not as bad as the 1930s I'll get attacked for being overly optimistic; if I say it is as bad I'll get attacked for being pessimistic; and if I say that I don't know I'll get attacked for being indecisive." As it turned out, the series of analyses he produced in *International Socialism* and elsewhere, at each stage of the crisis, walked this tightrope brilliantly.

26: Harman, 2000, was, like so many of Chris's articles, crucial in spelling out the implications of the political shift.

legacy he leaves includes a growing generation of articulate and active revolutionaries who can begin, collectively, to fill the gap created by his death. For one who devoted his life to building a socialist organisation imbued with the same passion and clarity he himself displayed, there can be no greater testament.

References

Cliff, Tony, 2003 [1948], "The Nature of Stalinist Russia", in *Selected Writings*, volume 3 (Bookmarks), www.marxists.org/archive/cliff/works/1948/stalruss

Choonara, Joseph, 2009, *Unravelling Capitalism: A Guide to Marxist Political Economy* (Bookmarks).

Harman, Chris, 1969, "The Inconsistencies of Ernest Mandel", *International Socialism 41* (first series), December 1969, www.marxists.org/history/etol/writers/harman/1969/12/mandel.htm

Harman, Chris, 1978, "Mandel's 'Late Capitalism'", *International Socialism 1* (summer 1978).

Harman, Chris, 1996, "Globalisation: A Critique of a New Orthodoxy", *International Socialism 73* (winter 1996).

Harman, Chris, 1999 [1984], *Explaining the Crisis* (Bookmarks).

Harman, Chris, 2000, "Anti-capitalism: Theory and Practice", *International Socialism 88* (autumn 2000), http://pubs.socialistreviewindex.org.uk/isj88/harman.htm

Harman, Chris, 2003, "Analysing Imperialism", *International Socialism 99* (summer 2003), http://pubs.socialistreviewindex.org.uk/isj99/harman.htm

Harman, Chris, 2007, "The Rate of Profit and the World Today", *International Socialism 115* (summer 2007), www.isj.org.uk/?id=340

Harman, Chris, 2008, "Theorising Neoliberalism", *International Socialism 117* (winter 2008), www.isj.org.uk/?id=399

Harman, Chris, 2009a, *Zombie Capitalism: Global Crisis and the Relevance of Marx* (Bookmarks).

Harman, Chris, 2009b, "State Capitalism—The Theory that Fuels the Practice", *Socialist Review*, November 2009, www.socialistreview.org.uk/article.php?articlenumber=11016

Kidron, Mike, 1970 [1968], *Western Capitalism Since the War* (Pelican).

Kidron, Mike, 1974, *Capitalism and Theory* (Pluto).

Kliman, Andrew, 2009, "Pinning the Blame on the System", *International Socialism 124* (summer 2009), www.isj.org.uk/?id=584

Marx, Karl, 1973 [1858], *Grundrisse* (Penguin), www.marxists.org/archive/marx/works/1857/grundrisse/

Not all Marxism is dogmatism: a reply to Michel Husson

Chris Harman

Michel Husson has criticised a number of Marxist economists, including myself, in the most stringent manner.[1] He writes that:

> The crisis has given rise in recent months to a series of contributions characterised by a counterproductive and discouraging dogmatism…What these contributions have in common are references to the orthodox interpretation of the law of the tendency of the rate of profit to fall.[2]

This, he claims, ignores the elementary fact that "there has been a very clear tendency for the rate of profit to rise in the principal capitalist countries. This evolution is sufficiently pronounced that one cannot expect it to be affected significantly by more or less appropriate correctives." He then provides a graph based on figures provided by the European Union for the US, Europe and the G8 that purport to justify his argument.

But there are big problems with coming to terms with these figures. First, he does not either provide information as to where the European Union got its figures from or explain in detail the methodology used to

---

1:   This paper was written for a recent conference in Amsterdam organised by the Fourth International.

2:   Husson, 2009.

construct the rate of profit from them (all he says is that they "relate the net excess from exploitation to the stock of capital"). Without such information it is impossible for those of us accused of "dogmatism" to subject his argument to scientific scrutiny.

Figure 1: Husson's figures for the US rate of profit
Source: Husson, 2009.

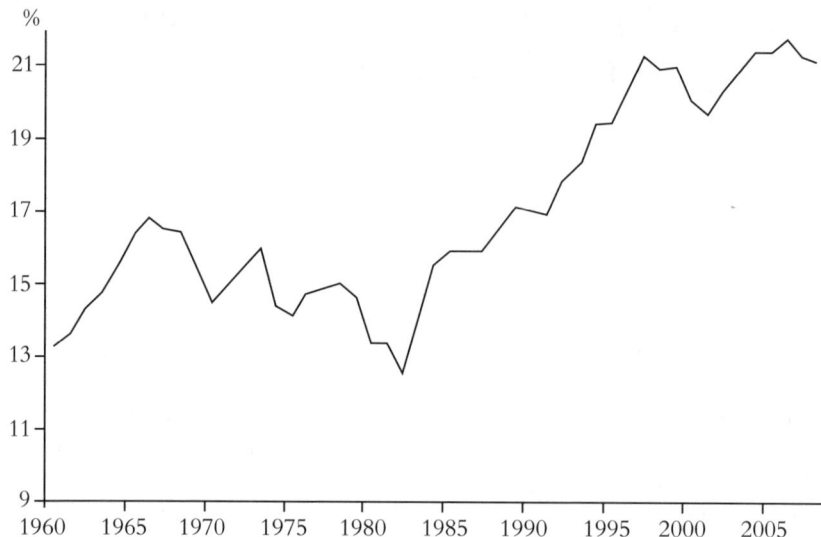

Secondly, his graphs differ very markedly from numerous other attempts to calculate the path of the rate of profit. This is most clearly the case with the US. Husson claims that in the decade 1998-2008 the rate of profit there not only recovered from a fall in the years after 1968-82 of about a quarter but rose to about 30 percent higher than the pre-1973 level.[3]

By contrast Robert Brenner, Fred Moseley, Simon Mohun, Alan Freeman and Andrew Kliman have all provided figures which, although differing to some degree with each other, show a pattern which is very different from the one Michel Husson portrays.[4] On the one hand they

---

3:   The figures I give here are based on the graph, since he does not provide the data.
4:   These graphs, and the others cited, are scattered throughout the article.

show a bigger decline up to 1982 than does Husson; on the other they show the recovery since to have been much more limited than Husson suggests, and not even reaching, let alone going 30 percent beyond, the figure for the late 1960s. Moseley, who shows the biggest recovery of profit rates in recent years, provides a pattern that nowhere approaches Husson's, while Brenner, Mohun, Freeman and Kliman all show recent profitability to have been substantially lower than during the 1960s. These figures are all based upon checkable statistics provided by the US Bureau of Economic Affairs in its NIPA tables. Arnaud Sylvain only provides figures up to 2000, but his graph certainly does not show the massive rise above the figures for the 1960s which Husson claims—rather it shows their peak in the late 1990s as being only about the level of 1973 and well below the level of the mid to late 1960s.[5] Gérard Duménil and Dominique Lévy's figures up to 1997 are similarly very different from Husson's.[6] Figures by Goldman Sachs only start in the 1980s and so do not show the decline in profits from the late 1960s. But the pattern of the recovery of US profits is very different from Husson's with the level in 1997 and 2007 only about 10 percent higher than in 1988.[7]

The same contradictions with Husson's figures are to be found with calculations for other countries. Brenner and Sylvain show a long-term fall in the rate of profit for Japan; as do Arthur Alexander,[8] and Fumio Hayashi and Edward C Prescott.[9] Mehmet Ufuk Tutan has carried out a meticulous study of profit rates for Germany. It only goes up to 1987 but shows a much less marked recovery than would be implied by Husson's graph for the four biggest European economies.[10] I have come across three studies of profit rates for China. One shows a sharp drop of more than a third between 1978 and 2000;[11] the second shows an even sharper drop of around 40 percent from the 1980s until 2003;[12] the third shows a fall for manufacturing until 1999 but a considerable rise after that.[13]

All these figures, it should be noted, are subject to enormous qualifications on at least two fronts.

5: Sylvain, 2001.
6: Duménil and Lévy 2002.
7: See Choonara, 2009.
8: Alexander, 1998.
9: Hayashi and Prescott, 2001.
10: Tutan, 2008.
11: O'Hara, 2006.
12: Felipe, Lavina and Fan, 2008.
13: Yu and Feng, 2006.

Figure 2: Moseley's figures for the US rate of profit
Source: Moseley, 2007.

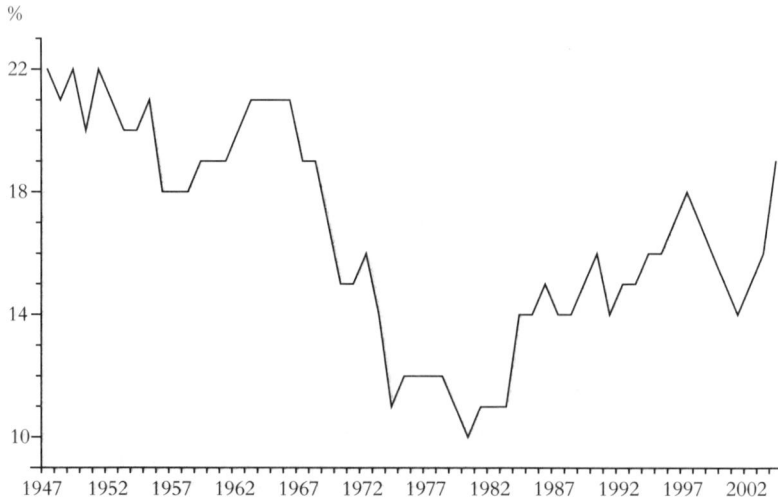

First there are problems deciding on how to measure capital investment—and then on finding the appropriate figures. Firms calculate the profitability of any investment by adding together the initial capital outlay on structures and equipment, adding the annual expenditure on raw materials, components and wages, and then dividing the total by their net profits, ie they divide what they laid out over a number of years by the profits made over those years. So with "conventional accounting procedures…the values of the capital stock and of capital consumption are measured at historic cost".[14]

But aggregating the different investments made at different times in a particular period is a necessarily complicated procedure, and most attempts to measure national rates of profit use a different procedure—that of current cost accounting. The profit made in a given year is measured against the market value (ie the replacement cost) of the structures and equipment used. This necessarily leads to a distortion in the figures since any increase in productivity since the investment was made will mean that its current market value is less than what was laid out on it: the rate

---

14: Bank of England Quarterly Bulletin, 1975.

of profit will appear higher than it actually was. The greater the speed of technological innovation the greater the discrepancy will be. This is very important in recent years given the rapid increase in computer-related productivity.[15] One would expect current cost calculations of the rate of profit to show recent profits relatively higher compared with those previously.

Figure 3: Brenner's figures for the US non-financial profit rate
Source: Calculated from BEA data

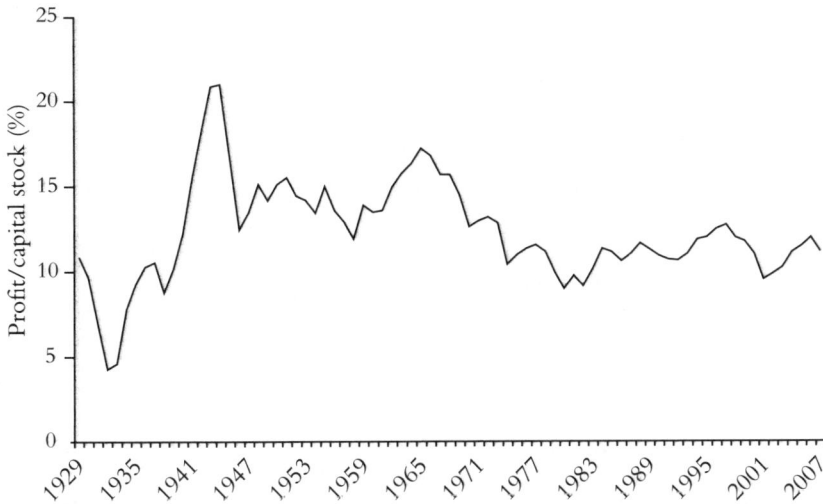

A second sort of distortion can affect the figures for historic cost calculations of the rate of profit in periods of rising prices of stocks of goods held by companies. Profitability can be magnified by the apparent increase in the value of these holdings as a result of inflation.[16]

Andrew Kliman has attempted to provide figures that eliminate both sorts of distortion, using historic cost calculations that attempt to remove the effect of inflation.[17] The overall pattern of his graphs is not

---

15: See, for instance, Tevlin and Whelan, 2003.
16: Bank of England Quarterly Bulletin, 1975.
17: He does so using normal mainstream inflation figures and his own approach based on the monetary equivalent of labour time (MELT).

completely dissimilar to that of Brenner, Mohun and Moseley—except that they show a much smaller recovery of profitability from the low point of the early 1980s.

Figure 4: Kliman's figures for the US rate of profit
Source: Kliman, 2009

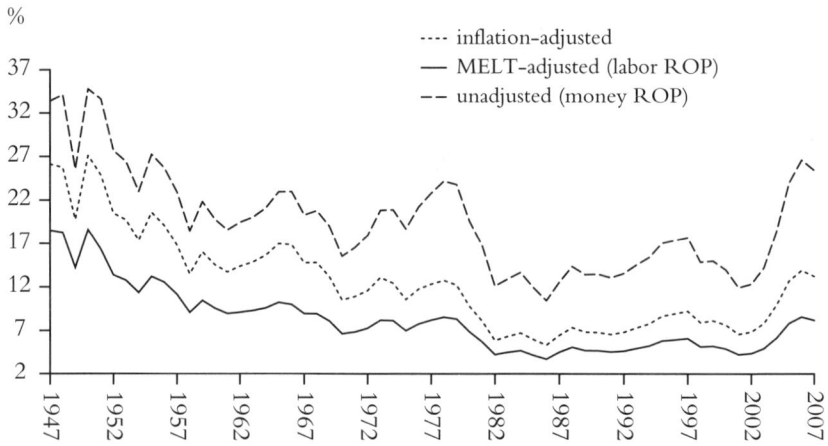

A third distortion in profitability figures can come from asset bubbles. These lead to firms asserting that their values have risen by more than any increase in real production (this is shown clearly in the US Flow of Funds accounts)—and in the case of financial transactions the increase can be recorded as part of the net increase in national output. Since profits in the national economy are usually calculated by deducting wage costs from the net national product its increase leads to profits seeming to increase more than they actually have.

The shock of the financial crash of the last two years is now leading some bourgeois economic commentators to recognise that there were "fictional profits"—and with them "fictional economic growth"—in the mid-2000s, if not earlier. Most calculations of profitability try to circumvent this problem by restricting themselves to non-financial corporations (or sometimes the non-financial business sector). But there are questions as to whether this completely eliminates the distortion since non-financial corporations like General Electric (the US's biggest manufacturing corporation), Ford and General Motors became increasingly dependent on financial operations from the 1990s onwards.

Figure 5: Mohun's figures for the US rate of profit
Source: Mohun, 2006

%

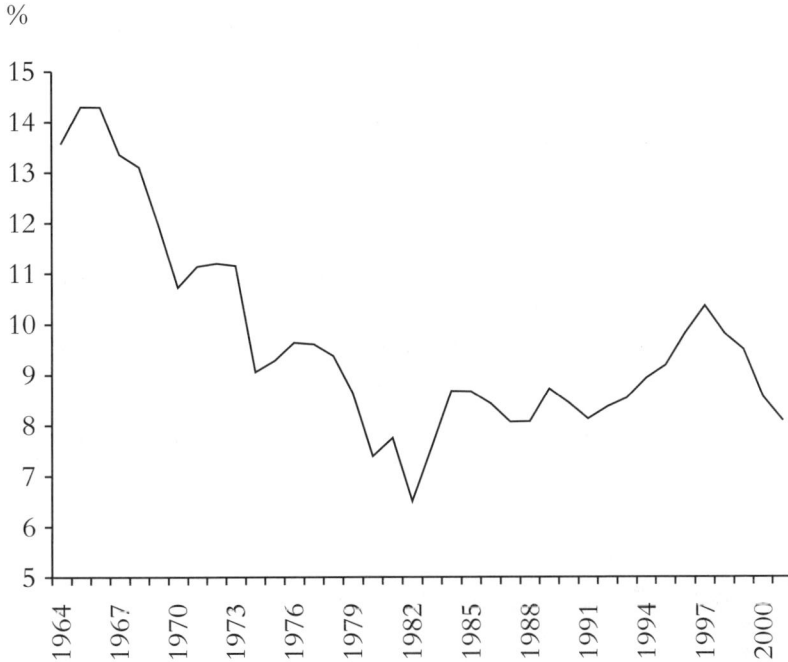

The *Financial Times* has reported that Andrew Smithers, the economic analyst, "has argued for some time that this is seriously distorted by inflation of asset values. He calculates that in 2007 changes in real estate values alone added a daunting $1,000bn-plus to non-financial corporate balance sheets".[18] Smithers calculates that asset appreciation of this sort "accounted for a rather staggering 22 percent of total earnings from non-financial corporations" in the last decade.[19] General Electric

18: Jackson, *Financial Times*, 26 November 2008.
19: Jackson, *Financial Times*, 30 March 2009.

was fined several million dollars in August for falsely inflating its profit figures.

There is every reason to think that Husson's figures will reflect all these distortions. The European site he refers to certainly estimates the value of investment undertaken by firms in terms of its replacement cost not its current cost. It also seems likely that the figures are for the whole economy including all of the bubble-inflated apparent profits for the financial sector. But without a detailed account of methodology and sources it is difficult to be more precise.

Faulty understanding of the theory

It is not only Husson's figures that are questionable so is his attempt to explain them in Marxist terms. He writes of Marx's "tendency of the rate of profit to fall":

> There is no *a priori* reason to think that the tendency systematically overcomes the counter-tendency. The productivity of labour is able to compensate, in a perfectly symmetrical manner, for rises in real wages and the increase in physical capital.

The accumulation of means of production does not have to mean, he insists, an increase in the organic composition of capital:

> The increase in the productivity of labour permits a reduction in the costs of machines. And this counter-tendency can compensate for the increase in the number of machines so that the evolution of the organic composition is indeterminate.

Under such circumstances an increase in the rate of exploitation of each worker can lead to a rising rate of profit. And this, he argues from his figures, is what has been happening over the last quarter of a century: "The numerator and denominator of the rate of profit can remain constant, and, consequently, the rate of profit."

There is, however, an important gap in his reasoning. He ignores an important point which has been made by various Marxists in controversies over the rate of profit in the last 40 years.[20] The controversy was

---

20: In English, the controversies first developed in the *Bulletin of the Conference of Socialist Economists* in the early 1970s, with contributions on different sides from Andrew Glyn, Robin Murray, Sue Himmelweit, Bob Rowthorn, Philip Armstrong, Ben Fine and others.

aroused by the theorem of the Japanese Marxist Okishio who argued that because capitalists would not introduce new technology unless it raised the rate of profit, rising capital investment could not reduce the rate of profit. Its effect would, in fact, be to raise productivity and so reduce the cost of new investment producing a general rise in the rate of profit. The only thing that could then reduce profitability would be a fall in the rate of exploitation (ie a rise in the share of output going to workers).

Figure 6: Freeman's figures for the US rate of profit
Source: Freeman, 2009

Index 1965=100

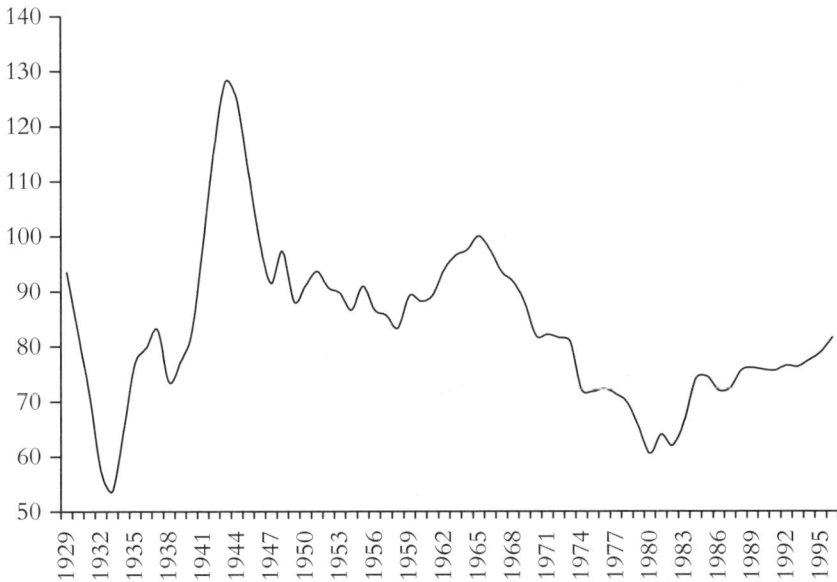

There is a simple and conclusive counter-argument which has been put in different ways by Robin Murray,[21] Ben Fine and Lawrence Harris,[22]

21: Murray, 1973.
22: Fine and Harris, 1979.

Guglielmo Carchedi,[23] Alan Freeman, Andrew Kliman[24] and myself.[25] It is that the effect of increased productivity in reducing the cost of future investments does not help individual capitalists profit from existing investment.

As the saying goes, "You cannot build the houses of today with the bricks of tomorrow." The fact that new machines will cost less to buy in a year or two's time does not somehow reduce the amount you have already spent on your existing ones. In fact, the more rapidly technological innovation takes place and productivity rises the more rapidly the machines suffer from "moral depreciation" and become obsolete. There is increased pressure not reduced pressure on profitability as a result.

Figure 7: Sylvain's figures for the rate of profit in various countries
Source: Sylvain, 2001.

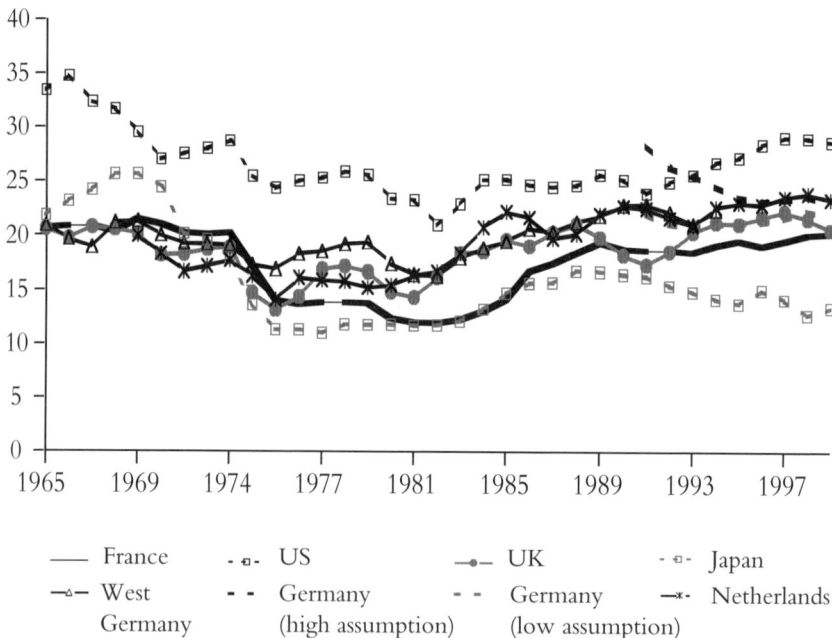

—— France	- ▫- US	—•— UK	- ▫- Japan
—▵— West Germany	- - Germany (high assumption)	- - Germany (low assumption)	—×- Netherlands

23: Carchedi, 1991.
24: Kliman, 2007.
25: Harman, 1984, pp20-34; Harman, 2009, pp68-75.

There is only one way this can work out in a way that counteracts the downward pressure on profit rates. That is if the cost of existing investments can somehow how be removed from the books (if capitals can be devalorised). But the individual capitalist cannot simply shrug off what he has spent already. If he does so he faces a reduction in his profitability every way he looks at it.

As I put it in my latest book, *Zombie Capitalism*:

> Investment…takes place at one point in time. The cheapening of further investment as a result of improved production techniques occurs at a later point in time. The two things are not simultaneous… When capitalists measure their rates of profit they are comparing the surplus value they get from running plant and machinery with what they spent on acquiring it at some point in the past—not what it would cost to replace it today… [The rate of profit] necessarily implies a comparison of current surplus value with the prior capitalist investment from which it flows. The very notion of 'self-expanding values' is incoherent without it.[26]

This means there is only one way in which the falling cost of new investment can overcome problems of profitability. It is if some capitals bear the losses due to devalorisation and are driven out of business while others benefit by buying up their structures, equipment and raw materials at less than their value. The crisis, by creating conditions under which some capitals cannibalise others, provides the conditions under which falling costs of new investment can serve to counter the long-term downward pressure on profit rates.

However, an important empirical fact about the economic crises of the last 40 years has been that there have been relatively low levels of business failures. The concentration and centralisation of capital means that the biggest firms are able to protect their less profitable divisions from going bust—a point already made by Preobrazhensky in 1931.[27] Other capitalists' fear of the damage which would follow if the really big firms themselves simply went bust has led in each crisis in recent decades to states stepping in to prevent that happening—what mainstream economic commentators now call the "too big to fail" problem. A study of

---

26: Harman 2009, pp74–75. The first version of this argument I have come across was that put by Robin Murray, using a corn model of production, in the *Bulletin of the Conference of Socialist Economists*: Murray, 1973.

27: Preobrazhensky, 1985, p137.

bankruptcies in the US concludes that they were very rare indeed until the 1990s. There were more in the short crisis of 2000-2 (Enron and WorldCom were the best known) but the turn to state bailouts since the collapse of Lehman Brothers—including the massive involvement of states in preventing a simple collapse of General Motors and Chrysler—shows the limits on the devalorisation of capital through crisis.

Figure 8: Duménil and Lévy's figures for the US business profit rate
Source: Duménil and Lévy, 2002

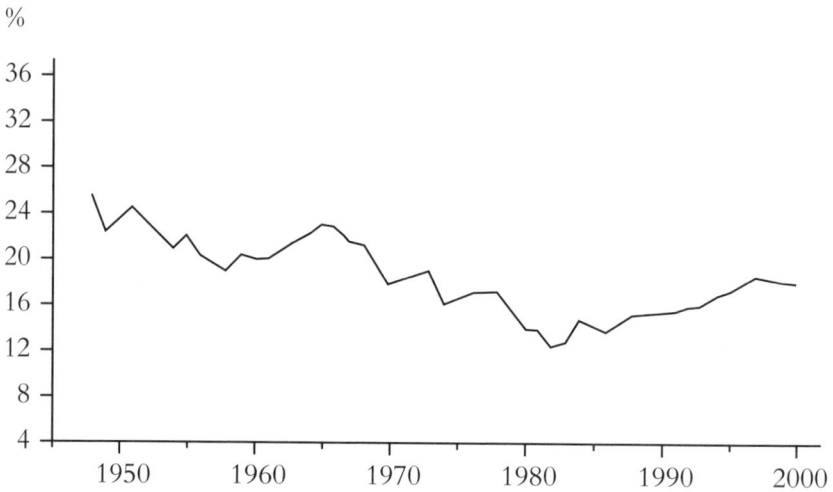

It is this which explains the dilemma faced by neoliberal economists in the current crisis. A pure Hayekian or neoclassical position would mean allowing many of the giant firms to go bust so as to provide a lease of life to the rest. But the reality is that the concentration and centralisation of capital has reached a point where the different elements of the system are so inter-tangled that unprofitable firms going bust can damage, rather than help, the remaining profitable ones.

The real roots of the crisis

Such reasoning enables us to see that the roots of the crisis do in fact lie in the downward pressure on profitability since the end of the 1960s. The attempts to deal with this have included all the means referred to by Husson—attacks on wages, the social wage, working conditions and so forth—that increase the rate of exploitation. A variety of different sources show an increase in the "share of capital" as opposed to wages for all the major capitalist countries. But in the absence of massive bankruptcies of the giant firms this has not been enough to restore the rate of profit to its old level. The result has been a long-term slowdown in the rate of productive accumulation even when the rapid accumulation taking place in China is taken into account.

In passing, it should be said that this downward trend in accumulation has one side-effect—the reduced tempo of accumulation can, at least at times, reduce the upward pressure on the organic composition of capital.[28]

But the most important effect of decreased accumulation at a time of increasing rate of exploitation is to open up a gap between the capacity of the system to produce goods and the capacity of the market to absorb them. This "overproduction" is not a result of "under-consumption" as such but of the failure of accumulation to take place on the scale necessary to replace lost consumer demand by an increased demand for investment goods.

The expansion of finance has taken place against this background. On the one side it has constituted an attempt by capitalists to get rates of profit higher than they could get from productive investment. This is a procedure that can work for some individual capitalists but not for the system as a whole since, at the end of the day, surplus value comes from productive investment. On the other side it has amounted to workers and members of the middle class being granted loans to buy things which created a short-term increased demand for the goods that could not have been sold otherwise. This "privatised Keynesianism" was positively encouraged by Alan Greenspan as head of the US Federal Reserve in the aftermath of the collapse of the telecoms and dotcom bubble of the late 1990s and the panic at the time of 9/11. But this too could not work beyond a certain point because workers could only have afforded interest payments on the loans sufficient to provide a continuing high level of profits to the finance sector if wages had been raised—which would then have reduced the rate of profit through the system as a whole. As even bourgeois economic commentators like Martin Wolf have recognised, the loans provided the means by which an important section of the US population became "the consumer of last resort" for the rest of the world system—and especially for Germany, China and, via Chinese demand, for Japan, the rest of East Asia and Latin America.

28: Figures for capital-output ratios and for capital-labour ratios suggest this has been the case at various times since the mid-1970s.

Figure 9: Goldman Sach's figures for yield on physical capital
Source: Daly, Kevin, and Ben Broadbent, 2009

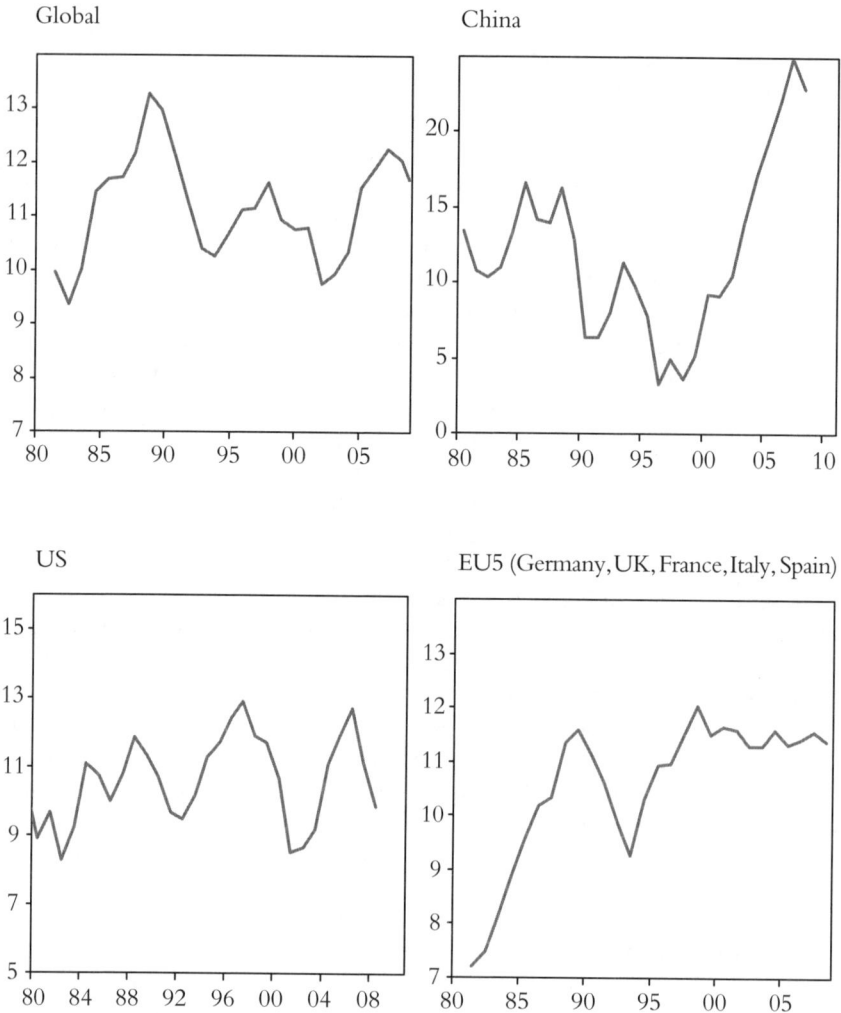

Global

China

US

EU5 (Germany, UK, France, Italy, Spain)

    The crisis can then be seen as a product of the "law of the tendency of the rate of profit to fall and its countervailing tendencies"—providing the counter-tendencies are seen as limited in their effects, raising the rate of profit from the very low level of the early 1980s but not sufficiently to boost accumulation on the scale needed to absorb everything produced by the system.

Figure 10: Tutan's calculation of the German non-residential rate of profit
Source: Tutan, 2008.

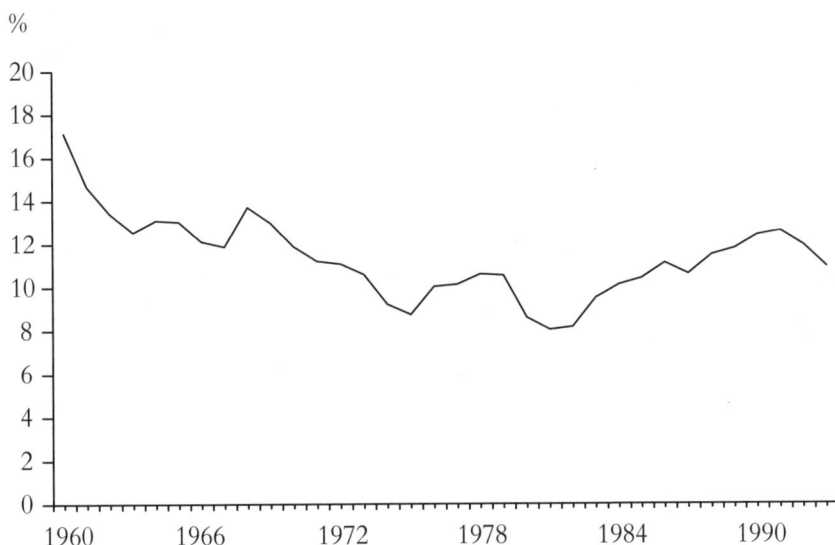

This resolves a mystery in Husson's picture—as to why his supposedly very high level of profit rates (higher than in the long boom or the "glorious 30 years") has not led to a level of productive investment sufficient to pull the whole global economy forward. Instead for 30 years we have had spells of accumulation in particular parts of the world system for a number of years at a time (sometimes very sharp spells as in Brazil in the late 1970s, China in the last decade or the US in the mid-1990s), but not a sustained global boom. His explanation seems to be that there are political forces preventing the system undertaking the Keynesian measures that would be good for it and instead leading to a diversion of accumulated money capital from productive investment into finance. It makes more sense to see the flow of money capital into finance as a response to productive profit rates that are deemed to be too low—something which is confirmed by all the calculations of profit rates except for the ones Husson supplies.

It should be added that Husson's own figures leave another question unanswered: what happens to the money capital that goes into finance? For only a portion of the money capital that flows into finance can stay there since finance (by definition) is not mainly concerned with converting money capital into commodities: some goes on building financial offices and on salaries but most flows back into the rest of the system. The financial system is a network of pipes connecting the different parts of the system that do convert money capital into commodities—or at best a sink which can only hold a certain amount of money capital before overflowing. The housing boom will have converted some of the money capital into commodities but not as much as might be thought, since most of it was absorbed by rising house prices, not by rising house construction (this was particularly clear in Britain, where house prices quadrupled in 12 years while housing construction remained at a historically low figure). In fact, the figures suggest that, in the US at least, it was only in the mid-2000s that finance did not eventually flow back into productive investment. In the mid to late 1990s there was net borrowing by industrial corporations. The problem was that even in this period capital globally did not feel confident enough about profitability to undertake investment on a scale necessary to produce a sustained boom.

References

Alexander, Arthur, 1998, "Japan in the context of Asia", SAIS policy forum series John Hopkins University.

Carchedi, Guglielmo, 1979, *Frontiers of Political Economy* (Verso).

Choonara, Joseph, 2009, "A Note on Goldman Sachs and the Rate of Profit", *International Socialism 124* (autumn 2009), www.isj.org.uk/?id=588

Daly, Kevin, and Ben Broadbent, 2009, "The Savings Glut, the Return on Capital and the Rise in Risk Aversion", Global Economics Paper No 185, Goldman Sachs Global Economics, Commodities and Strategy Research.

Duménil, Gérard, and Dominique Lévy, 2002, "The Profit Rate: Where and How Much Did it Fall? Did It Recover?", *Review of Radical Political Economy* 34, www.jourdan.ens.fr/levy/dle2002f.pdf

Felipe, Jesus, Edith Lavina, and Emma Xiaoqin Fan, 2008, "Diverging Patterns of Profitability, Investment and Growth in China and India during 1980-2003", *World Development*, volume 36, number 5.

Fine, Ben, and Lawrence Harris, 1979, *Rereading Capital* (Macmillan).

Freeman, Alan, 2009, "What Makes the US Rate of Profit Fall", unpublished paper, http://mpra.ub.uni-muenchen.de/14147/1/MPRA_paper_14147.pdf

Harman, Chris, 1984, *Explaining the Crisis* (Bookmarks).

Harman, Chris, 2009, *Zombie Capitalism* (Bookmarks).

Hayashi, Fumio and Edward C Prescott, 2001, "The 1990s in Japan: A Lost Decade", www.esri.go.jp/jp/prj21/forum04/pdf/summary4.pdf

Husson, Michel, 2009, "Le Dogmatisme n'est Pas Marxism", NPA website, http://bit.ly/husson-dogmatism

Jackson, Tony, 2008, "Recession Flames Fanned by Debt-Capex Combination", *Financial Times*, 26 November 2008.

Jackson, Tony, 2009, "Maybe Equities Rally, but My Money Stays Under the Mattress", *Financial Times*, 30 March 2009.

Kliman, Andrew, 2007, *Reclaiming Marx's Capital* (Lexington Books).

Kliman, Andrew, 2009, "The Persistent Fall in Profitability Underlying the Current Crisis: New Temporalist Evidence" (second draft), http://akliman.squarespace.com/persistent-fall

O'Hara, Phillip Anthony, 2006, "A Chinese Social Structure of Accumulation for Capitalist Long-Wave Upswing?", *Review of Radical Political Economics*, volume 38, number 3, http://hussonet.free.fr/rrpe397.pdf

Mohun, Simon, 2006, "Distributive Shares in the US Economy, 1964-2001", *Cambridge Journal of Economics*, volume 30, number 3.

Moseley, Fred, 2007, "Is the US Economy Heading for a Hard Landing?", www.mtholyoke.edu/courses/fmoseley/HARDLANDING.doc

Murray, Robin, 1973, "Productivity, Organic Composition, and the Falling Rate of Profit", *Bulletin of the Conference of Socialist Economists*, Spring 1973.

Preobrazhensky, Evgeny, 1985 (1931), *The Decline of Capitalism* (ME Sharpe).

Sylvain, Arnaud, 2001, "Rentabilité et Profitabilité du Capital: le Cas de Six Pays Industrialisés", *Économie et Statistique*, no 341-2, www.insee.fr/fr/ffc/docs_ffc/ES341G.pdf

Tevlin, Stacey, and Karl Whelan, 2003, "Explaining the Investment Boom of the 1990s", *Journal of Money, Credit and Banking*, volume 35, number 1, www.federalreserve.gov/pubs/feds/2000/200011/200011pap.pdf

Tutan, Mehmet Ufuk, 2008, *The Falling Rate of Profits in West Germany* (VDM Verlag Dr Mueller eK).

Yu, Zhang, and Zhao Feng, 2006, "The Rate of Surplus Value, the Composition of Capital, and the Rate of Profit in the Chinese Manufacturing Industry: 1978-2005". Paper presented at the Second Annual Conference of the International Forum on the Comparative Political Economy of Globalization, 1-3 September 2006, Renmin University of China, Beijing, China.

Zombie Capitalism and the origin of crises

Guglielmo Carchedi

*This is the second in a series of responses to Chris Harman's last book, **Zombie Capitalism: Global Crisis and the Relevance of Marx**. It was written shortly before Chris's death.*

The great merit of *Zombie Capitalism* is that it outlines the causes and consequences of the recurrence of crises while at the same time describing the challenges they pose for workers. Scholarly books on this subject are not generally known for their readability or their wider appeal. But this book stands out as one of the few fortunate exceptions. It is clearly written in as accessible a style as possible, given the inevitable complexity of much of its subject matter.

There are several features that recommend it, besides its accessibility. To begin with, Harman comes down squarely in favour of a temporalist approach (a term explained below). The choice of a temporalist versus a simultaneist approach would seem to be a quibble, a byzantine discussion diverting the attention from more fundamental issues. And yet it is a matter of the utmost importance. Marx computes the prices at which commodities (produced with the average technique within each sector) are tendentially sold—their prices of production—by adding the average rate of profit to the value contained in the inputs into their production (the constant and variable capital advanced). As far as this period is concerned, the values of the inputs are not transformed, while the values of the outputs are transformed into production prices. This in essence is Marx's transformation procedure, his price theory.

A critique of this was put forward by Eugen von Böhm-Bawerk shortly after the appearance of the third volume of *Capital*.[1] But by far the most influential attack on Marx's transformation procedure was mounted by Ladislaus von Bortkiewicz[2] and was brought to the attention of a modern readership by Paul Sweezy.[3] Essentially, the main criticism of Marx's approach is that, since any particular commodity is bought for the same price that it is sold for, some capitalists sell their output at its transformed value (their production price) but other capitalists buy the same products as inputs at their individual, untransformed value. If true, this would be a logical inconsistency undermining Marx's theoretical project. This inconsistency would mean that the purchasing power advanced to buy some inputs would be insufficient to start a new process of production, while the purchasing power advanced to buy some other inputs would exceed what was needed. Simple reproduction, repeated cycles of production on the same scale, would fail.[4] If the theory cannot show how the system reproduces itself, then the theory is called into question.

However, after the articles by Perez, Ernst and Carchedi in the early 1980s[5] it became clear that the critique is based on the incorrect assumption that the same commodities are both the inputs and the outputs for a particular period. For Marx, and in reality, inputs enter production at a certain point in time and outputs emerge at a different, later point in time. This is Marx's temporalist approach. From a temporalist perspective, the output of a period becomes the input of the following period. For example, a machine is bought at the same price for which it is sold. But while this is the production price for the seller it is the individual value for the buyer because that machine will realise more or less than the value paid for it when the output (created by the process for which the machine is an input) is eventually sold at its production price. As Marx writes, "Although [the inputs] entered the labour process with a definite value, they may come out of it with a value that is larger or smaller, because the labour time society needs

---

1:   Böhm-Bawerk argued that there is a contradiction between the first and the third volumes of *Capital*. See Böhm-Bawerk, 1973. For refutations of this critique see Ernst, 1982; Carchedi, 1984; Freeman and Carchedi, 1996; and Kliman, 2007.

2:   Bortkiewicz, 1971, p30.

3:   Sweezy, 1970 [1942].

4:   The same applies to expanded reproduction.

5:   Perez, 1980; Ernst, 1982; Carchedi, 1984.

for their production has undergone a general change".[6] From a temporalist perspective, which sees the economy as a succession of periods of production and realisation, the logical inconsistency melts like snow in the sun. Many Marxists who have ignored this simple point resort to simultaneous equations to determine the prices of the inputs and of the outputs of the *same* process.[7] Consequently, these authors theorise capitalism as a system in which time does not exist. It is not warranted to theorise capitalism timelessly even as a first approximation because conclusions reached on the basis of the opposite assumption are opposite and irreconcilable. Either I assume that time exists or I assume that time does not exist. All the conclusions reached on the basis of one assumption are invalid on the basis of the opposite assumption.

Without time there is no movement, without movement there is no change and without change there is equilibrium. Just as in orthodox economics, capitalism is seen as a system in or tending towards equilibrium, rather than a system in or tending towards crises, as in Marx. If capitalism is a system in equilibrium, it is also a rational system. But then the working class is deprived of the objective grounds upon which to base its struggle against capital. If the system is rational, the workers' struggle for the supersession of capital is irrational and voluntaristic because it is contrary to an objective, equilibrating movement. But if, as Marx argues, the system is irrational because it tends objectively towards crises and thus towards its self-destruction, the workers' struggle is grounded upon and becomes the expression of this objective movement; it is thus rational and not voluntaristic. Seen from a Marxist, temporalist perspective the system, then, is in a permanent state of non-equilibrium.[8] The issue of internal consistency, the battleground upon which both upholders and critics of Marx have been fighting over the decades, is certainly important. But the crucial point is not only that the so-called transformation problem is a non-existent problem once one reintroduces time in the analysis.[9] It is even more important to realise that the simultaneist alternative deals a deadly blow to workers'

6:   Marx, 1988.

7:   Harman points out that "the method of simultaneous equations assumes that the price of the inputs to production have to be equal to the prices of the outputs. But they do not" (p49). This is true. But the reason is that the inputs of a certain production process are not the outputs of the same process. This is the critical point from which Harman's argument is derived.

8:   This is not the same as disequilibrium because disequilibrium, being a deviation from equilibrium, implies the latter. But equilibrium and thus disequilibrium are ideological concepts with no scientific value whatsoever.

9:   As Harman stresses, "Marx's basic concepts survive all the criticisms once they are not interpreted through the static framework, ignoring the process of change through time that characterises the neoclassical system" (p53).

struggle by undermining the objective grounds upon which it is based. This point has escaped the commentators on both sides of the debate.[10]

There are other positive features in Harman's book such his development of the implications in Marx and Engels' theory of imperialism, and his emphasis on famine and environmental destruction as integral parts of capitalist development. This is the object of the final three chapters. Also of great interest is the detailed analysis of capitalism's course during the second half of the 20th century and of the crises that are the signposts of this course, the subjects of chapters 6 to 11. These are clearly written and informative. But aside from these positive features some critical comments are in order.

Harman rightly stresses that "the only source of value...is labour", so if constant capital invested grows proportionally more than variable capital, in other words if the organic composition of capital grows, the average rate of profit falls. This process takes place because technological competition gives a cutting edge to the innovators at the expense of the laggards (p70). However, there are four ambiguities in Harman's text that should be clarified. They concern more the exposition than the theoretical content of the book.

The first ambiguity is that Harman, after having pointed out that the rate of profit falls because technological competition expels labour and thus diminishes the source of value, seems to stress that this fall is due to lower prices following a rapid rate of accumulation "and this hits profits" (p60). Within a temporalist perspective lower output prices at the end of this period are also lower input prices at the beginning of the next period and all we have is a redistribution of value and a temporary fluctuation in the average profit rate. However, in terms of value analysis, a lower production of value during this period is also a lower realisation of value at the end of this same period so that less value can be invested in the subsequent period. On this account, lower prices reveal a fall in the production of value: the loss of profitability is permanent. But, as we shall see, lower unit prices (values) cannot be the cause of crises.

The second ambiguity, which is related to the first one, is that whereas the increase in the organic composition is identified by Harman as the ultimate cause of the fall in the average rate of profit, in the actual exposition of the argument the increase in the organic composition of capital seems to be one of the many factors affecting the course of the average profit rate. It might be worth recalling that the increase in the organic

---

10: For a more detailed exposition of the above, see Carchedi, 2009a. See also Carchedi, forthcoming.

composition of capital is the tendency, while the fall in that composition due to the cheaper means of production as a consequence of the same technological innovations is one of the counter-tendencies. The cheaper means of production reduce the value of the output produced. The producers still using the older and more expensive means of production can charge for their output only what it would have cost them to produce that output with the new and cheaper means of production. They therefore suffer a loss. For them it is as if some capital has been destroyed. But there is no destruction of capital for the economy as a whole because the value they fail to realise is, through the price mechanism, redistributed to the producers using the newer and cheaper means of production. The depreciation of the old means of production is thus no destruction of value and thus cannot be the factor (or one of the factors) that accounts either for the crisis or for the revival of the economy. To hold the contrary view would mean to hold onto an individualistic methodology, the opposite of Marx's method. Rather, if capital is a social relation, the destruction of capital is basically the termination of those relations that becomes manifest as unemployment.

The third ambiguity concerns the relation between Harman's analysis and the so-called "value form theory".[11] According to the author, "The concrete labour of the individuals is transformed through exchange...into a proportionate part of 'homogeneous', 'social' labour—or abstract labour" (p26; see also p117). This formulation could suggest that Harman adheres to value form theory, although in fact he does not.

Value form theory should be rejected not because it deviates from Marx but because, by deviating from Marx, it becomes logically inconsistent. First, use values are different by definition. Exchange cannot equalise them because equalisation or quantitative comparability presupposes that there is something that makes exchange possible. Two apples cannot be exchanged for one pear unless something establishes that exchange ratio prior to exchange, at the level of production. If this is not done, the exchange ratios become indeterminate. Money cannot fulfil the role of the homogenising factor. To express something common to the different use values, money must be the necessary form of existence of something common to those different use values. This something cannot be any concrete labour but must be the abstract labour contained in those commodities.[12]

11: This approach holds that concrete labour is converted to social, abstract labour through the process of exchange.

12: "Money is labour time in the form of a general object, or the objectification of general labour time, labour time as a general commodity"—Marx, 1973, p168.

Second, as Marx points out, at the moment of exchange the commodity sold has no use value for the seller for the simple reason that the seller cannot any longer use it, and it has no use value for the buyer because the buyer cannot yet use it. Exchange would conjure up value out of nothing, out of non-existent use values.[13] Third, if concrete labour is created in production and thus embodied in the product before exchange (an uncontentious point) and if abstract labour is socially validated concrete labour in exchange (the value form thesis), then the substance of abstract labour would be use values. The substance of value, then, would be embodied in the commodity before exchange, it would exist before social validation, contrary to the value form position. Finally, if abstract labour comes to life only at the moment of and through exchange,[14] if it does not exist before exchange, the difference between the production of value and its realisation is erased. Identity of production and realisation implies the cancelling out of time—simultaneism.[15]

The fourth ambiguity in Harman's analysis involves the relation between the law of the falling average rate of profit and underconsumption. Harman quotes Marx to the effect that "the antagonistic conditions of distribution...reduce the consumption of the bulk of society to a minimum" (p58). While this passage has been interpreted as if lower wages make it impossible for labour to consume all the produced wage goods, thus decreasing profits and contributing to the emergence or worsening of the crisis, Harman correctly rejects this interpretation. In a private correspondence, Harman points out that "cutting workers' wages or consumption can provide the conditions for preventing a fall in the rate of profit (or even increase the rate of profit), but do not guarantee that an increase in investment follows, and if there is no increase in investment there will be a crisis of realisation". But in his book Harman submits that if firms can force down real wages, some consumer goods will go unsold and profit rates will fall, thus "producing recession" (p76). This passage could

---

13: The commodity might have a subjective use value but this is irrelevant because at the moment of exchange the objective use value, the objective use to which that commodity can be put, is non-existent. The alternative is to step over to a subjectivist theory of prices, that is, to leave Marx definitively.

14: For Chris Arthur abstract labour has no material existence before exchange. See Arthur, 2004. For Patrick Murray general abstract labour is "nothing actual". See Murray, 2000. For Michael Heinrich "value can only exist if there is an independent and general form of value—money". See Heinrich, 2004.

15: For a much more detailed critique of value form theory and its many internal inconsistencies, see Carchedi, 2009b.

be interpreted as if lower wages would decrease the average rate of profit rather than increasing it. However, for Marx lower wages always increase profit rates. It is for John Maynard Keynes that lower wages can decrease profits through the workers' underconsumption. What follows shows the fallacy of this underconsumption thesis.

Let us consider the most favourable case for underconsumption. Suppose workers' wages are cut. This provides extra surplus value for the capitalist class. At the same time, workers' purchasing power falls by the amount of the wage cut. Commodities (consumption goods) with a value equal to the whole decrease in the workers' purchasing power go unsold. Suppose that the excess commodities cannot be purchased by the capitalists either. This is a loss for the capitalists producing consumer goods. Under these assumptions, the wage cut represents at the same time the maximum possible loss for the capitalist class. What is the effect on the average rate of profit? The extra surplus value accruing to capital due to lower wages is cancelled because of the unsold commodities: "the labourer has been indeed exploited, but his exploitation is not realised as such for the capitalist".[16] The extra profit and the loss due to lower wages cancel each other out and the numerator of the profit rate (the surplus value) returns to the level prior to the wage cut. But the average rate of profit does not return to this level because the denominator (the constant and variable capital) is now lower by the amount of the wage cut. Thus the average rate of profit is higher than its previous level even in the case of maximum loss (all the wage goods corresponding to the wage cuts are unsold). At the same time there is underconsumption. This is sufficient to reject the underconsumptionist thesis that crises (lower profit rates) are caused or aggravated by lower wages and thus by underconsumption.[17]

If underconsumption cannot cause the crisis, it must be a consequence of the crisis. For Marx the ultimate cause of crises should be sought in the introduction of new technologies. On the one hand, they

---

16: Marx, 1967, p244.

17: Suppose an initial situation: $80c+20v+20s = 120$, where c, v and s represent constant capital, variable capital and surplus value respectively. The rate of profit $p = 20/(80+20) = 20$ percent. Suppose now a wage cut reduces v by 5. In the new situation the output is given by $80c+15v+25s = 120$ and $p = 26.3$ percent. But if the wage cut is also a loss for the capitalists producing consumer goods, $80c+15v+20s = 115$ and $p = 20/95 > 20$ percent. In a two-sector economy an increase in the average rate of profit takes place at the cost of labour (due to lower wages and to lower purchasing power for wage goods) and at the cost of the capitalists producing wage goods. The average rate of profit rises because the gains in sector one more than compensate the loss in sector two. For rigorous proof, see Carchedi, forthcoming.

increase labour's productivity (units of output per unit of capital invested); on the other hand, they reduce the labour power relative to the means of production employed per unit of capital. If less variable capital and more constant capital are employed percentage wise, the average rate of profit falls. It falls, not "because labour becomes less productive, but because it becomes more productive".[18] This is the tendency that explains the origin of crises. There are counter-tendencies that hold back the tendential fall, even if only temporarily. But let us consider only the tendency in order to better evaluate the alternative theories.

Suppose an initial situation in the consumption goods sector such that $80c+20v+20s = 120$ is incorporated in 120 units of means of consumption. Abstracting from the sector producing means of production, the average rate of profit (ARP) is 20 percent. Suppose now that new technologies are introduced and that in the new situation $90c+10v+10s = 110$ is incorporated in 220 units of means of consumption. The ARP falls to 10 percent. The unit price falls from $120/120 = 1$ to $220/110 = 0.5$. Before the new technology was introduced the 120 units of consumption goods were distributed in equal parts between capital and labour (given that the rate of exploitation was $20s/20v = 100$ percent). After the introduction of the new technologies, each class receives 110 consumption goods and yet the ARP falls. Under the assumption that each unit of variable capital represents a worker, ten workers have lost their job. However, all consumption goods have been sold and the rate of exploitation has remained the same. Unemployment does not necessarily create underconsumption if the goods not bought by the unemployed worker are bought by those who are still employed. There is no underconsumption either if the rate of exploitation rises and the capitalists buy the goods that cannot be bought by the workers. There is underconsumption only if, as mentioned above, neither the capitalists nor the workers can purchase all the consumption goods. This is the crisis of underconsumption.

The question then is: what causes the lack of purchasing power? This, as mentioned above, can only be wages lower than 10v due to the capitalists' attempt to regain the lost profitability and to the capitalist's profits not higher or lower than 10s. But the stagnant or lower profits (and profit rates) indicate that the economy has already entered crisis (otherwise the capitalists could buy the commodities not purchased by labour with those extra profits). It also follows that crises are not due to a fall in prices either. In the example above, unit prices fall from 1 to 0.5

18: Marx, 1967, p240.

because productivity has increased. But this is an indication of crisis not so much because productivity has increased but because less value and surplus value have been produced. A fall in prices is a consequence and a manifestation of the crisis, not the cause.

The argument concerning the relation between underconsumption and crises can be summarised as follows. First, in and of themselves, lower wages do cause underconsumption but they increase the average rate of profit even in the case of maximum failed realisation (maximum underconsumption or overproduction). Second, they seem to cause a fall in the average profit rate (crisis) because they occur in parallel with lower profits, which are the manifestation of the crisis. Thus underconsumption is a consequence of the crisis (lower profits) rather than being its cause. Crises are caused not by the decreased consumption of use values but by the decreased production of surplus value. This is a consequence of technological competition and of the fall in the average profit rate and unemployment. In the final analysis the extent and depth of the crisis is measured by the rate of unemployment and of exploitation. This is the perspective of the collective labourer.

The fall in the average rate of profit obscures fundamental features of capitalism. Crises do not result in a general impoverishment but the impoverishment of the majority together with a concentration of wealth in the hands of a minority. Consider two capitalists within the same sector (a similar argument can be made in case of more than one sector). Originally, they both use the same basic technology, eg 70c+30v+30s = 130. The output is, say, 100 units of output. Subsequently, one of them introduces a new, more advanced technology, eg 80c+20v+20s = 120. This capital's output rises to 400 units. The ARP falls from 30 percent to 25 percent. But this average implies a redistribution of surplus value. The unit price (value) is now 250/500 = 0.5. The capital with the advanced technology realises 400x0.5 = 200 and thus a profit of 100 and a rate of profit of 100 percent. The capital still operating with basic technology realises 100x0.5 = 50 and thus loses 50 units of value. In this example, the capital using advanced technology appropriates not only the surplus value (30) but also a part of the value invested by the other capital (20). The movement expressing itself as the fall in the ARP causes an impoverishment of the capitalist class as a whole, but within this movement it causes a concentration of value in the hands of the most efficient capitalists at the cost of the less efficient capitalists (many of whom fold in times of crises).

Marx's approach has been challenged by Marxists and non-Marxists. Let us evaluate the most influential alternative explanations:

(1) Physicalist theories—basically the neo-classical, neo-Ricardian and Keynesian approaches—reach conclusions opposite to those of Marx. According to these theories, the profit rate rises instead of falling both because more use values are produced due to the new technologies and because labour is seen simply as a cost (the perspective of the individual capitalist) rather than also being value-creating activity (Marx's perspective). If more use values can be produced with lower costs, the average rate of profit can only rise. But if only use values are seen, labour is seen only as concrete labour. Physicalism then rejects the reality of abstract labour. But there is a problem here. Physicalism shipwrecks against the incommensurability problem. Simply put, use values are by definition different. In the absence of the homogeneous substance that is abstract labour, no quantitative measurement and comparison is possible. Unfortunately for physicalism, no solution exists for this internal inconsistency.

Keynes was aware of the problem. After having noted that "two incommensurable collections of miscellaneous objects cannot in themselves provide the material for a quantitative analysis", he comes up with a truly astonishing consideration: this "fact...need not, of course, prevent us from making approximate statistical comparisons".[19] As if two incommensurable quantities could be "approximately" measured and compared! They cannot, either exactly or approximately. The reason for this "oversight" is that no physicalist author can admit to this inconsistency for two fundamental reasons. First, to admit that there is a problem of incommensurability would mean to admit that the whole theory is built on quicksand. Second, if the theory is indefensible it becomes impossible to hold onto the position that technological innovation, the factor that accounts for capitalism's dynamism, increase the average rate of profit rather than decreasing it, that capitalism tends towards growth and equilibrium rather than towards crises, ie that it is a rational system.

(2) I have argued above that the attempt to single out the low level of wages as the prime cause of crises leads to a theoretical inconsistency. The opposite approach is the "profit squeeze" theory, which was popular within some Marxist circles in the 1970s and which seems to be enjoying a revival. This theory claims that crises are due to too high a level of wages. Given that wages and profits are in inverse relation, this approach seems to fit eminently well into Marx's paradigm. However, there are both empirical and theoretical explanations that invalidate the argument.

First of all, concerning the present crisis, one would expect that the

---

19: Keynes, 1964, p39.

world economy, and especially the US economy, would have embarked on a long period of economic growth, given that minimum wages in the US fell by no less than 25.7 percent from 1967 to 2005.[20] Second, the supporters of this view seem to ignore that Marx once remarked that "nothing is more absurd...than to explain the fall in the rate of profit by a rise in the rate of wages". The reason is that "the tendency of the rate of profit to fall is bound up with a tendency of the rate of surplus value to rise".[21]

Let us elucidate this important remark. In order to understand the origin of crises one has to start from a period of economic growth. According to the profit squeeze theory, in the upward phase of the cycle at a certain point wages start rising, thus eating into profits. Supposedly, this is where the crisis begins. However, in the upward phase profits increase, unless one wants to define this phase as one of falling profits. Thus, in terms of the theory, in this phase both profits and wages must increase. This is possible only if the mass of both value and surplus value increases. And this is exactly what happens. But this is the Achilles' heel of the theory. Suppose that surplus value increases by, say, 5 percent due to expanded reproduction. Any redistribution of this extra surplus value is theoretically possible. For example, 1 percent can go to wages and 4 percent to profits. Hence, in the upward phase higher wages do not necessarily decrease profits and crises do not follow. The theory is indeterminate and thus fails. A different explanation of the role of higher wages within a crisis theory must be sought. This is that the fall in the ARP causes first a rise and then a fall in wages.

The barometer of the capitalist economy's health is the average rate of profit, rather than the mass of surplus value. In a period of growth, technological innovations start pushing down the average rate of profit even though the mass of surplus value rises. This explains why the seeds of crises are already present in the upward phase of the cycle. For a while the increase in employment due to enlarged reproduction more than offsets the relative decrease in employment due to the increasing organic composition. In this phase increased competition by the capitalists for labour power leads to wage increases. The increased competition for labour power and thus the increase in wages can be reinforced by the attempt by the larger capitals to counter the fall in their rate of profit—inasmuch as the fall in the average rate of profit affects them too—by increasing the scale of production, and thus, potentially, the mass

---

20: Bernstein, Lawrence and Heidi, 2007, table 3.40.
21: Marx, 1967, p240.

of profits they receive.[22] It follows that, inasmuch as the fall in the ARP stimulates enlarged reproduction and thus higher wages, wage rises are the result of the fall in the average rate of profit, not vice versa. As the fall in the ARP continues inexorably, wage rises further decrease it, contributing to the bankruptcy of the weaker capitals and increased unemployment. At this point the mass of surplus value is also affected negatively. A decrease in the mass as well as in the rate of profits results in a crisis. It follows that the rise in wages can only strengthen a movement, the decrease in the average rate of profit, rather than cause it. At this point, wages begin to fall due to capital's attempt to recover its profitability.

There is a way one could try to rescue the profit squeeze theory—by assuming that the mass of surplus value falls instead of rising. In this case, higher wages would indeed necessarily dent profits. But this would mean stepping out of the frying pan into the fire. In fact, one would assume what has to be explained is a decreasing mass of profit, ie the downward phase, and thus the crisis.

One last point: this theory leads naturally to the conclusion that crises could be avoided if only the workers were to restrain their demands. The blame for the crises then falls squarely upon the workers' shoulders—music to capital's ears.

(3) While the theories discussed above focus on one element as the prime cause of crises, some Marxist authors reject what they see as "mono-causal" explanations, especially that of the tendential fall in the ARP. Instead, they argue, there is no single explanation valid for all crises, except that they are all a "property" of capitalism and that crises manifest in different forms in different periods and contexts. However, if this elusive and mysterious property becomes manifest as different causes of different crises, while itself remaining unknowable, if we do not know where all these different causes come from, then we have no crisis theory. Moreover, if it is agreed that crises manifest themselves as a falling ARP, if one resorts to the theories criticised above for an explanation of the peculiarities of each crisis, one is left empty-handed because—as argued—none of those theories can explain the origin of crises except the tendential fall in the ARP.

(4) All the theories discussed above have Marx as a reference point. But there are also theories of a different and opposite kind that submit that the cause of crises resides in the financial and speculative sphere, namely in extremely high levels of debt, rampant speculation, a permissive

---

22: Marx, 1967, p256.

monetary policy, the loosening of rules governing borrowing and lending due to deregulation, and so on. From here the crisis overflows into the real economy. In short, the crisis is due to mistakes in the financial and monetary sphere. The obvious question is: given that crises are a constant and recurrent feature of capitalism, if they are due in the last instance to the mistakes of the financial and monetary authorities as well as of the politicians, of governments, etc, why do they recur? In other words, why don't policymakers learn from their mistakes? Obviously, there must be structural, economic reasons that not only prevent them from learning from their past mistakes but that actually force them to repeat those mistakes recurrently. In fact, the origin of the financial and speculative crises should be sought in the real economy, in the production of value and surplus value, rather than, as is fashionable nowadays, turning the relation of cause and effect upside-down.

References

Arthur, Chris, 2004, *The New Dialectic and Marx's "Capital"* (Brill).

Bernstein, Jared, Mishel Lawrence and Shierholz Heidi, 2007, *The State of Working America* (Economic Policy Institute).

Böhm-Bawerk, Eugen von, 1973 [1896], "Karl Marx and the Close of his System", in Paul Sweezy (ed), *Karl Marx and the Close of his System* (Kelley).

Bortkiewicz, Ladislaus von, 1971 [1906], "Calcolo del Valore e Calcolo del Prezzo nel Sistema Marxiano", in Ladislaus von Bortkiewicz, *La Teoria Economica di Marx* (Einaudi).

Carchedi, Guglielmo, 1984, "The Logic of Prices as Values", *Economy and Society*, volume 13, number 4.

Carchedi, Guglielmo, 2009a, "Limits and Challenges of the Consistency Debate in Marxian Value Theory", *Research in Political Economy*, volume 25.

Carchedi, Guglielmo, 2009b, "The Fallacies of 'New Dialectics' and Value-Form Theory", *Historical Materialism 17*.

Carchedi, Guglielmo, forthcoming, *Behind the Crisis* (Brill).

Ernst, John, 1982, "Simultaneous Valuation Extirpated: a Contribution of the Critique of the Neo-Ricardian Concept of Value", *Review of Radical Political Economics*, volume 14, number 2.

Freeman, Alan, and Guglielmo Carchedi (eds), 1996, *Marx and Non-Equilibrium Economics* (Edward Elgar).

Heinrich, Michael, 2004, "Ambivalences of Marx's Critique of Political Economy as Obstacles for the Analysis of Contemporary Capitalism", *Historical Materialism*, annual conference, 10 October 2004, London, revised paper.

Keynes, John Maynard, 1964, *The General Theory of Employment, Interest and Money* (Harcourt, Brace and World).

Kliman, Andrew, 2007, *Reclaiming Marx's "Capital": A Refutation of the Myth of Inconsistency* (Lexington).

Marx, Karl, 1967, *Capital , volume three* (Progress), www.marxists.org/archive/marx/works/1894-c3/

Marx, Karl, 1973 [1939], *Grundrisse* (Penguin), www.marxists.org/archive/marx/works/1857/grundrisse/

Marx, Karl, 1988 [1861-3], "Economic Manuscript of 1861-3", in Karl Marx and Frederick Engels, *Collected Works*, volume 30 (Progress), www.marxists.org/archive/marx/works/1861/economic

Murray, Patrick, 2000, "Marx's 'Truly Social' Labor Theory of Value: part I, Abstract Labor in Marxian Value Theory", *Historical Materialism 6*.

Perez, Manuel, 1980, "Valeur et Prix: Un Essai de Critique des Propositions Néo-Ricardiannes", *Critiques de l'Economie Politique, nouvelle série*, 10.

Sweezy, Paul, 1970 [1942], *The Theory of Capitalist Development: Principles of Marxian Political Economy* (Monthly Review).

A whiff of tear gas

Andy Durgan

Upon joining the Dagenham and Ilford International Socialists in late 1972 I was offered a special bargain price package of reading material. I eagerly devoured what was a fairly mixed selection of work but one pamphlet stood out: Chris Harman's *How the Revolution was Lost*. Having flirted with Stalinism, here were all the arguments I had been looking for. Brilliantly succinct and, in contrast with most of the stuff masquerading as Marxist writing I had waded through until that point, it was understandable. It was this talent, what Pat Stack refers to as his "unfailing ability to make the complex seem clear and simple", that made Chris so special.

Despite being one of the outstanding Marxist theorists, historians and economists of the second half of the 20th century, he lacked any academic ambitions. As is known, he abandoned his doctoral thesis to dedicate himself full time to revolutionary politics. Less known is that the only copy of his thesis was stolen from the locker he had left it in. Explaining what for most people would have been an unmitigated disaster many years later he seemed only vaguely amused by his misfortune!

I first heard Chris at an IS day school in East London in early 1973 where he spoke on armed insurrection—not, as I would realise later, the normal fare of our public meetings or debates. Like others, I was initially disappointed in that his oratory style did not compare to his writing skills, but I would soon appreciate that, to cite Pat Stack again, you "never left one of [Chris's] meetings without feeling [you] had learned something new". This particular time it was the uprising of the Austrian *Schutzbund* in

1934. Over the years, of course, Chris's speaking style would improve and increasingly match the clarity of his writing.

Later when I got to know Chris I found that behind that shy, and at times awkward, exterior was a very likeable person. His lack of pretension and his sense of humour were what most struck you about him. It was, in fact, surprisingly easy (surprisingly for those who did not know him perhaps) to talk to him about more or less anything. But even on the most relaxed social occasions being with Chris was part of your political education.

Where we both shared a very specific interest was in relation to events in Spain. Chris followed developments during the transition from Francoist dictatorship to faltering democracy closely and had contact with various leading activists of the country's burgeoning far left organisations. The most promising of these was the *Organización de Izquierda Comunista* (Left Communist Organisation, OIC) which had emerged out of the mass struggles of the mid–1970s and had two or three thousand members, mainly workers. Their politics were fairly eclectic but, in contrast to much of the Spanish radical left, emphasised the centrality of working class self-emancipation and were clearly anti-Stalinist. Relations with the OIC had flourished after it was discovered that they had translated and published Chris's pamphlet analysing the denouement of the Portuguese Revolution.

In early 1976 Chris attended the still clandestine OIC's first congress. This took place in a monastery and, much to Chris's amusement, the delegates periodically interrupted proceedings to sing hymns and thus fool any passing would-be informant! On a more serious note, the subsequent collapse of the OIC is dealt with in his seminal piece on the crisis in the European revolutionary left that appeared in *International Socialism* in 1979. Like much of Spain's far left the OIC had not expected the mass radicalisation of the mid–1970s to give way to a stable bourgeois democracy.

More tenuous relations were now established with the ex-Maoist *Movimiento Comunista* (MC), which the remnants of the OIC had joined. The IS Tendency was only beginning to emerge as an organised tendency at this time and the SWP still maintained a fairly pragmatic relationship with a number of groups who rejected Stalinism, or at least claimed to, and were not afflicted by the peculiarities of orthodox Trotskyism. MC appeared to fit the mould and, moreover, was quite an impressive organisation both in terms of size and base. However, Chris became increasingly frustrated with MC's confused politics and expected them to eventually disintegrate. This was something we disagreed over but ultimately he would be proved right, of course.

In the 1990s with the near terminal crisis of the Spanish revolutionary left and the demise of the communist bloc, new opportunities arose and eventually led to the setting up of what would become *En Lucha*. From the group's foundation in 1994 through to his death Chris would play a decisive role in its evolution. The very nature of the group, its core of talented young activists and its rejection of simplistic formulae and "short cuts", had a lot to do with Chris's unassuming way of relating to the comrades. With his help we weathered the ups and downs that any young organisation inevitably faces.

At first comrades found Chris slightly disconcerting as he often appeared to fall asleep during the rather lengthy sessions of our conferences. They soon learnt that was merely a ruse as he would suddenly "wake up" and make some brief but extremely useful contribution to the debate! Over the years Chris became a popular and near permanent fixture at our annual gathering; only his presence in Egypt meant he missed this year's.

Above all Chris represented what was best about 1968. Having become politically active myself in the shadow of the 1960s, the superb *The Fire Last Time* has weighed heavily on my own political development. And although it was hardly May 1968, a favourite snapshot of Chris comes from Nice in December 2000 when we tried to "blockade" the EU summit. Showered by the CRS with tear gas canisters and as bravado turned into shambolic retreat I, literally, bumped into Chris still trying to go forward, a broad grin on his face. This is how I am sure he would like us to remember him: very much alive, fighting and enjoying every minute of it. *Gracias Chris por todo. La lucha continua.*

Chris Harman

Zombie Capitalism
Global Crisis and the Relevance of Marx

"A powerful, comprehensive and accessible critique of capitalism from one of the world's pre-eminent Marxist economists. It is a clear, incisive warning of the massive dangers posed by a 'runaway system' and the threat it poses for the future of humanity."
Graham Turner
Author of *Credit Crunch: Housing Bubbles, Globalisation and the Worldwide Economic Crisis*

"Essential reading for anyone who wants to understand the present crisis and its place in the history of capitalism, and an important contribution to Marxist political economy."
Alex Callinicos
Professor of European Studies, King's College London

Faced with the financial crisis that began in 2007 some economic commentators began to talk of "zombie banks"—financial institutions incapable of fulfilling any positive function but representing a threat to everything else. Capitalism in the 21st century is a zombie system, seemingly dead when it comes to achieving human goals and responding to human feelings, but capable of sudden spurts of activity that cause chaos all around. Chris Harman shows how Marxism is the essential point of departure for any explanation of how this world emerged and developed over the past century and a half.

Published by Bookmarks. Out now—£16.99

020 7637 1848
mailorder@bookmarks.uk.com
www.bookmarks.uk.com

Marxism and anarchism

Paul Blackledge

There is a striking paradox at the heart of contemporary anti-capitalism. Many within the movement deny what is undoubtedly one of its defining characteristics: the very fact that it is *political* at all.[1] The practical problems with this approach have been dissected in previous issues of this journal.[2] In this essay I provide some context for these debates by examining the roots of the anti-political perspective in earlier arguments between anarchists and Marxists. My hope is that by outlining the historical similarities and differences between anarchism and classical Marxism the contemporary encounters between these two tendencies might move beyond what is too often a caricatured non-debate. Specifically, I argue that the rational core of anarchism—its desire to immunise the movement against the malign influences of "statist" politics—is actually weakened by its anti-political position. Moreover, this weakness is reinforced by anarchist criticisms of what they call Marx's "statism". As we shall see, this claim involves a massive misunderstanding of classical Marxism which not only serves to conceal its essence as the theory of working class self-emancipation but also obscures the way this theory points beyond the practical limits of anarchism.

In 1871 both Karl Marx and Mikhail Bakunin, the most

1: Thanks to Colin Barker, Alex Callinicos, Joseph Choonara, Kristyn Gorton and, especially, Chris Harman for their comments on an earlier draft of this essay. Chris Harman's detailed comments were, as ever, both generous and superbly insightful. He was an inspirational mentor, and this essay is dedicated to his memory.
2: Most recently, for instance, Callinicos and Nineham 2007, p93.

prominent representatives of the international socialist and anarchist movements respectively, welcomed the Paris Commune as a practical realisation of their visions of socialism.[3] This fact would seem to confirm the claim made by Daniel Guérin in his classic history of anarchism that, beyond the sound and fury of sectarian wrangling, "anarchism is really a synonym for socialism".[4] If, additionally, we accept Noam Chomsky's comment that "the consistent anarchist...will be a socialist, but a socialist of a particular sort": a "libertarian socialist",[5] then perhaps we might be led to view anarchism as a variant of what Hal Draper called, from a classical Marxist perspective, the tradition of "socialism from below".[6]

However, whereas Draper insisted that anarchism was a variety of socialism from above while being scathing in his criticisms of claims that Lenin had built an "authoritarian" party,[7] Guérin suggests that Lenin was at best an "ambivalent" figure whose work combined libertarian and authoritarian elements,[8] while Chomsky insists that, in contrast to consistent anarchism, Marx's thought can be characterised by a tension between an earlier libertarian socialism and later "authoritarianism"; a tension which is reflected in the history of Marxism as a conflict between libertarian socialist tendencies, represented, for instance, by Rosa Luxemburg, and state socialist tendencies, above all associated with Lenin. Chomsky argues that although the ideas of the former "converge with elements of anarcho-syndicalism", the latter is so far removed from this tradition that "if the left is understood to include 'Bolshevism' then I would flatly dissociate myself from the left".[9]

Similar arguments are a commonplace within contemporary autonomist and anarchist circles,[10] and inform the animosity these groups tend to show towards classical Marxists generally and "Leninists" more specifically.[11] Typically, anarchists and autonomists are wont to criticise Lenin in

---

3:    On the Paris Commune generally and anarchist and Marxist interpretations of its significance more specifically see Gluckstein, 2006, especially pp181-207.
4:    Guérin, 1970, p12.
5:    Chomsky, 1970, pp xv, xviii.
6:    Draper famously distinguished between what he called the "two souls of socialism": the traditions of "socialism from above" (Stalinism and reformism) and "socialism from below" (classical Marxism)—Draper, 1992, pp2-33.
7:    Draper, 1992, pp6, 11; Draper, 1999, p187.
8:    Guérin, 1970, p86.
9:    Chomsky, 2005, pp182-184; see also Berkman's claim that Leninism leads only to "dictatorship and reaction"—Berkman, 1989, piv.
10:   On the parallels between class struggle anarchism and autonomist Marxism see Franks, 2006, p12; Day, 2005, p10.
11:   See, for instance, Franks 2006, p15.

particular as the main representative of the state socialist tradition which was tried and failed in the 20th century.[12] To the extent that they engage with Marxism, theoretical and political differences within this milieu usually focus on the relationship of Marx to Lenin, asking whether the latter made a qualitative "authoritarian" break with the former or if he merely extended some of Marx's "authoritarianism" to its logical conclusion. If autonomists attempt to "rescue" Marx from Lenin, anarchists tend to reject them both through reference to Bakunin's famous claim that Marx was an "advocate of state communism".[13]

As we shall see, Bakunin's criticism of Marx is "inept".[14] It does, however, cohere with a more widespread liberal critique of Marxism which damns it by association with Stalinism.[15] Thus, in Peter Marshall's massive history of anarchism he argues not only that Bakunin's criticism of Marx as a "state socialist" was "prophetic", but also that the experience of Stalinism meant that Bakunin, and not Marx, had been "vindicated by the verdict of history".[16]

Although this claim has a certain superficial plausibility, careful examination of Bakunin's perspective reveals it to be not only false but also reactionary. For Bakunin's argument was not simply a critique of what might happen if, as he caricatured it, Marx or the Marxists came to power. It involved a much more general rejection of the possibility that society could be democratised. This question, the problem of the possibility of real democracy, sits at the core of the political differences between classical Marxism and anarchism, and informs disagreements about the relationship between freedom and authority, the issue of political organisation, and the character of the ethical critique of capitalism. This aspect of Bakunin's thought reflects a widespread failing within anarchism to develop an adequate conceptualisation of democracy: a weakness which is rooted in an incoherent model of human

---

12: For instance, Franks, 2006, p226.
13: Bakunin, 1990, p143.
14: Callinicos, 2003, p299.
15: The rational kernel of the anarchist caricature of Marxism is the fact that the most powerful voices claiming to be Marxists in the 20th century were statists (of either the Stalinist or Maoist variety) who presided over brutal systems that were far from anything we would recognise as socialist. However, given both that Marx's vision of socialism provides the basis for an immanent critique of the socialist pretensions of the old Stalinist states (Thomas, 1980, p122), and that this journal has long been associated with the argument that the Stalinist and Maoist regimes were varieties of bureaucratic state capitalism which deployed bastardised versions of the ideas of Marx and Lenin to justify local dictatorships, I will not rehearse those arguments here (see, for instance, Harman, 1990).
16: Marshall, 2008, p305.

nature that fatally undermines the socialist side of anarchism's claim to be the most consistent form of libertarian socialism.

As we shall see, Marx provided the theoretical tools to transcend the limitations of anarchist theories of human nature, and Lenin most fully elaborated the political implications of Marx's vision of socialism from below. Far from standing in opposition to the tradition of libertarian socialism as Chomsky suggests, Lenin, once properly dissociated from his caricature at the hands of the Stalinists,[17] is best understood as making a fundamental theoretical and political contribution to the struggle for human freedom. This is not to say that Leninist organisations are without their faults: far from it. But because autonomists and anarchists misunderstand the social basis of these problems their critique of classical Marxism tends not only to be misguided but also to be politically debilitating.

Direct action and the state

In an "open Marxist" critique of Lenin's politics that shares common ground with anarchist and autonomist arguments, John Holloway suggests a link between Leninist, democratic centralist, forms of organisation and the claim that classical Marxists are state socialists. He argues that the problem with the "form of the party" is that it "presupposes an orientation towards the state" in a way that "impoverishes" the struggle itself. Consequently, even if these forms of organisation are successful, they are doomed to reproduce the kind of hierarchical and alienated power relations characteristic of the state.[18]

Taken as an account of reformist socialist political organisations Holloway's arguments are insightful: these parties do tend to undermine their own progressive roots by subordinating their activity to work within capitalist states. However, because he conflates reformist and Leninist parties, he too quickly slips from a critique of the former to a rejection of the latter. The obvious weakness with this argument is that it ignores the different content of these strategies: reformist parties aim to win the state while the Bolsheviks aimed to "smash" it! On this issue Lenin insisted that the anarchists were right: "we do not at all differ with the anarchists on the question of the abolition of the state as aim".[19]

To realise this goal Leninist parties have a fundamentally different mode of political activity to reformist organisations: if reformist organisations focus on winning parliamentary majorities, revolutionary socialist parties

---

17: Blackledge, 2006.
18: Holloway, 2002, pp11-18.
19: Lenin, 1968, p304.

must be rooted in the place where workers have the potential to overthrow the old order—their workplaces.[20] By using the label "state-centred" to describe both Leninist and reformist parties, anarchists elide the fundamental distinction between seizing and smashing the state in a way that blinds them to the emancipatory core of Lenin's contribution to socialism.[21]

For his part, Lenin argued that anarchism mistakenly generalised from a critique of the practice of reformist political parties to a rejection of any attempt to build *political* organisations.[22] Consequently, "anarchism was not infrequently a kind of penalty for the opportunist sins of the working class movement. The two monstrosities complemented each other".[23] This is not to say that classical Marxists dismissed the commitment of anarchists to the struggle for freedom. Thus Trotsky wrote of the death of an anarchist he had known in Paris that "his anarchism was the expression, though theoretically incorrect, of a profound, genuinely proletarian indignation at the villainy of the capitalist world and at the baseness of those socialists and syndicalists who crawled on their knees before this world".[24] Lenin and Trotsky did not doubt the honest "indignation at the villainy of the capitalist world" that anarchists shared with socialists; rather they argued that anarchist theory tended to undermine the promise of this activism.

Interestingly, anarchism's political weaknesses mirrored flaws Lenin diagnosed in reformism in his *What is to be Done?* This book was intended as a critique of reformist currents in the Russian socialist movement—a much more militant reformism than we are used to in the West. Electoral politics was not on the cards in Russia at the time, but trade union struggles against local bosses were. Lenin criticised Russian reformism not for its (non-existent) electoralism, but rather because it did not fight to raise the myriad of local struggles against various aspects of the Russian system into a broader national movement against the autocracy. To realise this project required a national political organisation which challenged the limits of localism by drawing links between these various struggles. This is the basis for Lenin's famous argument that the revolutionary socialist should act not as a simple trade unionist but more generally as the "tribune of the people".[25]

20: Molyneux, 1986, p76.
21: See especially Lukács, 1971, pp295-342.
22: As we shall see below, anarchists (or at least most of them) do not reject building organisations, but they do reject *political* organisations because they tend to define politics narrowly as pertaining to winning state power.
23: Lenin, 1993, p32.
24: Trotsky, 1921.
25: Lenin, 1961b, p423.

Lenin's convincing reply to those anarchists who rejected "political" activity was that, far from overcoming the problem of politics, they merely allowed the dominance of bourgeois politics to go unchallenged. He argued that within the workers' movement anarchism therefore, in a way that paralleled reformist trade unionism, led to the "subordination of the working class to *bourgeois* politics in the guise of negation of politics".[26] It was to counter this tendency that Lenin argued to build a national *political* party that aimed to link together all the local struggles across Russia into a general offensive against the state.

This challenge to the power of the state was placed on a firmer theoretical footing in the year before the October Revolution when Lenin broke with the last vestiges of Second International Marxism to argue, in stark contrast to anarchist claims that he and Marx aimed to "take over the state" and use it for their own ends,[27] that workers must be organised ideologically, politically and militarily (ie as a state) to smash the old (capitalist) state. This was not a case of taking over the old state, but of replacing it with a new organisation. And while workers' states are still in a sense states (as we shall see below they are states of a very peculiar type, and in recognition of this difference Lukács called the new organs of workers' power an "anti-government"),[28] they have a very different social content to the capitalist state. Whereas capitalist states deploy military and ideological powers to maintain capitalist social relations, workers' states mobilise their resources in the interests of suppressing the barriers to building a society based around meeting human needs. Because workers do not exploit any class below them, as these barriers are gradually overcome workers' states will tend to "wither away". Unfortunately, because anarchists are inclined to reify "the state" as *the* enemy of freedom, they are apt to underestimate both differences in the forms of class power (while liberal democracies and fascist dictatorships are types of capitalist states the differences between them are of the utmost importance) and more profound historical changes in the social content of state power (differences between feudal, capitalist and workers' states, for instance).[29] It is this tendency to reify something called "the state" as the enemy of freedom that undermines their conception of revolutionary politics.

While this is perhaps most apparent in the writings of those anarchists who imagine that they might be able to bypass the state, it is a much

---

26: Lenin, 1961a, p328.
27: Marshall, 2008, p25.
28: Lukács, 1970, p63.
29: For an overview of the importance of these distinctions to socialist politics see Hallas, 1979, chapter 3.

more general problem within anarchism. Thus the anarchist Ben Franks has suggested that, "despite the universal acceptance, in contemporary class struggle anarchist writings, of the need for revolution, there is a lack of clarity concerning its constituents and characteristics".[30]

To the extent that there is an anarchist model of revolution it tends to be rooted in the idea of direct action. There is not one form of direct action but rather a plurality of forms which, it is suggested, prefigure relations in a truly free (stateless)[31] society. Indeed, direct action is the practical implication of anarchist anti-statism,[32] and the plurality of forms of direct action is reflected in the plurality of anarchisms.[33]

Although support for and appeals to direct action of one sort or another are common on the left, for anarchism this tactic is much more than one weapon among many in an activist's armoury: it flows directly from their rejection of the state, and is explicitly counterposed to more traditional approaches to politics.[34] Indeed, anarchism tends to be self-consciously anti-political, and this perspective is best understood as a reaction against the idea that politics, as it has conventionally been defined, is concerned with the state. This type of anti-politics is, of course, political once we accept a broader conception of politics, and the arguments for direct action are obviously political arguments even if they are not state-centred arguments.

In opposition to what he suggests is traditional state-centred politics, David Graeber argues that "the very notion of direct action, with its rejection of a politics which appeals to governments to modify their behaviour, in favour of physical intervention against state power in a form that itself prefigures an alternative—all emerges directly from the libertarian tradition".[35] From this perspective it is argued that a multitude of different forms of direct

---

30: Franks, 2006, p262.
31: Randall Amster and his co-editors of a recent academic collection on anarchism have argued that "Proudhon's call for a stateless society became a hallmark of anarchist thought" (Amster and others, 2009, p3).
32: Woodcock 1962, p28. Franks describes direct action as being of "critical importance to current anarchist practice" (Franks, 2006, p17).
33: Colin Ward lists anarchist-communism, anarcho-syndicalism, individualist anarchism, pacifist anarchism, green anarchism, anarcha-feminism (Ward, 2004, pp2-3, see also Franks, 2006, pp12-18). Murray Bookchin from the libertarian socialist wing of anarchism penned a devastating critique of lifestyle anarchism which ended with a critique of "a state of mind that arrogantly derides structure, organisation, and public involvement; and a playground for juvenile antics" (Bookchin quoted in Gordon, 2008, pp25-26).
34: Franks, 2006, pp116-124.
35: Graeber, 2002, p62. See also Gordon, 2008, pp17; Woodcock, 1962, pp28; Franks, 2006, p115.

action are the living embodiment of non-state forms of social interaction that prefigure, in a myriad of ways, an alternative type of society. This approach to politics informs the types of organisations embraced by anarchists and autonomists. Whereas traditional parliamentary and revolutionary parties have oriented towards the states whose power they wished to capture or defeat, because anarchists reject these approaches in favour of prefiguring an alternative to the state they reject the form of centralised political parties that are necessary to confront states, often, though not uniformly, embracing instead supposedly non-hierarchical "horizontal" forms of organisation.[36]

In this sense at least anarchists are good Leninists. For Lenin argued, as Tony Cliff points out, that the organisational forms needed by socialists "derived from the nature of the political tasks" set.[37] If the structure of Bolshevism derived from the task of overthrowing the Russian autocracy, different tasks demand different structures. Anarchists argue that, because they reject the goal of winning state power, they have no need of the centralised political structures of those that do.

One problem with this claim is that it is parasitic on the bourgeois view of politics: if traditional political theory has focused on the state, anarchism tends merely to invert these concerns rather than to overcome their limitations. Marx's approach to politics is very different: just as *Capital* is a critique of political economy rather than a study of economics, Marx's politics are best understood as a critique of traditional political perspectives. So whereas traditional (liberal) approaches to the state conceive it as the corollary of an unchanging human nature, Marxists argue that states are historical phenomena, tied up with specific relations of production, and consequently the key to getting rid of them is to remove the relations of production which both underpin and are maintained by them.

With respect to the modern capitalist states, Marxists focus on the way they help sustain the capitalist system at the expense of human freedom. This involves an analysis of how states relate to those class struggles and other social movements which create the potential for developing the solidarity and socialist consciousness necessary to overcome capitalist alienation. On this issue it is clear that once these struggles reach a large enough scale, they will be confronted by states which act as the key organisational safeguard of the capitalist system. It is for this reason that any movement from below which becomes powerful enough to challenge capitalism will be forced to confront the state. As Alex Callinicos has written in an exchange with John

---

36: Franks, 2006, pp196-259.
37: Cliff, 1986, p84. See also Le Blanc, 1990, p44.

Holloway, "the trouble is that the state won't leave us alone".[38]

The truth of this statement was brought home recently in Britain by the death of Ian Tomlinson on the G20 demo in London. This incident acted as a lightning rod exposing the regular and systematic violence meted out by the police against not only political demonstrators but also large sections of the broader population. The fact that it occurred in the wake of the recent international state interventions to prop up the banking system, and in the context of those states' sustained and regular use of military power, serves to remind us of the intrinsic links between capitalism and the state system. Among numerous other functions, capitalist states act as instruments of political legitimisation, social control, economic regulation and military competition: they are "structurally interdependent" with capitalism, which cannot survive without them. And, whatever else the recent wars and economic bailouts have achieved, they should have laid to rest the idea that the forces of globalisation have broken the power of states.[39]

In the first instance, therefore, the concern Marxists show for the state flows not from some supposed statist predilections but rather emerges out of the needs of the movement from below: once social movements are strong enough to point towards a real alternative to the status quo, states will intervene with the aim of suppressing them. Marx's and Lenin's so-called statism therefore consists primarily of a realistic appreciation of the enemy of the struggle for freedom: the workers' movement requires a centralised military force to overcome its centralised military opponent. As Trotsky wrote, "To renounce the conquest of power is voluntarily to leave the power with those who wield it, the exploiters".[40]

Ironically, while many anarchists have gravitated towards similar conclusions at highpoints in the class struggle, even at these points their failure to distinguish between bourgeois and workers' states has proved fatal. For instance, in Spain in 1936 the main anarchist organisations felt compelled to join the Republican government so that the military opposition to Franco's fascists could be coordinated under a unified structure. While this policy made some sense from the military point of view, it unfortunately placed the anarchists atop a bourgeois state whose lifeblood was threatened by the social revolution their members were leading (and which offered by far the most powerful alternative to fascism). In government the revolutionary energy of the anarchists was weakened as they were caught between the needs of the

---

38: Callinicos and Holloway, 2005, p117.
39: Harman, 1991, p13, see also Harman, 2009, chapter 4.
40: Trotsky, 1973, p316.

revolution and the need to maintain unity with their bourgeois partners. By contrast, in a similar situation in 1917 the Bolsheviks did defend Kerensky's bourgeois government against Kornilov's proto-fascist forces, but did not join the bourgeois government, thereby retaining their independence.

Throughout this period they insisted that the most consistent and most powerful alternative to Kornilov was to be found in the workers' councils (soviets) which Kerensky, like his Spanish counterparts 20 years later, wanted to extinguish, but which the Bolsheviks saw as the embryo of a new workers' state.[41] These two approaches to revolutionary practice had very different outcomes. Whereas the actions of the anarchists in Spain helped demobilise their own support, the Bolsheviks' "united front" with Kerensky strengthened their hand and laid the basis for the successful socialist revolution in October—when they led the overthrow of Kerensky's government and replaced it with soviet rule. Despite differences in their rhetoric, both the Bolsheviks in Petrograd in 1917 and the anarchists in Barcelona in 1936 organised the "vanguard" of a revolutionary movement from below, and both recognised the need to build a unified military opposition to the counter-revolution. However, because the Bolsheviks recognised the difference between workers' and bourgeois states, they were better able to conceptualise differences between forms of unity that would strengthen the workers' movement and others which would weaken it. By contrast, when the Spanish anarchists recognised a similarly genuine need for unity, anarchism's one-dimensional view of the state meant that they ended up following the disastrous path of subordinating the revolutionary movement to the requirements of unity with their bourgeois partners.[42]

If Marxist concerns about the state do not reflect their supposed "statism", their focus on workers' councils as the basis for opposition to capitalism shows that it is also far too simplistic to counterpose prefigurative politics to Marx's supposed instrumental approach.[43] For classical Marxists do not deny a prefigurative dimension to socialist politics—in fact they insist that an element of prefiguration exists in the shape of the institutions and culture of working class self-organisation and solidarity. However, Marxists also recognise that capitalism both fragments the working class internally and divides it from other exploited and oppressed groups externally. Consequently, Marx and (especially) Lenin insisted that

---

41: On the importance of soviets to Marxism and on the relationship between soviets and revolutionary parties see Gluckstein, 1985, pp212-246.
42: Durgan, 2006, pp165-6; 1981, p104-110; 2007, p.88; Trotsky, 1977, pp646-668.
43: Franks, 2006, p100.

socialist politics includes taking up the struggle against these divisions, and this implies a distinction between the revolutionary party, as a relatively homogeneous group of socialist activists, and the working class, which is more or less fragmented depending on the level of class consciousness at any moment. The Marxist distinction between party and class is not a distinction between a fixed elite and the foot soldiers, but a simple recognition of the fact that there exist a variety of levels of class consciousness within the working class—from scabs to revolutionaries and all the variations in between. The point of the party is to help win a majority of the working class to socialism, and to build a workers' movement that offers a desirable model of liberation to other groups outside it. For the party to succeed in this task is to create the conditions for its own dissolution! Because socialism will be achieved once the divisions within the working class and between it and other oppressed and exploited groups are overcome, there will be no need for revolutionary parties in a mature socialist society. By their nature therefore revolutionary parties, as opposed to other forms of solidarity, cannot prefigure socialism: they are rather a (necessary and transient) instrument in the struggle for socialism.[44]

As to the key activity of revolutionary socialist parties—the attempt to win majorities to socialism—the guiding principle of Marxist politics is flexibility. Whereas real state "socialists" tend to reify one perspective (changing government either by insurrectionary or parliamentary means)[45] and anarchists another (direct action), Marxists focus on struggle at the point where we have the potential power to change the system—the workplace. But beyond this, Marxists aim to make concrete judgements of particular tactics at particular junctures, judging their applicability by a simple criterion: are they likely to increase the self-activity, confidence and political consciousness of working class people and other oppressed and exploited groups? So while Marxists will engage in electoral campaigns on the one hand, and forms of direct action on the other, this will be for different reasons than do reformists and anarchists. Marxists consider neither tactic to be sufficient for the tasks confronting the left, and certainly both can degenerate into variants of elitism. Neither parliamentary politics nor direct action can be the last word in revolutionary politics because neither represent a fundamental challenge to the system, and in both cases activists run

---

44: Harman, 1996.
45: To be fair to anarchists, their tendency to reduce Lenin to a 20th century Blanquist (see below) coheres with some of the best academic discussions of the issue. For instance, see Miliband, 1977, p155 and for my criticisms Blackledge, 2007, p78.

the risk of acting on behalf of, as opposed to alongside, ordinary people. Viewed from this perspective, a dogmatic commitment to direct action is best understood not as a solution to the problem of reformist statism but as the flipside of parliamentary elitism, and this explains why, despite its radical rhetoric, Draper claimed that anarchism is a form of socialism from above. It is not that Marxist parties are immune to the danger of elitism, but that this danger tends to have different roots: particularly when workers' struggles are at a low ebb there is tendency for organisations whose life-blood is the struggle to degenerate into sectarianism.[46] If anarchist groups are prone to a similar tendency, the problem with the reification of direct action as *the* radical tactic of choice—in which, as Franks revealingly argues, "a small part of an entity represents the whole thing"[47]—is that it is liable to reinforce rather than challenge the propensity to elitism and substitutionism: the tendency of activists to substitute their activities for broader social movements. This weakness illuminates another, and superficially surprising, problem associated with anarchism: its reticence about engaging with the broader concept of democracy.

If the demands of the struggle from below are one aspect of Marxist concerns with the state, another is the problem of democracy. In terms of the debate with anarchists this problem has two distinct sides: democracy within revolutionary organisations and democracy within (pre and post revolutionary) societies. Anarchist anti-authoritarianism might, at first glance, suggest a deep concern with democracy. And indeed the anarchist theorist Uri Gordon has argued that "there are major parallels between some of the values animating activists' collective process practices and those which feature in the more radical end of democratic theory".[48] However, as Gordon goes on to point out, because democracies allow for majority control whereas anarchism defends the absolute rights of the individual against the state, it is best understood as "not 'democratic' at all".[49] Similarly, in his classic survey of anarchism, George Woodcock argued that "no conception of anarchism is farther from the truth than that which regards it as an extreme form of democracy. Democracy advocates the sovereignty of the people. Anarchism advocates the sovereignty of the person".[50] More recently, Ruth Kinna has admitted that anarchists have had little of substance to say about democracy beyond a desire for consensus

46: Barker, 2001, p42.
47: Franks, 2006, p118.
48: Gordon, 2008, p69.
49: Gordon, 2008, p70.
50: Woodcock, 1962, p30.

decision-making which, as she rightly points out, is open to the criticism that it tends to repeat the characteristics Jo Freeman famously analysed in the American anarcha-feminist movement in the 1960s, what she called *The Tyranny of Structurelessness*:[51] the ability of the most articulate (usually middle class) members of structureless groups to hold de facto power within them.

For Marxists, the point of building democratic, and therefore centralist (if voting is to be meaningful majorities must get their way),[52] revolutionary organisations is intended in part to govern against this problem: leadership and policy can be changed through debate about the best way forward. Indeed, it is precisely because healthy revolutionary organisations bring together individuals from a wide spectrum of campaigns that they provide an arena for debate about the way forward both for the movement as a whole and for specific local campaigns. These debates are not only essential to the process of unifying various campaigns into a broader movement capable of challenging capitalism; they are also an invaluable mechanism through which members learn from each other's successes and failures and by which the party concretely embeds these lessons within the movement. But because debate is orientated towards action, decisions must be made, either by the kind of consensus that comes through sharp debate—which is very different to the kind of consensus achieved by going at the pace of the slowest—or by votes when debates do not reach a consensus.

The fact that revolutionary socialist parties are weapons of struggle rather than prefigurative forms entails that their internal structure is of secondary importance to their ability to act effectively. Nevertheless, because effective action requires open debate, internal democracy is an essential characteristic of these organisations—at least where external constraints allow. It is an unavoidable problem with this kind of structure that there will be a tension between debate and action. Unfortunately, the anarchist alternative of seeking consensus is only possible in relatively homogeneous groups, and can only be reproduced over time if those groups remain relatively immunised against the fragmentation of opinion in society more generally; that is if they are already, or degenerate into, a sect. It is not that the problems anarchists point to in democratic centralist organisations do not exist—Franks gives an unfortunately caricatured list of what are best understood as sectarian tendencies within Leninist parties[53]—it is rather that these problems are a necessary feature of socialist activity, and they are

---

51: Kinna, 2005, pp114-115; Freeman, 1970.

52: Löwy, 2005, p.23.

53: Franks, 2006, p212.

shared to a greater or lesser degree by *any* form of radical political organisation, including anarchist and autonomist organisations.

Human nature and socialism

The issue of democracy points to a deeper fundamental problem with anarchism: anarchist conceptions of human nature. On democracy itself, the 19th century French anarchist Proudhon complained that "universal suffrage is the counter-revolution", while his Russian counterpart, Bakunin, pointed to a rejection of democracy when he argued that "all political organisation is destined to end in the negation of freedom".[54] This is an important statement which if taken seriously is not a prescient warning of the dangers of Stalinism, but rather implies the impossibility not only of socialism but also of any form of democratic social organisation. To make sense of Bakunin's statement it is useful to examine the oft-repeated claim that anarchism involves a synthesis of "a socialist critique of capitalism with a liberal critique of socialism".[55]

Despite its superficial attractiveness there are fundamental difficulties with such a synthesis: liberals and socialists hold to very different models of human nature which point in very different political directions. Whereas liberalism assumes as its analytical point of departure the atomised egoistic individual, socialism, or at least Marx's socialism, recognises the social nature of human individuality.[56] From the liberal assumption that people are by nature individually egoistic it is difficult to conceive of social organisation except as an alien power (state) over them: the state is simultaneously a threat to, and the essential guarantor of, individual liberty. The state is for liberals therefore, in Tom Paine's felicitous phrase, a "necessary evil"! In a sense anarchism can be understood as a radicalisation of this perspective on the basis of a more optimistic view of human nature: it rejects the idea that the state, evil in any of its forms, is in fact necessary. Anarchist reticence about discussing democracy reflects the fact that from their perspective democratic political structures remain states and thus "the negation of freedom".

It is not that all anarchists embrace a simple egoistic and individualistic model of human nature—if this has been true of the dominant voices of American anarchism over the last century, European anarchism has tended to embrace a much more social conception of human nature. Thus Proudhon, Bakunin and especially Peter Kropotkin articulated "a

---

54: Marshall, 2008, p23, p296.
55: Goodway, 1989, p1; Chomsky 1970, pxii; Marshall, 2008, p639.
56: Marx, 1973b, p84.

broad belief in a society underpinned by a spirit of solidarity, a society perceived as an organic whole within which individual freedom is mediated through some notion of communal individuality".[57] However, as David Morland argues in his exhaustive analysis of classical anarchist accounts of human nature, social anarchism does not involve a successful synthesis of socialism and liberalism, but rather brings these two accounts of human nature together in an uneasy mix which, by universalising the liberal conception of the egoistic individual alongside more socialistic elements, results in an "irresolvable stalemate over the question of human nature".[58] Because Marx, by contrast, recognised that human individuality is shaped by the kind of society in which we live, he was able to grasp both the social and historical roots of modern individualism and that democratisation need not merely result in a new form of unfreedom, but rather expanded the space and nature of individual liberty.[59] Marx and Engels, therefore, agreed with Bakunin that organisation implies authority, but recognised that because society is an organisation it would be silly to imagine it without authority.

The struggle for socialism from this perspective is not so much a struggle against authority as it is a struggle to smash one undemocratic form of authority and replace it with a democratic alternative. Whereas liberalism and anarchism find it difficult to imagine the social aspect of humanity except as the alien form of the state, Marx argued that because workers are able to free themselves only through collective organisation their solidarity points towards a concrete democratic alternative to their alienation. Thus Engels comments that, while all revolutionary socialists agree "that the political state, and with it political authority, will disappear as a result of the coming social revolution", this would not mean the end of social organisation. Rather, he insisted, under socialism society would lose its (alienated) political character to take instead the form of the democratic control of administrative functions.[60] Consequently, the key question Marxists ask of any society is not is it characterised by some form of authority (the answer can only be yes), but rather is authority under democratic control and if not who is in control? As Herbert Marcuse comments, Marx looked not to the ending of authority but rather to its complete democratisation.[61]

57: Morland, 1997, p3.
58: Morland, 1997, pp188-189.
59: Collier, 1990, p41. See Blackledge, 2008, p134, for how Marx developed this historical conception of human nature through his critique of Max Stirner's anarchism.
60: Engels, 1988, p425; 1990c, p227; Marx, 1974b.
61: Marcuse, 2008, p87.

Moreover, because social structures evolve over time, society itself has a historical character: if we are to take democratic control of society, we must first examine its concrete nature at specific historical junctures. For prehistoric hunter gatherers, society might have been the small group to which an individual belonged. Today, by contrast, because we live in a world marked by an international division of labour, our society is global. Consequently, our social problems, and ultimately the solutions to those problems, are global: while local activity is an essential component of the struggle for a better world, final success can only be won by democratising society on a global scale. This, and not some statist predilection, is the material basis for another of Marx's crimes in the eyes of anarchists: his centralism.[62]

The fact that this centralism is rooted in the material transformation of society illuminates another anarchist myth: that Marx believed capitalist alienation can be overcome "simply by changing the form of government—by placing the control of government in socialist hands".[63] Marx cut his political teeth arguing precisely the opposite: that the successful struggle for liberation cannot come through a mere change in government but must be rooted in a much deeper social movement.

Towards Paris

The rational core of the myth that Marx thought that a change in government would suffice to bring about socialism can be traced to his debate with the anarchists in the First International over the issue of raising political demands, ie of demanding reforms from government.

Extrapolating from their views of human nature both Proudhon and Bakunin believed that there was a natural social harmony which could be regained only through the eradication of government and the state.[64] Consequently, whereas Marx, supported by English trade unionists, stressed the necessity of fighting for reforms—Marx insisted that when workers won reforms and acted to enforce the new laws they did not "fortify governmental power, on the contrary, they transform that power, now used against them, into their own agency"[65]—his anarchist critics believed that making demands of the state would only make matters worse. If the above statement opened Marx to reformist

---

62: Marshall, 2008, p305. In a comment in which he criticised Bakunin's "schoolboy stupidity", Marx wrote that "a radical social revolution depends on certain definite historical conditions of economic development as its precondition" (Marx, 1974b, 334).
63: Kinna, 2005, p31.
64: Kinna, 2005, p8.
65: Marx, quoted in Fernbach, 1974, p17.

misinterpretation,[66] it and others like it are best understood as part of a process whereby he sought to foster and strengthen socialist consciousness within the working class. As Collins and Abramsky point out in their seminal study of the First International, Marx believed that "trade union struggle represented a necessary phase through which the workers must pass on the road to full emancipation".[67] The demands on the state arose organically from within the workers' movement, and Marx supported reforms such as limitations on the working day both as a good in themselves and as part of the long-term process of socialist transformation which could only finally be realised through revolution.

This is most evident in his comments on the Paris Commune. Perhaps because Marx's analysis of the Commune explodes the myth that he was a "state-socialist" it is difficult to fit with anarchist preconceptions about his politics. Despite the fact that Marx argued that the Commune was an example of real living socialism which showed that "the working class cannot simply lay hold of the ready-made state machinery, and wield it for its own purposes",[68] Bakunin insisted that the Marxists "believe it is necessary to organise the workers' forces in order to seize the political power of the state".[69] And while anarchists such as Peter Marshall have dismissed Marx, Engels and Lenin's embrace of the Commune as an example of the dictatorship of the proletariat as an "irony of history",[70] in reality it is anarchism that has much more profound problems conceptualising the Commune.

In his analysis of the Commune, Marx pointed out that though the old structures of state power (in Paris at least) had been smashed, workers replaced them not with a negation of authority but with their own rule: the Commune was "a working class government" that held real (not sham parliamentary) power in Paris. This, he explained, is what he meant by the concept of the dictatorship of the proletariat,[71] or, more simply, the rule of the working class.[72] And although Marxists have described this situation as a workers' state, more properly, as Engels commented a couple of years later, the word "state" is misleading here: "All the palaver about the state ought to be dropped, especially after the commune, which has ceased to

---

66: Fernbach, 1974, p17.
67: Collins and Abramsky, 1964, p101; Compare Gilbert, 1981, p90.
68: Marx, 1974c, 206.
69: Bakunin, 1973, p263.
70: Marshall, 2008, p301.
71: Marx, 1974c, pp206, 208, 212,
72: Draper, 1987, p29.

be a state in the true sense of the term".[73] Because workers' states, unlike all previous states, are expressions of the rule of the majority rather than of a minority, they are no longer specialised coercive apparatuses maintaining exploitative social relations. And though the Commune did not survive long enough to show this, even these structures will wither away as the threat of bourgeois counter-revolution recedes.

It is difficult to understand how Bakunin, by contrast, could embrace the Commune given that he had declared himself the enemy "of every government and every state power".[74] Indeed, as Kropotkin argued a few years later from a perspective very close to Bakunin's, the Commune's key failing was its embrace of a representative structure which meant that it reproduced the typical vices of parliamentary governments. The weaknesses of the Commune, he insisted, were due not to the men who led it but to the "system" it embraced.[75] From an anarchist perspective it would appear that Kropotkin is the more consistent of the two: the Commune retained the form of representative government and was therefore merely another example of that which anarchists should oppose: the state. What Marx added to this mix was not a defence of "statism" but a recognition that, while aspects of the form of state and government had been retained by the Commune, their content had been radically transformed once a new class had come to power. This approach to the problem of revolution explodes another anarchist myth about classical Marxism: that it is a form of Jacobinism.

Jacobinism, Blanquism and Marxism

The claim that Marx was a statist who believed a simple change in government would suffice to bring about socialism is related to the charge that he failed to escape the limits of the Jacobinism of the revolutionaries of the most extreme phase of the French Revolution. For instance, in his *Statism and Anarchy*, Bakunin argued that "by education and by nature [Marx] is a Jacobin, and his favourite dream is of political dictatorship".[76] Leaving aside Bakunin's silly rhetoric about Marx's supposed will to power, the charge of Jacobinism is important and deserves to be refuted.

For a year in 1793-4 the Jacobins were at the forefront of the French Revolution. Led by Robespierre, they rode a contradiction during their time at the head of the government. On the one hand they believed they

---

73: Engels, 1989b, p71.
74: Bakunin, 1990, p136.
75: Kropotkin, 2002, pp237-242.
76: Bakunin, 1990, p182.

were acting as the instrument of Rousseau's "general will". On the other hand, however, they never adequately addressed the problem of how a common good could exist and be represented in a class divided society. In fact, far from representing the general will, the Jacobins came to power through support from, and effectively represented the interests of, the so-called *sans-culottes* of urban "small shopkeepers and craftsmen (both masters and journeymen), servants and day-labourers".[77] Because Robespierre de facto recognised the limited nature of his social base, even if he was unable to provide an adequate theoretical account of it, he came to believe that the common good would have to be imposed on society as a correction against "the shortcomings and defects of individual men".[78] So, despite his fervent advocacy of democracy, he held to a more or less implicit belief not only that "democracy had to be directed from above" but also that "no reliance could be placed on the spontaneous revolutionary ardour of the people".[79] It was the contradiction between his formally democratic politics and the limited social basis of his support which, in the context of external military intervention against the Revolution, gave rise to The Terror.

Although Guérin rejected the idea that revolutions necessarily degenerated into tyranny, he nevertheless agreed that Marx had not fully overcome the tension between the "communal" and "Jacobin" aspects of his politics, and that Lenin went further along the Jacobin path.[80] The reference to Lenin is an allusion to his famous comment that "a Jacobin who wholly identifies himself with the *organisation* of the proletariat—a proletariat conscious of its class interests—is a *revolutionary Social-Democrat*".[81] This phrase has often been cited as evidence that Lenin at least failed to escape the limits of Jacobinism, and that because of this the Russian Revolution, like its French predecessor, was doomed to end in terror. However, from the context within which Lenin wrote it is clear that reference to Jacobinism was first made by the reformist critics of Marxism who sought to jettison revolutionary politics altogether, and that Lenin was pointing out that like the Jacobins, but in very different conditions, the Marxists were the most resolute opponents of the ruling order.[82]

As a keen student of Marx, the difference between the conditions

---

77: Rudé, 1988, pp94-5.
78: Israel, 2001, p717.
79: Soboul, 1977, p107.
80: Guérin, 1989, p.121.
81: Lenin, 1961c, p383.
82: Le Blanc, 1990, p83. For contemporary reformist criticism of Marx's supposed Jacobinism see Bernstein, 1993, p36.

that gave rise to Jacobinism and those that underpinned the emergence of modern socialism would have been ABC to Lenin. Michael Löwy points out that while Marx obviously admired Robespierre's "historical greatness and revolutionary energy", he explicitly rejected Jacobinism "as a model or source of inspiration for socialist revolutionary praxis".[83] Indeed, from his earliest writings, Marx drew on Hegel's critique of Jacobinism. According to Hegel, Robespierre's Terror was the necessary counterpart of his attempt to impose a vision on society from the top down that was not rooted in a prior transformation of the nation's "dispositions and religion".[84]

Marx recognised the power of Hegel's argument, but disagreed that Jacobinism exposed the limits of the revolutionary project.[85] Rather he argued that this gap between the revolutionary leadership and the mass of the population was not a general characteristic of revolutions, but rather reflected the bourgeois nature of the French Revolution. He distinguished this type of revolution from modern proletarian revolutions in a way that pointed to the qualitative difference between his politics and Jacobinism.[86] According to Marx, bourgeois revolutions were born of developing contradictions between emergent capitalist relations of production and existing pre-capitalist states, and where they were successful resulted in the removal of fetters to further capitalist development. Although these revolutions were generally marked by a progressive break with pre-capitalist hierarchies, they were characterised by the transfer of power from one ruling class to another and involved at best a contradictory relationship between their leadership and the mass of the population. For instance, bourgeois revolutions "from above" such as Bismarck's unification of Germany involved no mass action at all, whereas bourgeois revolutions "from below" in England, America and France were won through the involvement of the lower classes but ended similarly with the exclusion of the poor from power. Proletarian revolutions, by contrast, because they are made for and by the working class—"the emancipation of the working classes must be conquered by the working classes themselves"[87]—were necessarily qualitatively more democratic in both their execution and their outcome.

Marx's distinction between bourgeois and proletarian revolutions points to a fundamental problem with the claim that there was an unbroken

---

83: Löwy, 1989, p119.
84: Hegel, 1956, pp446, 450, 449. Compare Marx, 1975, p413.
85: Taylor, 1975, p437.
86: Marx, 1973a.
87: Marx, 1974a, p82.

trajectory to him from Robespierre. Unlike Robespierre, Marx was absolutely clear that there could be no commonly accepted idea of what is good in a class divided society, but equally that workers' collective struggles were uniquely able to point towards a systemic alternative to capitalist alienation in a way that could appeal far beyond their own ranks. If modern socialism only became a possibility therefore with the emergence of the modern working class, to realise this potential requires at least a two-sided struggle by socialists for leadership within the movement: Marxists struggle for the hegemony[88] of socialism within the working class itself, while simultaneously struggling to win working class socialist hegemony across society more generally. At its core, therefore, Marx's revolutionary strategy was founded upon the emergence of new social forces—the growth of capitalism and with it the modern working class. For this reason it is very different from previous (top-down/statist) attempts to realise a better world, and goes some way to explaining why Marx believed it was important for revolutionaries to have a sure grasp of history: if a socialist revolution was possible only in specific historical circumstances, it was important to recognise what these were and how they differed from the conditions that had given rise to other revolutionary moments.

By contrast with Marx, there were 19th century socialists who continued the Jacobin tradition—and Marx distanced himself from their politics. For instance, the French socialist Blanqui envisioned revolution as an act won by a small elite of revolutionaries who would act on behalf of the workers.[89] Commenting on the Blanquists in the wake of the Commune, Engels argued that this group were "socialists only in sentiment", because their model of socialism was not underpinned by anything like an adequate account of either the class struggle or the historical basis for socialism itself. And in stark contrast to the claim that he and Marx were closet Jacobins he dismissed Blanqui's proposal that the revolution be a "*coup de main* by a small revolutionary minority*", and claimed that the Blanquist (Jacobin) approach was an "obsolete" model of revolution as "dictatorship".[90]

In a sense Marxism transcended the distinction between anarchism and Blanquism: like the former it was rooted in the real movement from below, but like the latter it recognised the crucial role of socialist leadership in overthrowing the old state. The point was that socialist leadership must

---

88: For a terrible anarchist critique of this concept see Day, 2005, pp6-7, and for a devastating Marxist reply see McKay, 2009.
89: Draper, 1986, pp37-8.
90: Engels, 1989a, p13. See also Lenin, 1964, p47, on the differences between Marxism and Blanquism.

be rooted in the real movement rather than imposed upon it from above. As Trotsky argued, it is a mistake to counterpose spontaneity to leadership for they are better understood as two sides of the same coin.[91]

This approach to the problem of revolution filled out one side of the general model which Marx and Engels had elaborated in 1845. Revolution was necessary, they argued, not only because "the ruling class cannot be overthrown in any other way", but also because "the class overthrowing it can only in a revolution succeed in ridding itself of all the muck of ages and become fitted to found society anew".[92] This idea of "socialism from below" is the defining characteristic of Marxism which distinguishes it not only from any forms of state socialism, but also from anarchist anti-statism. It is only partially true, as some anarchists have argued, that Marx and (class struggle) anarchists are fighting for the same goals by different means:[93] for Marx fought for the democratisation of social authority in a way that escapes the limitations of anarchist theory. While this means that, like anarchists, Marxists fight to "smash" capitalist states, we also recognise that sometimes steps towards greater democracy require more state activity: one only has to think of the anti-statist rhetoric used by the opponents of healthcare reform in America to recognise that "it is absurdly unhistorical to suggest that at all times and in all places it is the state which is 'the main enemy of the free individual'".[94]

Whereas the liberal aspect of anarchist theory portrays the relationship between freedom and authority as a zero-sum trade off, Marxists argue that because individual freedom is shaped by social organisation it can only be realised in some form of organisation. From this perspective, far from being in opposition each to the other, freedom and authority are best understood as complementary concepts: the former can expand if the latter is democratised. If our goal of democracy is therefore a form of authority, the alternative is not no authority but undemocratic authority.

This argument illuminates Bakunin's famous prediction that if the Marxists came to power their state would be "nothing but the highly despotic government of the masses by a new and very small aristocracy".[95] As we have noted, this comment has been seized upon by numerous anarchists,[96] and (strangely enough) some Marxists,[97] as an eloquent warning of the dangers of

---

91: Trotsky, 1977, p1017.
92: Marx and Engels, 1970, p95.
93: Kinna and Prichard, 2009, p272; Guérin, 1989, p119.
94: Arblaster, 1971, p181.
95: Bakunin, 1990, pp178-179.
96: Chomsky 1970, pp ix-x; Ward, 2004, p5; Marshall, 2008, p305.
97: McNally, 2006, p348.

bureaucratisation. However, it is no such thing. Rather it is best understood as a precursor to Robert Michels' famous "iron law of oligarchy", according to which all organisations inevitably generate ruling elites.[98] Duncan Hallas comments that when applied to democratic centralist organisations, this type of argument smells of "a secularised version of the original sin myth",[99] and, just as the original sin myth condemns us to a life of hardship, despite its formal radicalism the anarchist idea that all organisation negates freedom leaves little hope for a progressive alternative to capitalism.

Conclusion

It is because Marxists and anarchists have different goals that they fight for these goals by different means. As we have seen, whereas anarchists tend to envision a natural (ahistorical) social harmony beyond the state, for Marxists socialism is conceived as the complete democratisation of society based upon the emergence of historically novel social relationships. While anarchists therefore attempt to prefigure freedom through direct action, Marxists fight for socialism within the working class and for an orientation towards the working class among anti-capitalist activists. If direct action does not require anything but a loose federal organisational structure, the struggle to democratise society against the state requires a democratic and centralised combat organisation that maximises its chances of success by focusing its resources. Despite anarchist claims to the contrary this does not entail a top-down model of leadership. Rather, to be successful the party must both give voice to the movement from below, while simultaneously struggling against the sectionalism of the movement. This model of leadership is best understood, as Cliff argued, neither as a variety of managerialism nor as a form of intellectual elitism, but as rooted in comradeship in struggle:

> "The revolutionary party must conduct a dialogue with the workers outside it. [It] should not invent tactics out of thin air, but put as its first duty to learn from the experience of the mass movement and then generalise from it... Marxists [should] give a conscious expression to the instinctive drive of the working class to reorganise society on a socialist basis".[100]

Cliff did not pull this model of leadership out of thin air, but learned it by studying the renewal of Marxism that occurred for a brief period

---

98: Thomas, 1980, p252.
99: Hallas, 1996, p40.
100: Cliff, 1996, pp73-74.

around the First World War. This movement had similar roots to the syndicalist current that emerged within the workers' movement before the war as a reaction against reformism. Syndicalism was underpinned by a renewal of class struggle from below and drew on Proudhon's and Bakunin's conceptions of direct action as an alternative to bourgeois politics, alongside Marx's conception of socialism as working class self-emancipation.[101] Like more recent anti-capitalists, the syndicalists had "nothing but contempt for 'politics' in the form of compromise and opportunism which characterised parliamentary affairs".[102] Although the renewed Marxist movement shared syndicalism's distaste for the opportunistic politics of the reformist left, by re-engaging with Marx's broader conception of the political they pointed beyond the limits of syndicalism. Associated with the writings of Lenin, Trotsky and Luxemburg, this movement found its highest political expression in Lenin's 1917 work *The State and Revolution,* which traced the intellectual origins of the international socialist movement's evolution towards reformism to a wilful misrepresentation of Marx's critique of the state within the Second International.

The trajectory taken by Antonio Gramsci highlights both the differences and similarities between this renewed Marxism and anarcho-syndicalism in the early 20th century. In response to the accusation that he and the rest of the group around the socialist newspaper *L' Ordine Nuovo* in Turin in 1919 and 1920 had acted in a syndicalist fashion, he replied that, yes, like the syndicalists and against the increasingly reformist interpretation of Marxism dominant with the Second International, his grouping had attempted to root their socialism in the real spontaneous movement of workers from below instead of offering an "abstract" model of leadership. However, the weakness with this approach, which for Gramsci pointed to a more general weakness with syndicalism, was that *L'Ordine Nuovo* failed to articulate a strategy that was able to link the demands of the Turin workers with the peasants in the South of Italy into a project that could make concrete the aim of overthrowing the Italian state and replacing it with a democracy based upon workers' councils.[103]

Over the next few years Gramsci sought to overcome these weaknesses while building on the strengths of the *L'Ordine Nuovo* period. Like the anarcho-syndicalists, he rooted his practice in the day to day struggles of ordinary workers, but unlike them he extended this approach into a

---

101: Darlington, 2008, pp74-75.
102: Portis, 1980, pp44-45.
103: Gramsci, 1971, pp197-198; Williams, 1975, pp145-168.

political strategy that aimed not only to "smash" the capitalist state as part of a broad anti-capitalist movement but also to replace it with a democratic alternative.[104] This goal, and the Leninist means by which he sought to achieve it, has nothing in common with the label "state socialism".

It does, though, presuppose Marx's conception of human nature and its corollary, his positive model of democracy. Lenin's contribution to the tradition of socialism from below was to show that in order both to win a majority across society and to smash the old state the left requires a democratic and centralised political party. It was from Lenin that Gramsci learned his politics, and their contribution to Marxism was not only built upon Marx's critique of anarchism's incoherence, but also remains a rich source of lessons for anti-capitalist and socialist activists to this day.

104: Gramsci, 1978, p369.

References

Amster, Randall and others, 2009, "Introduction", in Amster, Randall and others (eds), *Contemporary Anarchist Studies* (Routledge).

Arblaster, Anthony, 1971, "The Relevance of Anarchism", *Socialist Register 1971* (Merlin), http://socialistregister.com/index.php/srv/article/view/5336

Bakunin, Mikhail, 1973 [1871], "The Paris Commune and the Idea of the State", in Sam Dolgoff (ed), *Bakunin on Anarchy* (Allen and Unwin), www.marxists.org/reference/archive/bakunin/works/1871/paris-commune.htm

Bakunin, Mikhail, 1990 [1873], *Statism and Anarchy* (Cambridge University Press), www.marxists.org/reference/archive/bakunin/works/1873/statism-anarchy.htm

Barker, Colin, 2001, "Robert Michels and the 'Cruel Game'" in Colin Barker and others (eds), *Leadership and Social Movements* (Manchester University Press).

Berkman, Alexander, 1989, *What is Communist Anarchism?* (Phoenix Press), http://tinyurl.com/comanarcho

Bernstein, Eduard, 1993 [1899], *The Preconditions of Socialism* (Cambridge University Press).

Blackledge, Paul, 2006, "What was Done", *International Socialism* 111 (summer 2006), www.isj.org.uk/?id=218

Blackledge, Paul, 2007 "On Moving On from 'Moving On': Miliband, Marxism and Politics", in Clyde Barrow and others (eds), *Class, Power and State in Capitalist Society: Essays on Ralph Miliband* (Palgrave).

Blackledge, Paul, 2008, "Marxism and Ethics", *International Socialism* 120 (autumn 2008), www.isj.org.uk/?id=486

Callinicos, Alex, 2003, "Marxism and Anarchism", in Baldwin, Thomas (eds), *The Cambridge History of Western Philosophy* (Cambridge University Press).

Callinicos, Alex, and John Holloway, 2005, "Can We Change the World Without Taking Power?", *International Socialism* 106 (winter 2005), www.isj.org.uk/?id=98

Callinicos, Alex, and Chris Nineham, 2007, "At an Impasse: Anti-capitalism and Social Forums Today", *International Socialism* 115 (summer 2007), www.isj.org.uk/?id=337

Chomsky, Noam, 1970, "Introduction", in Daniel Guérin, *Anarchism* (Monthly Review).

Chomsky, Noam ,2005, "Anarchism, Marxism and Hope for the Future", in Noam Chomsky, *Chomsky on Anarchism* (AK Press), http://www.ditext.com/chomsky/may1995.html

Cliff, Tony, 1986, *Lenin: Building the Party* (Bookmarks).

Cliff, Tony, 1996, "Trotsky on Substitutionism", in Tony Cliff, and others, *Party and Class* (Bookmarks), http://www.marxists.org/archive/cliff/works/1960/xx/trotsub.htm

Collins, Henry, and Chimon Abramsky, 1964, *Karl Marx and the British Labour Movement* (Macmillan).

Collier, Andrew, 1990, *Socialist Reasoning* (Pluto).

Darlington, Ralph, 2008, *Syndicalism and the Transition to Communism* (Ashgate).

Day, Richard, 2005, *Gramsci is Dead* (Pluto).

Draper, Hal, 1986, *Karl Marx's Theory of Revolution Vol. III* (Monthly Review).

Draper, Hal ,1987, *The Dictatorship of the Proletariat: From Marx to Lenin* (Monthly Review).

Draper, Hal, 1992, *Socialism from Below* (Humanities Review Press).

Draper, Hal, 1999, "The Myth of Lenin's 'Concept of the Party'", *Historical Materialism 4*, www.marxists.org/archive/draper/1990/myth/myth.htm

Durgan, Andy, 1981, "Revolutionary Anarchism in Spain", *International Socialism* 11 (winter 1981).

Durgan, Andy, 2006, "Seventy Years after the Spanish Civil War", *International Socialism* 111 (summer 2006), www.isj.org.uk/?id=220

Durgan, Andy, 2007, *The Spanish Civil War*, (Palgrave).

Engels, Frederick, 1988 [1872], "On Authority", in Marx and Engels, *Collected Works, vol. 23* (Progress), www.marxists.org/archive/marx/works/1872/10/authority.htm

Engels, Frederick, 1989a[1874], "Programme of the Blanquist Commune Refugees", in Marx and Engels, *Collected Works, vol 24* (Progress), www.marxists.org/archive/marx/works/1874/06/26.htm

Engels, Frederick, 1989b [1875], "Letter to August Bebel 18th-28th March 1875", in Marx and Engels, *Collected Works, vol. 24* (Progress), www.marxists.org/archive/marx/works/1875/letters/75_03_18.htm

Fernbach, David, 1974, "Introduction" to Karl Marx, *The First International and After*, (Penguin).

Franks, Benjamin, 2006, *Rebel Alliances* (AK Press).

Freeman, Jo, 1970, *The Tyranny of Structurelessness*, http://struggle.ws/pdfs/tyranny.pdf

Gilbert, Alan, 1981, *Marx's Politics* (Martin Robertson).

Gluckstein, Donny, 1985, *The Western Soviets* (Bookmarks).

Gluckstein, Donny, 2006, *The Paris Commune: A Revolution in Democracy* (Bookmarks).

Goodway, David, 1989, "Introduction", in David Goodway (ed), *For Anarchism* (Routledge).

Gordon, Uri, 2008, *Anarchy Alive* (Pluto).

Graeber, David, 2002, "The New Anarchists", *New Left Review, II/13*, www.newleftreview.org/A2368

Gramsci, Antonio, 1971, *Selections from the Prison Notebooks* (Lawrence and Wishart).

Gramsci, Antonio, 1978, *Selections from Political Writings 1921-1926* (Lawrence and Wishart).

Guérin, Daniel, 1970, *Anarchism* (Monthly Review), http://www.infoshop.org/library/index.php/Daniel_Guerin:Anarchism

Guérin, Daniel, 1989, "Marxism and Anarchism", in David Goodway (ed), *For Anarchism* (Routledge).

Hallas, Duncan, 1979, *Trotsky's Marxism* (Pluto), www.marx.org/archive/hallas/works/1979/trotsky/index.htm

Hallas, Duncan, 1996, "Towards a Revolutionary Socialist Party", in Tony Cliff and others, *Party and Class* (Bookmarks), http://www.marxists.org/archive/hallas/works/1971/xx/party.htm

Harman, Chris, 1990, "The Storm Breaks", *International Socialism 46* (spring 1990), http://chrisharman.blogspot.com/2009/10/storm-breaks-crisis-in-eastern-bloc.html

Harman, Chris, 1991, "The State and Capitalism Today", *International Socialism 51* (summer 1991), www.isj.org.uk/?id=234

Harman, Chris, 1996, "Party and Class", in Tony Cliff and others, *Party and Class* (Bookmarks), http://www.marxists.de/party/harman/partyclass.htm

Harman, Chris, 2009, *Zombie Capitalism* (Bookmarks).

Hegel, Georg, 1956, *The Philosophy of History* (Dover).

Holloway, John, 2002, *Change the World without Taking Power* (Pluto).

Israel, Jonathan, 2001, *Radical Enlightenment* (Oxford University Press).

Kinna, Ruth, 2005, *Anarchism* (Oneworld).

Kinna, Ruth, and Alex Prichard, 2009, "Anarchism, Past, Present, and Utopia", in Randall Amster and others (eds), *Contemporary Anarchist Studies* (Routledge).

Kropotkin, Peter, 2002 [1880], "Revolutionary Government", in Roger Baldwin (ed), *Peter Kroptkin: Anarchism* (Dover), http://dwardmac.pitzer.edu/anarchist_archives/kropotkin/revgov.html

Le Blanc, Paul, 1990, *Lenin and the Revolutionary Party* (Humanities Press).

Lenin, Vladimir, 1961a [1901], "Anarchism and Socialism", Lenin, *Collected Works, vol 5* (Progress), www.marxists.org/archive/lenin/works/1901/dec/31.htm

Lenin, Vladimir 1961b [1901], "What is to be Done?", in Lenin, *Collected Works, vol 5* (Progress), www.marxists.org/archive/lenin/works/1901/witbd/index.htm

Lenin, Vladimir 1961c [1904], "One Step Forward, Two Steps Back", in Lenin, *Collected Works, vol 7* (Progress), www.marxists.org/archive/lenin/works/1904/onestep/index.htm

Lenin, Vladimir, 1964 [1917], "Letter on Tactics", in Lenin, *Collected Works, vol 24* (Progress), www.marxists.org/archive/lenin/works/1917/apr/x01.htm

Lenin, Vladimir, 1968 [1917], "The State and Revolution", in Lenin, *Selected Works* (Progress), www.marxists.org/archive/lenin/works/1917/staterev/

Lenin, Vladimir, 1993 [1920], *Left Wing Communism an Infantile Disorder* (Bookmarks), www.marxists.org/archive/lenin/works/1920/lwc/index.htm

Löwy, Michael, 1989, "The Poetry of the Past: Marx and the French Revolution", *New Left Review*, I/177.

Löwy, Michael, 2005, "To Change the World We Need Revolutionary Democracy", *Capital and Class*, 85.

Lukács, Georg, 1970 [1924], *Lenin: A Study in the Unity of his Thought* (New Left Books), www.marxists.org/archive/lukacs/works/1924/lenin/index.htm

Lukács, Georg, 1971 [1923], *History and Class Consciousness* (Merlin), www.marxists.org/archive/lukacs/works/history/index.htm

Marcuse, Herbert, 2008, *A Study on Authority* (Verso).

Marshall, Peter, 2008, *Demanding the Impossible: A History of Anarchism* (Harper).

Marx, Karl, 1973a [1852], "The Eighteenth Brumaire of Louis Bonaparte", in Marx, *Surveys from Exile* (Penguin), www.marxists.org/archive/marx/works/1852/18th-brumaire/index.htm

Marx, Karl, 1973b [1857], *Grundrisse* (Penguin), www.marxists.org/archive/marx/works/1857/grundrisse/

Marx, Karl, 1974a [1867], "Provisional Rules of the International" in Marx, *The First International and After* (Penguin), www.marxists.org/archive/marx/iwma/documents/1867/rules.htm

Marx, Karl, 1974b [1874], "Conspectus of Bakunin's 'Statism and Anarchy'", in Marx, *The First International and After* (Penguin), www.marxists.org/archive/marx/works/1874/04/bakunin-notes.htm

Marx, Karl, 1974c [1871], "The Civil War in France" in Marx, *The First International and After* (Penguin), www.marxists.org/archive/marx/works/1871/civil-war-france/index.htm

Marx, Karl, 1975 [1844], "Critical Notes on the Article 'The King of Prussia and Social Reform by a Prussian'", in Marx, *Early Writings* (Penguin), www.marxists.org/archive/marx/works/1844/08/07.htm

Marx, Karl, and Frederick Engels, 1970 [1845], *The German Ideology* (Lawrence and Wishart), www.marxists.org/archive/marx/works/1845/german-ideology/

McKay, Ian, 2009, "The Many Deaths of Antonio Gramsci", *Capital and Class 98*.

McNally, David, 2006, *Another World is Possible* (Merlin).

Miliband, Ralph, 1977, *Marxism and Politics* (Oxford University Press).

Molyneux, John, 1986, *Marxism and the Party* (Bookmarks).

Morland, David, 1997, *Demanding the Impossible? Human Nature and Politics in Nineteenth-Century Social Anarchism* (Cassell).

Portis, Larry, 1980, *Georges Sorel* (Pluto).

Rudé, George, 1988, *The French Revolution* (Phoenix).

Soboul, Albert, 1977, *A Short History of the French Revolution 1789-1799* (University of California Press).

Taylor, Charles, 1975, *Hegel* (Cambridge University Press).

Thomas, Paul, 1980, *Karl Marx and the Anarchists* (Routledge & Kegan Paul).

Trotsky, Leon, 1921, "Vergeat, Lepetit and Lefebvre", www.marxists.org/archive/trotsky/1924/ffyci-1/app07.htm

Trotsky, Leon, 1973, *The Spanish Revolution* (Pathfinder), www.marxists.org/archive/trotsky/spain/index.htm

Trotsky, Leon, 1977 [1930], *The History of the Russian Revolution* (Pluto), www.marxists.org/archive/trotsky/1930/hrr/

Ward, Colin, 2004, *Anarchism: A Very Short Introduction* (Oxford University Press).

Williams, Gwyn, 1975, *Proletarian Order* (Pluto).

Woodcock, George, 1962, *Anarchism* (Penguin).

CAPITAL & CLASS

The journal of the Conference of Socialist Economists

Special 100th edition: 33 years of *Capital & Class*

Since 1977 *Capital & Class* has been the main independent source for a Marxist critique of global capitalism. Pioneering key debates on value theory, domestic labour, and the state, it reaches out into the labour, trade union, anti-racist, feminist, environmentalist and other radical movements. It analyses the important political, economic and social developments of our time and applies a materialist framework unconstrained by divisions into economics, politics, sociology or history. Each issue includes both in-depth papers and an extensive book reviews section.

Issue 100 will be a special issue which celebrates 33 years of *Capital & Class*.

Subscribers receive three issues of *Capital & Class* per year, plus access to the journal's online electronic archive containing the entire back catalogue An easy-to-use search engine makes it possible to search the full text of more than 1400 articles and over 700 book reviews, and subscribers can download high quality printable .pdf files.

But *Capital & Class* is not just a scholarly left-wing journal. Its editorial board members are elected representatives of a democratic membership organisation. Individual subscribers become members of the Conference of Socialist Economists with the right to vote at the AGM, elect members to the executive committee and editorial board, and influence policy.

Capital & Class to be published on behalf of CSE by SAGE!

From February 2010, beginning with Issue 100, *Capital & Class* will be published by SAGE. SAGE has over 40 years of journals publishing experience and, amongst other things, subscribers will benefit from access to the various 'Web 2' digital technologies used by Sage. *Capital & Class* will of course maintain its editorial and scholarly independence.

Subscriptions:
ou will be sent a renewal invoice from SAGE. In order to continue subscribing all you need do is return payment with the remittance slip to SAGE in the pre-paid envelope that will be provided.

An institutional subscription includes electronic access as well as print copies, which means that everyone within the institution is able to access the journal at any given time. For full details visit: www.uk.sagepub.com.

Capital & Class / CSE
Unit 5
25 Horsell Road
London N5 1XL
cseoffice@pop.gn.apc.org
www.cseweb.org.uk
Tel & Fax: 020 7607 9615
Skype: cseoffice

The sex work debate

Jane Pritchard

The debate on "sex work" has divided the trade union movement. While the GMB has tried to organise women who work in lap dancing clubs, in 2009 the Trade Union Congress (TUC) Women's Congress voted against a motion which supported the decriminalisation of the sex industry and the unionisation of sex workers. Instead a motion was passed in favour of the criminalisation of the purchase of sex. Over the last two years the University and College Union (UCU), the Communication Workers Union (CWU) and Unison have taken different positions on this debate. Within feminist thinking there are opposed views on sex work and violence against women. Radical feminists in alliance with neoconservatives campaign for the abolition of prostitution and, in the interim, are supporting legislation that proposes the criminalisation of men. Other feminists, many of them academics who research in this area, as well as sex workers' organisations themselves, demand the decriminalisation of prostitution. They argue that, while the long-term aim is to eliminate the conditions that breed prostitution, in the short term the priority is to keep women safe.

The language itself is highly problematic and emotive. The use of the term "prostitute" is regarded as a denigrating word used for women who are forced into selling sex through poverty and exclusion, while the use of the term "sex worker" is seen as dignifying an activity which reflects and compounds women's oppression. This article does not suggest that sex work is "a job like any other"—however, the term sex work will be used, first because it avoids the moral condemnation often attached to the word prostitute. Second, this term is used because women who directly sell sex on the streets, in flats or in brothels are only a subset of a much larger number of women who work in the sex industry.[1] The modern sex industry is a multibillion dollar industry, which generates huge profits for both transnational corporations and criminal gangs. The sex industry is difficult to define because it encompasses a huge range of diverse activities. According to the writer Elisabeth Bernstein:

> The scope of sexual commerce has grown to encompass: live sex shows; all variety of pornographic texts, videos, and images, both in print and on line; fetish clubs; sexual "emporiums" featuring lap-dancing and wall-dancing; escort agencies; telephone sex and cyber-sex contacts; "drive through" striptease venues; and organised sex tours of developing countries.[2]

Accurate figures are hard to come by, but there is a general consensus that the last two decades have seen a resurgence in the international sex industry, including street prostitution, the voluntary or forced migration of women to work in the sex industry and the proliferation of lap dancing clubs. What is certain is that the sex industry is hugely profitable. A European Parliament report from 2004 estimated the global sex industry to be worth $5,000 billion to $7,000 billion.[3] Some of the transnational corporations involved, such as Hugh Heffner's Playboy and lap dancing chains owned by Spearmint Rhino and Foxy Lady, are well known. However, many apparently more respectable companies make huge profits from providing telephone lines and cable and satellite programmes, and being the internet providers for the sex industry. These include GM Motors (through DirecTV), Time Warner, News International (EchoStar satellite, AT&T) and hotel chain Marriot International.

In a world where everything is for sale, activities such as lap dancing, which were once viewed as oppressive to women, are now accepted as mainstream leisure opportunities. Pole dancing lessons, which require stilettos and skimpy shorts, are widely advertised as the new way of keeping fit. Soft porn is routinely displayed at the counters of supermarkets and garages, and prostitution is glamorised on TV in programmes such as *The Secret Diaries of a Call Girl*. At the same time there was widespread revulsion at the murder of five young women working on the streets of Ipswich in 2007. This

---

1: *Times Higher Education*, 11 December 2008, reviewing the work of Dr Teela Sanders.

2: Bernstein, 2001.

3: Gall, 2006.

combination of increased visibility, normalisation and brutal violence has revitalised a debate about how to respond to prostitution and the sex industry, about whether sex workers are criminals or victims, and whether the industry should be tolerated, reformed to improve women's lives or totally opposed as the institutionalised oppression of women. Two of the main debates have coalesced, first around whether working in the sex industry is fundamentally the same as working in other industries with the consequence that "sex workers" should organise in unions just like other workers, and second, whether clients should be criminalised as a way of reducing the demand for paid sex. These debates are the focus of this article.

It is argued here that understanding prostitution and the wider sex industry has to be rooted in understanding the specific oppression of women within the capitalist family unit and the increasing commodification of sex as the marketplace intrudes into the most intimate aspects of human existence. In the wider sense these phenomena have to be located in the context of the dynamics of capitalist expansion, in the vast growth in the global reach of capitalism in the late 19th century and again over the last 30 years in what is loosely termed globalisation. In these two periods the factors which drive women (and much smaller numbers of men) to sell sex have been transformed.

The sex as work debate

The notion of "sex work", that selling sex is a job like any other, emerged in the 1970s through prostitution advocacy groups in the US such as Cast Off Your Old Tired Ethics (COYOTE). It is predicated on the idea that, as all sex is commodified under capitalism, what can broadly be termed erotic labour is another service that can be bought or sold like any other. The result of this analysis is to argue against the criminalisation of prostitution and against attempts to eradicate prostitution altogether. Some contemporary campaigners go beyond arguing that "sex work" is a job like any other and argue that "sex work" is actually superior to other jobs that are available for women. They point to benefits in terms of working hours, autonomy, self-direction and even job satisfaction.

Some celebrate "sex work" as an inherent human right and, in particular, as a women's right of sexual expression and an arena in which women can exercise disproportionate control over men. At this end of the spectrum of theories about "sex work", what began as an understanding of how economic necessity drives women into the sex industry has become a celebration and expression of women's empowerment. For example, Ana Lopez of the GMB union and the International Union of Sex Workers

(IUSW), calls prostitution a "positive choice" for women. The IUSW website argues that prostitution can be empowering for women:

> People gain personal strength from selling their bodies because their clients worship and admire them, they have as much sex as they want and defy traditional mores and roles imposed on them. Often prostitutes are extremely healthy, playful, creative, adventurous and independent women.[4]

Such arguments are accepted by academic Gregor Gall who claims of the "sex work" discourse:

> [It] has been shown to be sufficiently robust to allow the generation of sex, sexual services and sexual artefacts as commodities under capitalism to be categorised not just as work but as wage labour...[therefore] sex wage labour under capitalism may be expected to be subject to the same broad impulses and dynamics of the process of capitalist accumulation that other wage labour is subject [to].[5]

Gall concludes that as "sex work" is fundamentally the same as other forms of employment, it generates the potential for a unionisation project and the possibility of sex workers exercising collective influence in order to defend and advance their interests.

At the other end of the spectrum there is abolition feminism which alleges that all commercial sex is violence against women. Proposals to improve safety for sex workers by legitimising their working situations are rejected as legitimising violence against women. In this view there is no qualitative difference between the "violence" of a society which "forces" a woman to become a lap dancer, and violence that expresses itself in beatings, rape and murder.

Between these polar ends of the spectrum socialists and feminists take a range of views. However, in order to consider these arguments it is important to understand the relationship between capitalism, prostitution and the sex industry and the specific oppression of women in capitalist society.

Capitalism, prostitution and the sex industry

Although it has been dubbed the oldest profession, prostitution has not been found in all societies. Historian N J Ringdal suggests that prostitution

---

4:    www.isuw.org
5:    Gall, 2006, p35.

was a unique cultural phenomenon first developed in Mesopotamia and later spread to surrounding cultures in Egypt, Greece and India.[6] However, from ancient times, many societies in North America, the old East India and Polynesia had a high degree of freedom for women and were unacquainted with prostitution.[7] Therefore prostitution was not an inevitable feature of early human societies. Leading Bolshevik Party member Alexandra Kollontai helped to develop a Marxist analysis of prostitution after the Russian Revolution of 1917. She drew a distinction between prostitution in other eras, such as ancient Greece and Rome, and prostitution under capitalism.[8] In ancient times the number of prostitutes was small and prostitution was seen as a legal complement to exclusive family relationships. In the Middle Ages, under artisan production, prostitution was accepted as lawful and unproblematic. Prostitutes had their own guilds and took part in festivals and local events just like any other guilds.[9]

With the rise of capitalism that changed. Prostitution in the 19th century occurred on a much greater scale than in previous societies. It was fed by the massive social dislocation as people were driven from agriculture into the manufacturing system. The urbanisation, poverty and large scale migration which characterised 19th century capitalism produced conditions in which brothels sprang up around the globe. In his book *London Labour and the London Poor*, written in the 1850s, Henry Mayhew described how women in seasonal and insecure trades were frequently driven into prostitution at certain times of the year.[10] Thus milliners, whose skills were only in demand during the London society "season", became particularly associated with prostitution. Socialist anarchist Emma Goldman quoted a study called *Prostitution in the Nineteenth Century* to describe the conditions that fuelled the growth of prostitution:

> Although prostitution has existed in all ages, it was left to the 19th century to develop it into a gigantic social institution. The development of industry with vast masses of people in the competitive market, the growth and congestion of large cities, the insecurity and uncertainty of employment, has given prostitution an impetus never dreamed of at any period in human history.[11]

6: Ringdal, 2004.
7: Ringdal, 2004.
8: Kollontai, 1921 in Holt, 1977.
9: Kollontai, 1921 in Holt, 1977.
10: Mayhew, 1861.
11: Goldman quoting Blaschko in Innes, 2000.

In 1921 Kollontai claimed that in Berlin there was one prostitute for every 20 "honest" women. In Paris the ratio was one to 18 and in London one to nine.[12]

Then as now there was a strong relationship between the migration of women and prostitution. At the end of the 19th century around 80 percent of prostitutes in Rio de Janeiro and Buenos Aires were first generation immigrants from Europe.[13] This was true of major cities from Italy to India, with the majority of migrants being from Central and Eastern Europe.[14] Hysteria and moral panic focused on the growth of a "white slave trade". The claim that white women were being defiled by foreign and non-white men brought forth an alliance of reactionaries encompassing the church and politicians. However, there was little evidence that women had been kidnapped or coerced. Rather they were attempting to escape from desperate poverty and to some extent gain economic independence.

International capitalist development in the 19th century transformed prostitution into an international sex industry. The most recent period of globalisation and restructuring of capitalist production, from the 1970s onwards, has again reshaped the sex industry as it has wreaked havoc with the lives of ordinary people, women in particular. In developing countries structural adjustment programmes imposed by the International Monetary Fund (IMF) have increased displacement in rural areas, increased unemployment in urban areas and led to wage cuts and increases in poverty. In new production zones of South East Asia transnational corporations ride roughshod over minimum wage and health and safety laws, leaving women working in hazardous conditions. The booming sex industry fills the gap left by wages paid below subsistence levels or the lack of any secure, paid employment.

Neoliberal policies have produced a huge polarisation between super rich elites and the marginalised and desperately poor who are often driven into the informal economy and sex industry to make ends meet. For example, Russia today is a major source of migrant sex workers and a major destination for sex workers. One writer has described the "erotisation of Russian culture", in the post-Soviet era. The new Russian super-rich have fuelled a commercial sex boom in which "prostitution was fully incorporated into both the public and private life of the post-Soviet elites, who were

12: Kollontai, 1921.
13: Ringdal, 2004.
14: Gibson, 1986.

often to be found in expensive night clubs surrounded by call girls".[15] This has coincided with the dramatic collapse of the economy and the drying up of any alternative sources of employment. A survey in the 1990s ranked prostitution eight out of the twenty most common jobs in the country.[16]

The Iraq War, which has brought in its wake the destruction of the Iraqi economy and social structures, has increased the sex industry. The *Independent* newspaper reported that an estimated 50,000 Iraqi women refugees were being driven into prostitution in Syria. Nihal Hassan reported from a sex club in Damascus, "The make up can't disguise the fact that most are in their mid-teens. It's a strange sight in a conservative Muslim country, but this is the sex business, and it's booming as a result of the war in Iraq".[17] The sex industry lies at the heart of complex international networks of poverty, legal persecution and economic exploitation which force women into prostitution. However, these networks could not have developed in this way were it not for the continuing oppression of women in contemporary society.

The expansion of international capitalism at the end of the 19th and early 20th centuries had many similarities to the current period of capitalism in terms of the internationalisation of finance, trade and investment and the sex industry. However, one important distinction must be made. There was a virtual absence of immigration restrictions up until the end of the First World War, while since the Second World War increasingly repressive and pervasive immigration legislation has been introduced in the developed world. Anti-immigration legislation means there is no possibility for poor and unskilled women to travel independently and work legally, so they become dependent on recruiting agencies and criminal networks. While some find low paid jobs looking after other people's families, or cleaning and catering, others get enmeshed in the complex web of the sex industry.

Migrant women working in the sex industry are at risk from deportation, imprisonment, harassment and abuse. Deportation means they end up with disastrous debts that they will never be able to pay and often face rejection by their families. In the UK government agencies consider trafficked women above all else as undesirable aliens. The fact that they may be victims of sexual violence and exploitation is completely subordinate or even irrelevant to their immigration status. Refugee organisations have accused the Home Office of choosing them as soft targets to boost deportation targets because migrant sex workers are an easy catch. Therefore

---

15: Avgerinos, 2007.
16: Avgerinos, 2007.
17: *Independent on Sunday*, 24 June 2007.

although New Labour politicians pay lip service to the plight of trafficked women, it is their government's repressive immigration legislation that leaves women vulnerable to criminal gangs and treats the victims of sex traffickers at illegal immigrants to be deported against their will.

The roots of oppression and the commodification of sex

The scale and nature of prostitution and sex work have been and are conditioned by the poverty, polarisation and dislocation endemic to global capitalism. However, prostitution is not just another dimension of exploitation, but has to be understood in the context of women's oppression. Women have not always been oppressed. According to Frederick Engels women's oppression developed with the emergence of private property and was later transformed by the rise of the bourgeois family, which became the mechanism for transferring property from one generation to the next.[18] Modern women's oppression was also shaped by the separation of the home from the workplace during the industrial revolution and the resulting creation of a separate sphere of private life.

Along with Engels, Bebel argued that prostitution was the flip side of marriage and a "necessary social institution of bourgeois society".[19] Prostitution played a specific role because sexual interest was removed from the bourgeois family and assigned to prostitutes. Women within the family were expected to endure sex as a means of procreating, whereas men were deemed to have desires that could only be satiated outside the confines of the family. Some Victorian moralists justified the existence of prostitution on this basis. As historian Leonore Davidoff has written:

> Defenders of prostitution saw it as a necessary institution which acted as a giant sewer, drawing away the distasteful, but inevitable waste products of male lustfulness, leaving the middle class household and middle class ladies pure and unsullied.[20]

Alexandra Kollontai wrote that prostitution was "the inevitable shadow of the official institution of marriage designed to preserve the rights of private property and to guarantee property inheritance through a line of lawful heirs".[21] This attitude helps to explain why prostitution was

---

18: Bebel, 1879, and Engels, 1972.
19: Bebel, 1879, and Engels, 1972.
20: Davidoff, 1995.
21: Kollontai, 1921, in Holt, 1977, p20.

morally condemned but tolerated and in some countries, such as France, highly regulated by the state.

Marxist accounts of the roots of women's oppression were revived by some strands in the women's liberation movement of the 1960s and 1970s. In its early days the women's movement sought to challenge the economic exploitation of women with campaigns against discrimination and for equal pay in the workplace. The movement also campaigned for 24-hour childcare, equal access to education and jobs and the extension of women's control over their own fertility through access to contraception and abortion. Women challenged stereotypes about their appearance and the double standards applied to their sexuality, which sanctioned men's sexual activity while castigating women who exercised the same freedom.

However, the gains made by the women's movement were not sustained. One wing of the movement retreated into the politics of the personal and substituted individual lifestyles for collective struggle while the other, the socialist-feminists, harnessed themselves to the Labour Party. The result of this was to seriously weaken the movement's ability to challenge inequality in the workplace and women's oppression in general. The demise of the women's movement, coupled with the increased marketisation of sex, laid the way open for a resurgence in new forms of sexism, the so-called ironic sexism which has led to the normalisation of "lads' mags", pornography and lap dancing clubs.

Today women participate more widely in the workforce than ever before, and although some gains have been made, genuine equality is a long way off. Although the ideology of the nuclear family is stronger than the reality, the family remains central to capitalism in terms of reproducing labour and fulfilling welfare functions. The oppression of women and the continued existence of the family are generated by the interests of capitalism which is best served by pushing the burden of social welfare onto individual families. Women are left to cope with a post-feminist ideology that tells them that they are equal and liberated, whereas the reality is one of unequal pay, responsibility for childcare and sexist discrimination.

Capitalism in the 21st century has increased the objectification of women and the commodification of sex. Sex is used everywhere, to sell everything. The social relationships that create the possibility of an industry for sex are deeply rooted in the structures of capitalism itself. The dominance of market competition over personal relationships creates a situation where human desires are transformed into commodities which can be sold for a profit. In his early writings Marx described how, in capitalist society:

Each attempt to establish over the other an alien power, in the hope of thereby achieving satisfaction of his own selfish needs...becomes the inventive and ever calculating slave of inhuman, refined, unnatural and imaginary appetites. He places himself at the disposal of his neighbour's most depraved fancies, panders to his needs, excites unhealthy appetites in him, and pounces on every weakness, so that he can then demand the money for his labour of love.[22]

Today we have become so used to a situation where all our human needs have been transformed into commodities that it seems almost natural. In their rapacious search for new markets to exploit, capitalist organisations probe more and more deeply into all aspects of our lives and in the process transform them further. Thus money can buy anything, including the simulation of love, but on the other side of the coin, all our human desires and abilities contract into a focus on consuming or what Marx called a sense of having:

Private property has made us so stupid and one-sided that an object is only ours when we have it, when it exists for us as capital or when we directly possess, eat, drink, wear, inhabit it, etc, in short, when we use it.[23]

Our ability to experience sexual pleasure is alienated from us and turned into a commodity which we then desire to consume. But this process transforms sexual confidence and satisfaction into goals which recede further and further from our reach. In her book *Female Chauvinist Pigs: Women and The Rise of Raunch Culture*, Ariel Levy shows how the growing commodification of sex and objectification of women's bodies has become increasingly divorced and disconnected from sexual pleasure and fulfilment.[24]

The sex industry now appears to be setting the agenda for numerous TV programmes, which show how women are encouraged to seek personal happiness by being surgically, cosmetically and sartorially tweaked into conforming to certain sexual stereotypes. In the US breast augmentation rose by 700 percent between 1992 and 2004. In some South American countries this procedure is a standard gift for a daughter at 18.[25] Increasingly,

---

22: Marx, 1975, p356.
23: Marx, 1975, p351.
24: Levy, 2006 p22.
25: Levy, 2006 p158.

women are even prepared to undergo a "vaginoplasty" in which their vulva and labia are surgically altered to make them look like those of porn stars in *Playboy*. There could be no more graphic example of how women in particular are alienated from their bodies to such an extent that they are prepared to pay for someone to cut and stitch them into a shape they are told will make them desirable to others.

Sex is not immune from the conditions which shape all aspects of our lives. All sexuality is shaped by the material conditions and social priorities of the society we live in, but the open treatment of sex as a commodity to be sold on the market is not just another aspect of that process. Sexuality is regarded as one of the last intimate aspects of ourselves. Sex is a part of our human nature, an experience that can be fulfilling and a central part of an individual's identity. As one economist put it:

> Prostitution is the classic example of how commodification debases a gift's value and its giver, as it destroys the kind of reciprocity required to realise human sexuality as a shared good and the mutual recognition of each partner's needs.[26]

Openness about sex and expectations of sexual fulfilment were key demands of the women's liberation movement. However, the sexual freedom fought for in the 1960s and 1970s has been distorted and repackaged as commodities. The selling of sexuality to clients transforms the body into an object, a thing for someone else to use. All aspirations to autonomy and personal satisfaction are brutally stripped away by commercial sex which degrades both women and men and reinforces the most backward prejudices against women.

Organising sex workers

After the Russian Revolution of 1917 the Bolsheviks believed that prostitution was incompatible with the aspiration for sexual equality. They revoked all laws concerning prostitution and the first All Russian Congress of Peasants and Working Women adopted the slogan "A woman of the Soviet Labour Republic is a free citizen with equal rights, and cannot be and must not be the object of buying and selling." Despite these proclamations prostitution in Russia grew after 1917, mainly due to the harsh economic circumstances that prevailed. It was dealt with inconsistently with brothels operating openly in some areas, while in others prostitutes were arrested.

26: Anderson, 1993, quoted in Van der Veen, 2001.

Kollontai's view was that prostitution was wrong, not on moral grounds, but because it stopped women contributing to the socialist society. Further, she argued that prostitution represented a threat to the new socialist morality because it destroyed solidarity and comradeship in the working class. Therefore the struggle against prostitution took place on two fronts: the first to secure economic equality for women and their participation in the labour force, the second to undermine the existence of the family as the source of women's oppression by introducing collective canteens, laundries and nurseries.[27]

There was also a lively exchange on the issue of prostitution and sexuality between German socialist and campaigner for women's rights Clara Zetkin and Lenin. Lenin recognised that prostitutes were double victims of bourgeois society—"victims, first of its accursed system of property and secondly of its accursed moral hypocrisy". However, he condemned the efforts by a Communist woman in Hamburg to organise prostitutes as a "morbid deviation". He argued that socialists should focus on organising women where they had collective power, in the workplaces, and thus transform the whole of society. Zetkin was herself contemptuous of the "empty chatter of bourgeois women" who moralised about the evils of prostitution—she argued that without well paid work for women, any discussion of abolishing prostitution was nonsense.[28]

Some campaigners and academics argue that prostitution is a job like any other in that sex workers negotiate rates of pay for the service they perform, and have control over their working conditions and exercise more autonomy than women in many other low-paid, low-status jobs. However, the possibility of collective organisation at work rests on the sharing of conditions, a common employer, and shared grievances, which can be opposed.

Sex workers face massive barriers in their capacity to organise collectively to improve pay and conditions. Women involved in street prostitution are marginalised, isolated and desperate, where there is little possibility of fighting for collective rates for the job, of negotiating collectively with clients or contributing to pension schemes. In the UK women who work on the streets are mostly those excluded from society, such as runaway teenagers, drug addicts and undocumented migrants turning to prostitution as a means of survival. It is by no means clear that they would wish to be incorporated into civil society as a "sex worker", even if this option was open to them. Not everyone who sells sex thinks of themselves

---

27: Kollontai, 1921, in Holt 1977.
28: Quoted in Ringdal, 2004, p267.

as a "sex worker" or wishes to be recognised as such.[29]

While this may be the case for women working on the streets of the UK historically, in parts of the developed world the situation may be more complex. During the 19th century and first part of the 20th century there were many examples of prostitutes organising and protesting against maltreatment. The current Uruguayan sex workers' organisation has the seeds of its history in the struggle of Polish prostitutes during the 19th century. Everyday resistance is documented from the mid-19th century in Lucknow (India), and Guatamala, and in colonial Kenya in the 1920s and 1930s.[30] There were significant waves of sex workers' organising in the 1970s and then in the early 1990s in response to HIV/AIDs. A third wave of organising appears to be emerging significantly in India and Argentina. The Karnataka Sex Workers Union, established in India in 2006, has specifically constituted itself as a trade union, affiliating to the New Trade Union Initiative (NTUI) which has organised other informal workers. They have assisted in enrolling women in the electoral register, struggled against the criminalisation of clients and lobbied the government about violence against sex workers.[31]

In 2001 in Argentina the *Asociación de Mujeres Meretrices de la Argentina* (AMMAR) sex workers' organisation became an official affiliate member of the *Central de los Trabajadores de la Argentina* trade union federation (CTA). Although subject to debate in the movement, their membership went beyond a token gesture. The CTA used resources to support women against abuse, while AMMAR branch secretaries took on responsibilities as elected members of the CTA.[32] There was no suggestion that sex work was desirable or fulfilling, but as (often) single parents it was the best option available to feed themselves and their families. In the words of one of the members of AMMAR their aspiration was:

> That one day there are no more women that exercise this work for necessity, however, as we are not the owners of the truth we leave open the discussion as to whether—in the future we dream of—there will be women that all the same want to do this work.[33]

29: O'Connell Davidson, 2006.
30: Downe, 1999; Kempadoo and Doezema, 1998.
31: Hardy, 2010. Also see www.blogger.com/profile/10868366661389533397
32: Hardy, 2010.
33: Hardy, 2010.

The rise of lap dancing clubs

The sex industry extends beyond the direct exchange of money for sex. Lap dancing clubs are a concrete manifestation of the sex industry which socialists need to address. First, these have been the very places in which there is deemed to be "erotic" labour and which have been targeted for union recruitment by the GMB trade union. Second, as socialists or activists in our communities, we have to take a view as to whether it is acceptable that these are located in our areas.

Lap dancing clubs are an important aspect of the industry because they are presented as its respectable face. Clubs like Spearmint Rhino have managed to gain an air of respectability, thanks to slick marketing and celebrity endorsements. Whereas strip clubs and brothels are seen as sordid and distasteful, lap dancing clubs are seen as an essential part of "lad" culture—somewhere that "city boys" can spend their bloated bonuses. Even worse is that taking staff to a club, buying drinks and paying for women to dance are legitimate business expenses and companies can claim back 15 percent VAT.[34] This reflects the entrenched discrimination and sexism in the financial sector. In this "ironic" and post-feminist culture attendance is not exclusive to men. Women are dismissed as puritans and spoilsports if they do not join in.

Lap dancing has been described as "the fastest growing area in Britain's sex industry". There are 150 clubs in the UK and 20 in London and they are estimated to generate £1 billion per year.[35] One factor in the proliferation of these clubs is the 2003 Licensing Act, which introduced the one size fits all premises licence, meaning that strip clubs are no longer required to get special permission for nudity. Some have suggested that lap dancing is completely separate from the sex industry and is simply one among many leisure activities open to ordinary people. The previous owner of For Your Eyes Only, Alan Whitehead, dismissed criticisms of his contribution to the sex industry and argued, "Sure they take their clothes off, but they're not strippers. They're dancers".[36]

Lap dancing is promoted as a job where women can make lots of money and have some power and autonomy. For the vast majority of women this is sheer nonsense. All lap dancers in clubs are self-employed, relying on tips and income from private dances. Dancers pay between £35 and £100 per night to the club management to "rent" facilities such as poles, cabaret areas, private dance booths and VIP suites. This

---

34: *Independent*, 20 September 2009.
35: *London Evening Standard*, 17 August 2007.
36: *Daily Mirror*, 9 July 2003.

self-employment is not liberatory but keeps women permanently insecure and subservient. The women are not in control, autonomous or empowered—they are strictly monitored and controlled.

Changes in the law reclassifying lap dancing clubs as "sex encounter institutions" should be welcomed, albeit cautiously. Radical feminists such as Julie Bindel have been prepared to make alliances with right wing groups to call on the state to get lap dancing clubs banned. Socialists should have no truck lining up with such people. Beyond opposing moralistic arguments we do not see the solution as giving more power to the state, as the state is a means of oppression, not liberation. For example, in 1984, the Obscene Publications Act (1959) was used to raid the Gay's the Word bookshop and seize hundreds of books as part of the moral backlash under Margaret Thatcher's Conservative government.

The impact of lap dancing clubs on localities goes far beyond what actually takes place inside them. It means that women who live and work in these areas are more likely to be subject to abuse and harassment. In 2006 the Respect group in Tower Hamlets council argued against the extension of licences for lap dancing clubs on the grounds that they degraded and exploited women and were part of New Labour's idea of regenerating inner cities by repackaging them as playgrounds for the rich. The City of London Corporation does not allow sex clubs or lap dancing venues. Instead taxi loads of stockbrokers from the City head to disadvantaged areas on the edge of the City, like Tower Hamlets.

Lap dancing clubs are symptomatic of the wider way in which the sex industry has been normalised and come to be viewed as acceptable. Before 2003 Jobcentre Plus (the UK government employment agency) did not advertise vacancies from within the "adult entertainment" industry. It would have meant that people not considering this type of employment could have risked their benefit entitlements. After a legal challenge from Ann Summers Ltd in 2003 this decision was reversed. Between 2006 and 2007, 351 jobs were advertised in government job centres, including pole dancers, "adult" chat line workers, masseuses and escorts.[37]

Some campaigners for rights for sex workers argue that erotic dancing is adult entertainment, not a sexual service, and that this group of workers should have access to the same employment rights and protection as other workers in the economy. In 2001 "erotic dancers" and others working in the sex industry were invited to join the GMB. The GMB has adopted the International Union Sex of Workers (IUSW) definition, which encompasses

37: Jobcentre Plus.

"any workers who use their body and/or their sexuality to earn a living".
In 2004 it had a branch of 150 members, mainly lap and table dancers. The
unions signed a recognition agreement with two lap dancing clubs and maintain that working conditions and terms of employment have since improved.
Codes of conduct and grievance procedures have been introduced, and
union representatives been elected in those two clubs. However well inten-
tioned the GMB, it is not clear that such organising has gone beyond a token
presence in the industry. If the women who work in these places are able
to organise to improve their wages and working conditions, then of course
socialists must support them. Our quarrel is not with the women who work
in them, but with the big firms and individuals who make vast sums for
commodifying sex and trading on the objectification of women.

Socialists should oppose lap dancing clubs because they are an integral part of the sex industry. Their very existence helps to perpetuate the
oppression of women. Lap dancing clubs are not normal workplaces,
and attempts to characterise them as such must be resisted. Whether the
dancers have union rights or not, the clubs function on the basis of the
objectification of women and package them as objects available for the
sexual gratification of others. The existence of lap dancing clubs makes it
harder to fight against the idea that women should be valued according to
how well they conform to physical stereotypes or how sexually available
they are.

Criminalising men?

Rather than criminalising sex workers themselves, some governments have
sought to criminalise the men who solicit or pay for sexual services. One of
the contentious clauses of the UK's Police and Crime Bill (2009) has been
the proposal to criminalise men who buy sex. The argument is that shifting
the burden of blame to clients will bring about a reduction in prostitution. This has been strongly opposed by a wide range of organisations and
representatives of sex workers as making things more dangerous as it drives
activity underground where women are less protected.[38]

In Sweden a 1998 law criminalised the buying of sex, a strategy
which embodied elements of a feminist approach that sees prostitution
as a violation of women akin to rape. Street prostitution in Sweden has
fallen, but prostitution via the internet has risen, which some suggest could
have happened independently of the legislation. Furthermore, sex worker

---

38: http://www.prostitutescollective.net/PolicingandCrimeHowToOppose.htm and
www.womeninlondon.org.uk/2009/11/notice-ecp-2/

organisations have pointed out that the criminalisation of their clients only pushes them into darker, less frequented areas, making them more vulnerable. Women who work on the streets are the most marginalised of all sex workers and they suffer the most from such legislation. O'Connell Davidson suggests that calling on the state to penalise buyers of sex has encouraged some feminists to forge alliances with repressive forces of the state and reactionary forces. She argues that this has involved:

> Police chiefs calling for more extensive police powers and tougher sentencing policy, anti-immigration politicians calling for tighter border controls, and moral conservatives urging a return to "family values".[39]

It is very difficult to identify the factors which propel men into paying for sex: their motives are diverse and there are many obstacles to any open discussion of the subject. The "punter" of popular myth is the sad, inadequate figure who cannot relate to women. However, *Paying the Price*, a 2004 government consultation paper, found that the typical customer was "a man of around 30 years of age, married, in full-time employment, and with no criminal convictions".[40] Today the number of men visiting prostitutes, or admitting to it, is increasing. The *Independent* quotes a 2005 study published in the *British Medical Journal* which found that the proportion of British men paying for sex had gone up from 5.6 percent in 1990 to nearly 8.8 percent in 2000. Dr Helen Ward, lead author of the report, points to growing divorce rates, sex tourism like stag holidays and the increasing availability of commercial sex through such means as the internet as reasons for the growth in male participation:

> It's far more acceptable to visit a prostitute. The sex industry is far more visible. Anyone with a WAP phone or a computer can find sex to buy. It's part of the commercialisation of everything—these days we expect to buy anything we want when we want it.[41]

Men may turn to buying sex because they work long hours, are isolated from social networks or are part of a transient population. But they are also encouraged to think that they should be having sex and that women's bodies are just another commodity that can be bought, like a car

---

39: O'Connell Davidson, 2003, p55.
40: *Paying the Price*, 2004, government consultation document.
41: *Independent*, 8 April 2007.

or a plasma TV. There is nothing inevitable about this situation. As Julia O'Connell Davidson has argued:

> Human beings are not born wishing to buy commercial sex services or visit lap dancing clubs, any more than they are born with specific desires to play the lottery or drink Coca-Cola. They have to learn to imagine that it would be pleasurable to pay a stranger to dance naked for them; they have to be taught that consuming such services is a signifier of the fact that they are having fun, a marker of their social identity and status as "a real man", "adult", "not gay" or whatever.[42]

It is capitalist society, with its sexist social structures and rampant consumerism, that is the educator.

State accommodation or repression

State responses to the sex industry have historically combined the repression of prostitutes with a tacit acknowledgement that prostitution cannot be eradicated and so must be regulated. One of the most notorious examples of the former came in 1864 when the British government passed the first of three Contagious Diseases Acts which applied to 11 garrison and port towns. The acts were a response to soaring levels of venereal disease in the armed forces which were so crucial to the British Empire. The acts permitted police officers to arrest women they thought might be prostitutes and force them to endure a humiliating and painful internal examination for signs of venereal disease. Women with such diseases could be confined in a "lock hospital" for up to three months. All working class women in the designated towns were vulnerable to abuse and arrest. A national campaign forced the repeal of the Contagious Diseases Acts, but the attitudes they embodied were enshrined in further legislation which followed.

Today most state responses are framed by two opposing political perspectives. The first sees prostitution as morally reprehensible and an affront to moral decency, which must be eradicated, and the second sees sex as a commodity like any other and seeks to regulate the sex industry. Neither works to reduce the exploitation involved in the sex industry.

Some campaigners, such as the English Collective of Prostitutes, point to New Zealand's decriminalisation of prostitution in 2003 as the model to be emulated. Campaigners point to how decriminalisation benefits sex workers by improving their ability to access health services or police protection and

---

42: O'Connell Davidson, 2006.

general attitudes towards them. However, the results of experiments with a more tolerant attitude to the sex industry have been the subject of bitter dispute. On the other hand, the Swedish model of criminalising clients, which has been hailed as a great success in greatly reducing visible prostitution, has simply driven these activities underground, making them more hazardous for the women who work in them. Although we should fully support the decriminalisation of prostitution, this does not mean that we support it being regulated and controlled by the state. State intervention in the sex industry is not ultimately the way to overcome the raunch culture and sexism that exist in society, or the material conditions which make women choose prostitution or lap dancing as the best alternative open to them.

In the UK the New Labour government treats prostitution as anti-social behaviour, issues prostitutes with Anti-Social Behaviour Orders (Asbo) and regularly declares "zero tolerance" for street prostitution. All attempts at helping or rehabilitating sex workers are formulated within this punitive framework. Police have been encouraged to work more closely with charities running safe houses, sexual health outreach programmes, and drug and alcohol treatment programmes to help women get out of the sex trade. However, as part of this process, women can be bound by Asbos to attend programmes designed to encourage them to get help with drink or drug problems. Breaching an Asbo can incur a prison sentence of up to five years, and a criminal record makes it even harder for women to leave the sex trade.[43]

The New Labour Government has purported to be concerned about the plight of "trafficked" women. The Poppy Project was set up in 2003 with funding from the Office for Criminal Justice Reform. A report they published, "Big Brothel", has been hugely criticised by 27 academics who research on the sex industry as well as organisations who represent or work with sex workers. They argue that it is seriously flawed and has produced sensationalist results, which are being used to introduce legislation that puts migrant and non-migrant women who sell sex at risk.[44]

More recently, the Policing and Crime Bill (2009) has been sold as a benevolent feminist project by politicians such as Harriet Harman. However, our attitude to this legislation should be based on whether it protects sex workers and their families—which it does not. The harsher definition of persistent soliciting (with "persistent" redefined as twice in a three-month period), the forced "rehabilitation" of those arrested, the

---

43: *Observer*, 12 August 2007.
44: *Guardian*, 20 October 2009; Murray, 1998.

targeting of brothels for raids and closures will drive prostitution further underground, increasing the vulnerability of those involved. Fear of arrest deters women from reporting violence or gaining access to health and other services. The majority of sex workers are mothers who worry about protecting their children from the stigma attached to criminalisation and the separation that results from a prison sentence. The legislation would penalise women who work from a flat. In May 2009 the Royal College of Nursing voted 93 percent in favour of up to four sex workers being allowed to work together legally on the grounds that decriminalisation would remove the stigma of prostitution, enabling sex workers to access the health services they need.

Measures that prevent men from buying sex from street prostitutes are increasingly presented and justified as anti-trafficking measures. However, huge objections have been made by groups concerned with the safety, human rights and civil liberties of women who work on the street.[45] With regard to "trafficked" women, the regulation of commercial sex does nothing in itself to counteract racism, xenophobia or prejudice against migrants and minority ethnic groups. An end to draconian immigration controls, and granting asylum to these women would, however, immediately undercut "trafficking".

Conclusion

Those who are exploited have the potential to challenge their alienation through collective struggle, which lays bare the hidden realities of how the market dominates our lives and where the real power for change lies. Ultimately, workers have the potential to create a socialist society in which human beings exercise democratic and collective control over their society and every aspect of their lives, including their sexual relationships.

The exploitation of women who work on the street could be ameliorated by rehabilitation programmes with real resources and treatment for drug addiction. Jail does not cure drug addiction and it certainly does not give women a route out of prostitution. To reduce the number of women involved in prostitution, the government should develop initiatives which offer training and employment to women, and provide rehabilitative counselling and support to women who are emotionally damaged and addicted to drugs and alcohol. Women who work on the street should be released from the burden of convictions for soliciting, enabling them to apply for jobs outside prostitution. Decriminalising prostitution and offering

---

45: www.prostitutescollective.net/PolicingandCrimeHowToOppose.htm

all trafficked women asylum would have a huge impact on many of these women's lives.

A real alternative for women who work in the wider sex industry cannot be divorced from the fight for real opportunities in the labour market and the struggle for good quality, affordable childcare and free higher education. Women may "choose" to work on adult chat lines or as exotic dancers, because the reality of their everyday lives is that this fits better with looking after families or study than the badly paid or inflexible alternatives on offer.

However, while reforming the industry could help women, the aim of such reforms should be to reduce women's dependence on selling sex and sexuality, not normalising or legitimising that exchange. "Sex work" is not a job like any other. It is not only a symptom of the most degrading and alienated aspects of life under capitalism, but also reinforces that degradation and alienation. Many jobs that people do today would still have to be done in a socialist society, but we believe that the poverty, alienation and oppression that create the conditions in which the sex industry flourishes would wither away. The commodification of sex deprives people of choice and fulfilment in their sex lives. The representation of sexuality displayed in lap dancing clubs or "lads' mags" does not promote sexual freedom—it makes that freedom harder to achieve. Human beings have the potential to establish genuinely fulfilling and free sexual relationships. As Frederick Engels put it:

> What we can now conjecture about the way in which sexual relations will be ordered after the impending overthrow of capitalist production is mainly of a negative character, limited for the most part to what will disappear. But what will there be new? That will be answered when a new generation has grown up: a generation of men who never in their lives have known what it is to buy a woman's surrender with money or any other social instrument of power; a generation of women who have never known what it is to give themselves to a man from any other considerations than real love or to refuse to give themselves to their lover from fear of the economic consequences. When these people are in the world, they will care precious little what anybody today thinks they ought to do; they will make their own practice and their corresponding public opinion about the practice of each individual—and that will be the end of it.[46]

46: Engels, 1972, p145.

References

Anderson, Elizabeth, 1993, *Value in Ethics and Economics* (Harvard University).

Avgerinos, Katherine P, 2007, "From Vixen to Victim: the Sensationalisation and Normalisation of Prostitution in post-Soviet Russia", *Vestnik, The Journal of Russian and Asian Studies*, 7.

Bebel, Augustus, 1879, *Women and Socialism*, www.marxists.org/archive/bebel/index.htm

Bernstein, Elisabeth, 2001, "The Meaning of the Purchase: Desire, Demand and the Commerce of Sex", *Ethnography*, volume 2, number 3.

Davidoff, Leonore, 1995, *Worlds Between: Historical Perspectives on Gender and Class* (Blackwell).

Downe, Pamela J, 1999, "Laughing when it hurts: Humour and Violence in the Lives of Costa Rican Prostitutes", *Women's Studies International Forum* 22.

Engels, Frederick, 1972 [1884], *The Origin of the Family, Private Property and the State* (New York), www.marxists.org/archive/marx/works/1884/origin-family/

Gall, Gregor, 2006, *Sex Worker Union Organising: An International Study* (Palgrave).

Gibson, Mary, 1986, *Prostitution and the State in Italy* (Rutgers University).

Hardy, Kate, 2010, "(Sex) Working Class Subjects: Incorporating Sex Workers into the Argentine Labour Movement", *International Labour and Working Class History* (forthcoming).

Innes, Christopher, 2000, *A Sourcebook on Naturalist Theatre* (Routledge).

Jobcentre Plus (no date) "Advertising Employer Vacancies from the Adult Entertainment Industry", www.jobcentreplus.gov.uk/JCP/stellent/groups/jcp/documents/websitecontent/dev_016084.rtf

Kollontai, Alexandra, 1977 [1921], "Prostitution and Ways of Fighting It", in A Holt, *Selected writings of Alexandra Kollontai* (Allison & Busby), www.marxists.org/archive/kollontai/1921/prostitution.htm

Levy, Ariel, 2006, *Female Chauvinist Pigs: Women and the Rise of Raunch Culture* (Simon & Schuster).

O'Connell Davison, Julia, 2003, "'Sleeping with the Enemy'? Some Problems with Feminist Abolitionist Calls to Penalise Those Who Buy Commerical Sex", *Social Policy and Society*, volume 2, number 1.

O'Connell Davidson, Julia, 2006, "Men, Middlemen and Migrants", *Eurozine*, 27 July 2006.

Paying the Price, 2004, government consultation document.

Marx, Karl, 1975, *Early Writings* (Penguin).

Mayhew, 1861, *London Labour and London Poor*, http://etext.virginia.edu/toc/modeng/public/MayLond.html

Murray, Alison, 1998, "Debt-bondage and Trafficking; Don't Believe the Hype", in Kamala Kempadoo and Jo Doezema, *Global Sex Workers: Rights Resistance and Realities* (Routledge).

Ringdal, Nils Johan, 2004, *Love For Sale: A World History of Prostitution* (Grove).

Van der Veen, Marjolein, 2001, "Rethinking Commodification and Prostitution: an Effort at Peacemaking in the Battles Over Prostitution", *Rethinking Marxism*, volume 13, number 2.

Jewish intellectuals and Palestinian liberation

John Rose

A review of Shlomo Sand, **The Invention of the Jewish People** *(Verso, 2009), £18.99 and Avi Shlaim,* **Israel and Palestine** *(Verso, 2009), £16.99*

I'll risk a prediction. Shlomo Sand's book, already a best seller in Israel and France, will accelerate the disintegration of the Zionist enterprise. Of course Israel's military force as well as its usefulness to Western governments can allow it to hang on for some time, but its ideological credibility, already severely shaken, will now shatter more quickly. Furthermore Sand is immune to any accusation of anti-Semitism. His book, with tremendous elan and gusto, is a celebration of an unknown early history of the Jewish religion.

Yet the November Verso UK launch of the English edition of his book missed this. Jacqueline Rose as interlocutor concentrated instead on the "67/48" question. Rose, along with Avi Shlaim, also present to promote his book, are two of Israel's most creative critics. They have even been called "Jews for Genocide" by ardent Zionist Melanie Phillips because of their prominent support for Independent Jewish Voices. Phillips is understandably bitter with the pair: in January 2005 over 600 people saw her team lose to their team in a debate, "Zionism is the Main Enemy of the Jews".

Yet Rose and Shlaim do not consider themselves "anti-Zionist"; hence the "67/48" question, meaning, do you favour two states along the

1967 border or one state on the 1948 borders? Rose seemed determined to "out" Sand on this matter. And indeed we learned that he was also for two states if only because one state, however desirable, was simply not practical. But it was a wasted evening. Do Rose and Shlaim agree with Sand that conversion rather than "exile" is a defining moment in Jewish history—the basis for the book's title? It was not properly discussed either by the panel or with the audience. Fortunately, though, queues for his book continued long after the meeting had finished.

Still a further thought lingers, which we will return to later. Was there an unspoken worry that evening for the fate of a Jewish minority in an Arab Palestine?

In 1670 Baruch Spinoza helped ignite the Enlightenment when he denied that Moses had received the Ten Commandments from god. Rather they had been written "by someone long after Moses".[1] Three centuries later Israeli archaeologists were reluctantly drawing the same conclusion. In Sand's pithy phrase, "the earth rebelled against mythistory".[2] Positioning himself firmly within the radical "minimalist" school of biblical criticism, Sand argues that archaeological discovery increasingly demands that we see the Bible:

> not as a book but a grand library that was written, revised and adapted in the course of three centuries, from the late 6th to the early 2nd BCE. It should be read as a multilayered literary construction of a religious and philosophical nature or as theological parables… The…ancient authors sought to create a coherent religious community… They invented the category of Israel as a sacred chosen people… This self-isolating literary politics, which began to develop between the little province of Yahud[3]…and the centres of high culture in Babylonia accorded well with…the policies of the Persian empire.[4]

The challenge this poses to the Zionists' manipulation of fictitious "biblical" Israel cynically servicing Jewish nationalist claims on Arab land is obvious. In addition the argument is rapidly going mainstream. The British Museum's recent Babylon exhibition tentatively drew similar conclusions, supported by grouping together fabulous artefacts from ancient

---

1:    Sand, 2009, p65.
2:    Sand, 2009, p115, pp123-5. See also Rose, 2004, pp20-25.
3:    ie Judah, today's West Bank and East Jerusalem.
4:    Sand, 2009, p126.

Babylonia and Persia, like the massive black stone Old Babylonian Code of Hammurabi (1792-1750 BCE), illustrating the evolution of monotheistic thinking over a thousand years before Judaism.

It was the Roman Empire as well as the period immediately preceding it, the epoch of Hellenistic culture, the culture of classical Athens, that boosted Judaism and transformed it into such a "dynamic, propagative religion" that it would "mount the Greek eagle and traverse the Mediterranean world".[5]

And here we come to the spectacular core of Sand's argument where he demolishes the entire Zionist ideological lexicon by replacing one single word with another single word, yet both so emotionally and politically loaded: conversion, not exile.

But surely "the distinguishing characteristic of the Jews has been their Exile", as David Vital wrote in his three-volume history of Zionism, hailed by the *Times Literary Supplement* as setting "new standards" for historians. This may constitute an ideological success story but it has little to do with real life Jewish history.

Bible sources are sometimes hostile, sometimes ambiguous about conversion, though one authoritative text, the "Book of Isaiah", predicts "all nations shall flow into...the Lord's house", and another source has the whole world adopting the "religion of Moses".[6] Philo, the great Jewish philosopher of Alexandria, who would struggle to make Plato compatible with Moses, had no doubts: Jewish laws would "shine" for the benefit of all.[7] The issue here is whether the God of the Jews is the God of all humanity (tribal or universal); if so then the pressures for conversion are implicit in the theology.

In any event there can be no doubt that conversion was the decisive factor "for the vast presence of Jewish believers throughout the ancient world before the fall of the Second Temple".[8] And Zionist historians know and admit it even though they then "sideline" the argument, preferring the "oppressive" narrative of expulsion, displacement, dispersal to account for the numbers outside Judea. Prior to Rome consolidating its rule, the Maccabee state even imposed Judaism on its neighbours by force.[9] This is the background to "Herod the Great", the legendary "half-Jewish" king, imposed by Rome, who, with his grandiose building work schemes, transformed the Second Temple in Jerusalem.

5:   Sand, 2009, p161.
6:   For a full discussion see Sand, 2009, pp150-154.
7:   Sand, 2009, p162.
8:   Sand, 2009, p150.
9:   Sand, 2009, pp154-161.

A critical moment in the spread of the Jewish religion was the translation of the Bible into Greek. Israeli historians reject the view that this must have been a trigger for conversion, arguing that many Jews knew no Hebrew and so the translations were intended for them. But this begs far more questions than it answers—not least why so many Jews did not know their national language. It is at least as likely that the Greek Bibles were for Hellenist converts.[10]

The reality is that Judaism spread rapidly throughout the Roman Empire, to such an extent that it laid the foundations for the "Rise of Christianity" captured so brilliantly as a chapter in Chris Harman's *A People's History of the World*. Judaism became nothing less than "the universal religion of the urban masses of empire".[11]

The city of Rome itself would feel the pressure. Judaism had "become seductive in broad circles... The crisis of the hedonistic culture, the absence of an integrating belief in collective values, and the corruption...appeared to call for a tighter normative system and a firmer ritual framework".[12]

Headlines here will have to suffice for several of Sand's fascinating accounts of a Judaism erupting almost everywhere. Women leading the conversions in Damascus and the reasons for it; the Berber conversions and the famous Berber Queen in North Africa, and their base for the eventual spread of Judaism to Spain; the conversion of a state in South Arabia in pre-Islamic Yemen, which led to bitter, bloody internecine Jewish-Christian warfare, with implications for the origins of nearby Ethiopia; and the conversions "in reverse"—the Islamisation of Palestine's Jewish peasantry who, most certainly, did not go into "exile".[13]

But the conversion of an entire early medieval European state, Khazaria, situated between the Black Sea and the Caspian Sea, requires closer attention because here is the potential base for modern European Jewry and hence the majority of Israelis.

Sand begins his exhaustive analysis of the evidence for Jewish Khazaria with an exchange of letters written in the 10th century between a Jewish representative of the court of the Islamic caliph of Cordoba, Spain, Abd ar-Rahman III, and the king of the Khazars, Joseph ben Aaron. The letters confirm that this was indeed a Jewish kingdom. Ten centuries later,

---

10: Sand, 2009, p161.
11: Harman, 2008, p92.
12: Sand, 2009, p170.
13: See Scharf, 2009.

in the early to mid-20th century, Jewish scholars mobilising all the techniques of established historical inquiry, subjecting to scrutiny a bewildering variety of sources in a range of different languages, drew an identical conclusion. Then something strange happened. We entered what Sand calls the "Realms of Silence", the title of his chapter on Khazaria, and the official Jewish memory forgot all about it.

Tracing this peculiar aspect of the 20th century evolution of Zionist historiography allows us simultaneously to give at least a superficial outline of Khazaria and the extraordinary panic it then subsequently posed for Zionist ideologues.

In 1944 Abraham Polok published in Hebrew his *Khazaria: The History of the Jewish Kingdom in Europe*. It was the first comprehensive work on the subject and it won a prize from the city of Tel Aviv. Polok was in many ways the perfect scholar for this subject. Born in Kiev, he knew Russian, Turkish, classical Arabic, ancient Persian, Latin and probably Greek. Nevertheless several reviewers began to have their doubts. What worried them was that Polok stated categorically that the great bulk of Eastern European Jewry originated in the territories of the Khazar empire. The ethno-biological "ancient Israeli" basis of Zionism was under threat. "I cannot imagine what greater joy and honour he grants us with this Turkish-Mongolian genealogy than our Jewish origin," cursed a critic.[14]

A further edition of the book was published in 1951 and then never re-issued. Furthermore not a single historical work about the Khazars has ever appeared in Hebrew since that date. There have been many books on the subject in English and other European languages. But only one of them was ever translated into Hebrew, Arthur Koestler's *The Thirteenth Tribe*. Koestler's work did not have the same academic foundations as Polok's but the line of argument was the same. The reaction was hysterical. "An anti-Semitic action financed by the Palestinians," said Israel's ambassador to Britain. "Perhaps the cosmopolitan has begun to wonder about his own roots," declared the World Zionist Organisation.[15]

Mainstream Israeli academia concurred. Yet as they did so they conveniently ignored the prestigious line of Jewish scholars stretching back to the 19th century who had developed the argument. Abraham Harkavy stated in 1867 that the first European Jews came "from the Greek cities on the shores of the Black Sea and from Asia, via the mountains of the Caucasus". Yitzhak Schipper, historian and prominent Zionist in Poland,

14:   Sand, 2009, p234.
15:   Sand, 2009, p234.

argued that the "Khazar thesis" accounted well for the massive demographic presence of Jews in Eastern Europe. Salo Baron, the great 20th century American Jewish historian, described the Khazars sending "many offshoots into the unsubdued Slavonic lands, helping ultimately to build up the great Jewish centres of Eastern Europe".[16]

An intriguing question is, of course, why Khazaria converted to Judaism. One possible answer is suggested by its much sought after geographical location:

> The Khazars were typical rice growers and regular consumers of fish and wine, though the bulk of the kingdom's income came from tolls. Khazaria straddled the Silk Road and also dominated the Volga and the Don rivers, which were major transportation routes… The Khazars were known for their flourishing trade especially in furs and slaves, and their growing wealth enabled them to maintain a strong and well trained military force that dominated all of southern Russia and today's eastern Ukraine.[17]

Pressed by the surrounding and competing empires, the Orthodox Christian Byzantine and the Abbasid Muslim Caliphate, Judaism might have seemed attractive as a form of ideological, theological defence. "Had the Khazars adopted Islam, for example, they would have become subjects of the Caliph…Christianity would have subordinated them".[18]

Khazaria as a trading Jewish nation suggests the interesting question of the alternative thesis for Jewish history—namely that of Abram Leon. I raised this in conversation with Shlomo Sand while he was in London. He agreed that the Leon argument—that the Jews also developed as a mobile trading community—could be compatible. A fascinating article by Aleksander Gieysztor explicitly links the Khazar empire to an independent group of long distance 10th century Jewish traders, known as the "Radanite" Jews.[19]

This is one line for further inquiry that flows directly from Sand's book.[20] Another is his discussion of the metamorphosis of the Jewish religion

---

16: Sand, 2009, pp241-242.
17: Sand, 2009, pp217-218.
18: Sand, 2009, p222.
19: Gieysztor, p16, also Rose, p47.
20: The debate about the origins of the Jewish "East European" language, Yiddish, with its German roots, is important here. German and other Western European Jewish medieval migration eastwards and Leon's explanations, need to be incorporated. Sand points to the significance of the Turkish roots of Yiddish, even the word to pray, *davenen*—Sand, 2009, p244.

into Jewish nationalism, Antonio Gramsci and the role of intellectuals.

As monotheistic religions spread around the ancient Mediterranean region they:

> gave rise to broader intellectual strata. From the ancient Essenes through the missionaries, monks, rabbis and priests, to the ulema, there were increasing numbers of literate individuals who had extensive…contact with the masses of agricultural producers—one reason that religion survived through the ages while empires…fell.[21]

It is the mediating role of these religious intellectuals, between the authorities and the masses, as well as, or so it seemed, between Heaven and Earth, that enhanced their stature. Sand regards nationalism in the modern world as having the same ideological force that religion had in the ancient and medieval world. Using the work of Benedict Anderson, Eric Hobsbawm, Ernest Gellner and Gramsci, among others, he explores how modern intellectuals helped create and sustain modern nationalism. But here there is unusual confusion in his argument. In particular, he misuses Gramsci's concept of the "organic intellectual", ignores or at least minimises the significance of the social class base of modern intellectuals and ends up mixing praise for Gramsci with a frankly embarrassing and gratuitous attack on him:

> It is not necessary to believe in Gramsci's political utopia—designed to justify his work as an intellectual in a workers' party—to appreciate his theoretical achievement in analysing the intellectual function that characterises the modern state.[22]

There is in fact a concealed hint here of Sand's own disappointed Marxist past. This issue clearly requires more discussion than is possible here,[23] but by junking Marxism he fails to distinguish two types of modern intellectuals, the middle class mediating intellectual who vacillates between differing social class interests and the intellectual who unambiguously declares for one social class. The social class background is not necessarily relevant. For sure, the upper class background of the Socialist Workers Party's Paul Foot made him a rarity, but his work as a professional intellectual was

---

21: Sand, 2009, p56.
22: Sand, 2009, p58.
23: In conversation he agreed to an interview about Gramsci and the issues raised here for *International Socialism* or *Socialist Review*.

devoted to working class interests and in that sense he re-made himself as an "organic" intellectual by consciously tying his own interests in that way.

And this argument brings us full circle back to the role of Shlomo Sand, Jacqueline Rose and Avi Shlaim as intellectuals. As outstanding critics of Zionism, are they, can they be, part of the Palestinian and wider Arab movement? How does a Jewish intellectual relate to an Arab movement? A satisfactory answer here will contribute to a debate about the place of Jews in an independent Palestine.

Shlaim knows the answer. And it is a great pity that his book of essays misses this question. There is of course, as always with Shlaim, a great deal of enormous value in this book, particularly his blistering assault on the Balfour Declaration and Britain's thoroughly nauseating record in creating the Zionist state. But his essays on the Arab world are disappointing—a review of an Arab author with a deeply negative view of Arab nationalism, and a record of Shlaim's interview with Jordan's King Hussein, implying that he regarded the king as part of the solution rather than being part of the problem. In fairness, though, his essay on Edward Said acknowledges the Arab intellectual's greater stature and recognises that Said saw the hollow core of the Oslo peace accords in a way that Shlaim readily admits he missed.

But Shlaim knows another history that is more important than any of this: his own. For he is an Iraqi Jew and elsewhere he has written:

> Judaism was a ritual. My parents used to attend the synagogue once a year, at home we spoke Judeo-Arabic, we listened to Arabic music. Nor was Zionism important, my parents had no empathy for it. There were Zionist agents who tried to create propaganda, but it didn't impress the Jewish elite and the middle class. There was no tradition of persecution or anti-Semitism in Iraq.

One of the great untold Jewish tragedies of the 20th century was the destruction of the Iraqi Jewish community, one of the oldest in the world and one which probably defies Sand's law of conversion with roots back to ancient Babylonia.

Not only that, Iraqi Jewish intellectuals really did help create Iraqi national culture in the early 20th century and a wonderful example is the fact that a third of Iraq's top musicians were Jewish.[24]

So, however bleak the intellectual and political landscape may be today, we should take a lesson from another great Jewish intellectual, Walter Benjamin, and "fan the sparks of hope from the past".

24: Rose, 2004, p180.

References

Gieysztor, Aleksander, 1986, "The Beginnings of Jewish Settlement in Polish Lands", in Chimen Abramsky, Maciej Jachimczyk and Antony Polonsky (eds), *The Jews of Poland* (Blackwell).

Harman, Chris, 2008, *A People's History of the World* (Verso).

Rose, John, 2004, *The Myths of Zionism* (Pluto).

Sands, Shlomo, 2009, *The Invention of the Jewish People* (Verso).

Scharf, Miriam, 2009, "Review: The Invention of the Jewish People", *Socialist Review* (November 2009), www.socialistreview.org.uk/article.php?articlenumber=11026

Shlaim, Avi, 2009, *Israel and Palestine* (Verso).

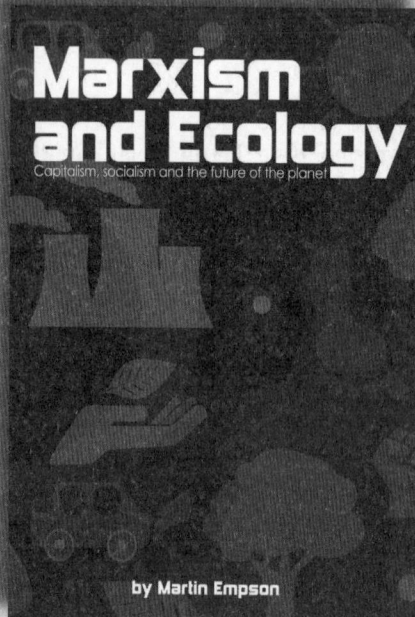

Get the new *Socialist Worker* pamphlet:

Marxism and Ecology: Capitalism, Socialism and the Future of the Planet

by Martin Empson

What did Karl Marx contribute to our understanding of our environment?

The answer, suggests this new pamphlet, is a great deal, despite being largely overlooked. Marx condemned capitalism not just for its exploitation of men and women but for producing a dangerous "metabolic rift" between humans and nature.

Marx's approach offers vital insights for all those who want to go beyond tinkering with the present set-up of society to stave off the threat of devastating climate change.

Available from Bookmarks, £1.50

Bookmarks—the socialist bookshop

1 Bloomsbury Street
London
WC1B 3QE

020 7637 1848

mailorder@bookmarks.uk.com

www.bookmarks.uk.com

Struggle, continuity and contradiction in Bolivia

Jeffery R Webber

*A review of John Crabtree and Laurence Whitehead (eds), **Unresolved Tensions: Bolivia Past and Present** (University of Pittsburgh, 2008), £24.50*

Bolivia has long been marginalised from mainstream international political discussion and affairs. Even the rest of South America has often forgotten the existence of its landlocked indigenous core. However, the poorest country in South America entered the spotlight in December 2005 when Evo Morales won an electoral majority and became the country's first indigenous president. He was elected on the back of an incredible tide of left-indigenous insurrection that began with the Cochabamba Water War against privatisation in 2000 and crested with the ousting of neoliberal presidents Gonzalo Sánchez de Lozada and Carlos Mesa in 2003 and 2005 respectively.

Morales, who has led the *Movimiento al Socialismo* (Movement Toward Socialism, MAS) since the party's creation in the mid-1990s, quickly embarked on a whirlwind post-election tour of the globe. More international attention was focused on Bolivia in the wake of that tour than at any time since at least Che Guevara's fateful demise in 1967, and perhaps as far back as the 1952 National Revolution.

Conservative Latin American pundits, such as Mexico's ex-leftist Jorge Castañeda, lined up behind the Bush administration to brand Evo as the latest addition to a disconcertingly immoderate current within the wider left turn gripping regional politics. Incipient fissures in neoliberal legitimacy broke wide open in the midst of a serious Latin American recession in the late 1990s and early 2000s.

The economic downturn of that period gave birth to a series of system-shaking revolts in countries such as Argentina, Ecuador and Bolivia itself. Extra-parliamentary struggles were later accompanied by a sea change in electoral politics as left and centre-left parties took office in country after country. Whatever the actual character of the various new governments once elected, it is undeniable that they were supported initially because they promised the masses an alternative to the two-decade old neoliberal assault and the destitution it wrought.

Morales, with humble rural origins and a political formation rooted in the anti-imperialist struggle of the coca growers' movement of the 1980s and 1990s, symbolically played up his ties to Venezuela and Cuba from the outset. The conservative hawks in Washington latched on to this imagery to demonise the new Bolivian president.

The same symbolism that triggered the ire of the dinosaur Cold Warriors in Washington simultaneously captured the imagination of large sections of the international left. Too often this has meant neglecting a careful assessment of the actual record of the Morales government during its time in office and the historical trajectory of class struggle and indigenous resistance in Bolivia over the past decade. Few have seriously taken into account, for example, the revolutionary anti-capitalist aims of the protest wave between 2000 and 2005, and the fact that Morales and MAS played an important part in channelling this energy out of the streets and into the constitutional channels of electoral politics and populist reformism.

As it turns out, both conservatives and uncritical leftists have exaggerated the extent to which the December 2005 elections transformed the political and social structures of Bolivia. Deep continuities with the inherited structures persist under Evo, and his government has never shared the revolutionary anti-capitalist and indigenous-liberationist ambitions that characterised the protest movements that emerged in the first five years of the current decade.

If anything, as we approach Morales's second term in office—he won a landslide victory in December's elections—the platform of MAS signals that a further strengthening of its inclination towards modest reformism and conciliation with foreign and domestic private capital. Vice-president Álvaro García Linera has described the government's development plans as building Andean-Amazonian capitalism for the next 50 to 100 years. His view is that a transition towards socialism is an impossible dream without an extensive intermediate stage of industrial capitalist growth.

The conjuncture of a new electoral cycle is an ideal time to take stock of the chasm between image and reality in contemporary Bolivian political economy. Such an undertaking was ostensibly the motivation behind John Crabtree and Laurence Whitehead's recently released edited volume, *Unresolved Tensions: Bolivia Past and Present*. Unfortunately, these seasoned British observers of Bolivian affairs have produced a wildly uneven and unsatisfactory book. What is more, despite the calculated pretences of distanced objectivity—the book is "not designed to promote any one particular standpoint" and is compiled by "sympathetic but uncommitted outsiders"[1]—the bulk of its content lies within the parameters of acceptable left-liberal opinion. With the honourable exceptions of the chapters by Luis Tapia and Carlos Arze, the debate is largely circumscribed by a left-right spectrum ranging from moderate supporters of the conservative wing of the MAS government to polite academic defences of the neo-fascist right in the eastern lowland departments, or *media luna* (half moon) formed by Tarija, Santa Cruz, Beni and Pando.

Nevertheless, a careful reading of the text in its entirety can produce important insights into the ideological framing of the study of Bolivian politics, as well as occasional bits of useful empirical data on the state of the economy and the specificities of the country's natural resource wealth.

Ethnicity

Unresolved Tensions is organised around the themes of ethnicity, regionalism, state-society relations, constitutional reform, economic development and globalisation.

Part one, on ethnicities, features a debate between Xavier Albó, Carlos Toranzo and Diego Zavaleta Reyles. Albó, a Jesuit priest and well-regarded cultural anthropologist, is in an entirely separate league to his interlocutors. Even when one takes account of the near-total absence of political economy from his analysis, Albó's work remains incomparably richer in historical depth and nuance than that of Toranzo or Zavaleta Reyles.

Albó takes as his point of departure the results of the 2001 national census. People over the age of 15 were asked which ethnic group they felt they belonged to: "Around 31 percent considered themselves to be Quechua, 25 percent Aymara (the largest populations of both groups found in the western Andean region of the country), and a further 6 percent identified themselves as belonging to one of 31 smaller indigenous (*originario*) groups and Mojeños (0.9 percent). In other words, nearly two thirds (62

1:     Crabtree and Whitehead, 2008, p255.

percent) of the population said they belonged to one or another of these ethnic groups".[2]

Bolivia, accompanied only by Guatemala, stands out in Latin America as having maintained a majority indigenous population into the early years of the 21st century. This is an extraordinary story of survival, rooted in centuries of resistance. Consider, for example, what officials carrying out the 1900 census had to say on the matter of the indigenous population in that period: "In a short space of time, in view of the progressive laws of statistics, the indigenous race will be, if not removed entirely from the scene, at least reduced to a small fraction".[3]

Albó provides a useful historical panorama of the political struggles around ethnicity and, at least cursorily, their interaction with simultaneous processes of class conflict and state formation since the colonial period. Against standard views of uncontested colonial and neocolonial rule over a passive indigenous majority, Albó stresses the importance of waves of indigenous rebellion (and also indigenous elite collaboration with colonialists) stretching back centuries. Indigenous people did not "simply [adopt] a passive, prepolitical posture" in the face of domination, but rather were the agents behind "continuous struggles and rebellions" against the different authority structures of the colonial and republican periods.[4]

Albó is at his weakest when he introduces a cliched trajectory of Bolivia in the post-1989 world, in which the "class based approach" to popular struggle has been abandoned in favour of "a more ethnic paradigm".[5] In fact, struggles for socialism from below and indigenous liberation were deeply intertwined in the most powerful popular movements of the 21st century, exhibiting what I have called "combined oppositional consciousness".[6]

He is also far too lenient towards the small number of indigenous elite who abandoned their mass movement bases and cynically adapted to the neoliberal multiculturalism adopted as official state policy over the course of the 1990s. The most glaring example is Victor Hugo Cárdenas, who became the first Aymara vice-president of Bolivia during the height of neoliberal restructuring.

Finally, Albó falls considerably wide of the mark when he suggests the MAS government has perhaps been insufficiently conciliatory in its dealings with the neo-fascist right of the *media luna* departments. "Arguably," Albó

2:    Crabtree and Whitehead, 2008, p13.
3:    Crabtree and Whitehead, 2008, p13.
4:    Crabtree and Whitehead, 2008, pp16-17.
5:    Crabtree and Whitehead, 2008, p24.
6:    Webber, forthcoming 2010.

suggests, the differing agendas of the eastern bourgeois and left-indigenous blocs have been "unnecessarily exacerbated by some of the [overly assertive] positions adopted by the MAS government".[7] The opposite is true. The MAS has allowed neo-fascist right wing vigilantes to flourish and the departmental governments of the eastern lowlands supporting them have also operated with impunity.

Regionalism

The important question of the uneven and combined development of capitalism across different geographical regions of Bolivia over the course of the last two centuries is far from adequately addressed in part two of the book on regionalism.

A significant mark against the project as a whole is that it treats the work of José Luis Roca as serious scholarship. Unimpeded by the actual historical record, Roca's chapter maintains that regionalist conflict in Bolivian history effectively subsumed class and ethnic tensions under its umbrella, and continues to define the central axis of division in the country to this day. Roca lines up ideologically behind the separatist forces of the *media luna* against the alleged centralism of La Paz. The solution to pervasive regionalist conflict is, for him, to devolve autonomous powers to each of the nine departments, as the eastern bourgeois bloc of the *media luna* has demanded. This will supposedly result in the long-desired decentralisation of political power and perhaps ensure the ongoing viability of Bolivia as a unified country.

This ignores the massive concentrations of natural gas deposits, large agro-industrial landholdings, and industrial and financial capital in the departments of Santa Cruz and Tarija. A radical redistribution of the country's wealth down the social hierarchy, along geographical, ethnic and class lines, is one of the urgent necessities of the day. The demands for autonomy emanating from the eastern lowlands reflect a political campaign to halt through destabilisation each and every modest movement by the Morales government towards that end.[8]

Roca cites approvingly the notoriously racist *Pueblo Enformo* (*Sick People*), written by historian Alcides Arguedas in the early 20th century. Roca agrees with Arguedas that the imaginative and creative qualities of some subsections of the Bolivian population can be celebrated, but that we must simply lament "the obstinacy of the Aymaras of La Paz". Roca's chosen people of the *media luna* are refreshingly modern, broadly supporting "neocapitalist

---

7: Crabtree and Whitehead, 2008, p29.
8: See, among other sources, Weisbrot and Sandoval, 2008.

development and market economics". The largely indigenous departments of the West, by contrast, are "strongly influenced by traditionalism", desiring a retrogressive "return to pre-Hispanic societal modes across Bolivia".[9]

This analysis is roughly as sophisticated as that of Gabriela Oviedo, a former Miss Bolivia, who infamously intervened in public affairs several years ago. She remarked to the beauty pageant press that she hated the fact that outsiders think of Bolivia as a country populated merely by short Indians. Ovieda wanted us to know that she is from the eastern side, where the elite are tall and white, and very often have a brilliant command of the English language.[10]

The author of the other chapter in this section of the book is, in sharp contradistinction, a serious historian, Rossana Barragán. She puts to rest many of Roca's simplistic formulations, especially the view that Santa Cruz was a victim of central state neglect until the late 20th century. "We suggest", Barragán argues, "that it was the central government which financed the regions, while to some extent giving rise to cruceño regionalism at the end of the 20th century. We argue that if there was a single state policy that was constant, sustained, and enduring, it was the policy that favoured Santa Cruz, a policy that came at the cost of serious internal balances".[11] While Barragán's piece is an important corrective, it focuses narrowly on the geographic origins and distributional patterns of fiscal resources going to and from the central state in Bolivian history. We still require a much more comprehensive study of uneven and combined capitalist development, and the particular complexities of regional, class and ethnic interlacing in the Bolivian context. Without this kind of investigation we cannot pretend to understand "regionalism" in Bolivia.

State-society nexus

It should not be surprising that in the context of effervescing mass movements in recent years in Bolivia the central concern for mainstream sociologists and political scientists has been the spectre of revolution and the concomitant necessity of containing the rebels from below and re-establishing order from above.

George Gray Molina, head of the United Nations development programme in Bolivia and author of the lead chapter in this section of *Unresolved Tensions*, writes, "In recent years much attention has shifted to the relative

---

9:     Crabtree and Whitehead, 2008, p74.
10:   Fuentes, 2005.
11:   Crabtree and Whitehead, 2008, p83.

strength of social movements and the weakening of traditional political parties, democratic institutions, and the rule of law, among other dimensions of the state-society balance".[12] According to Gray Molina, a UN survey published in 2007 found that "Bolivians feel that laws are not enforced, because most feel that 'laws are unjust' and that 'unjust laws may be broken'." He goes on to note that "Bolivian public opinion has identified the worst transgressors as 'the rich' and 'politicians'." Gray Molina is also concerned that "most Bolivians continue to advocate 'universal' enforcement of laws while at the same time reserving the right to transgress, protest, overturn law".[13]

For revolutionaries the question arising from this has been how ideological discontent with the reigning order, and its expression in the rising cycle of protest in the first five years of the 21st century, might be channelled into a fully-fledged societal and political transformation of the country's structures in the interests of the indigenous proletarian and peasant majority.[14]

For liberals such as George Gray Molina, the priority is constructing and preserving the correct institutional apparatus of state-society relations to dampen the rising tide and consolidate the status quo—a status quo necessarily reconfigured cosmetically but with an unaltered foundation. The best bet for liberals might be a degree of "institutional pluralism", allowing the persistence of "state holes", "places where bureaucratic or legal state presence is tenuous...where authority, legitimacy and sovereignty are continuously contested"[15] by unions, indigenous communities and social movements—so long as they are ultimately contained, so long as the overarching system of liberal capitalist rule is not threatened at its core. By and large, Gray Molina concludes, state-society relations under Evo Morales express many continuities with the preceding model and seem to be functioning to meet basic liberal ends.

The Bolivian ruling class and its organic intellectuals are, of course, divided on this point. Conservatives such as Franz Xavier Barrios Suvelza believe, in the style of conservative American political scientist Samuel Huntington, that a praetorian society such as Bolivia's cannot survive the sort of "politicisation", ie increasing involvement in democratic politics of the popular classes, that is occurring under Morales. A reassertion of explicitly "apolitical" and "a-democratic" realms of the state is

---

12: Crabtree and Whitehead, 2008, p109.
13: Crabtree and Whitehead, 2008, p120.
14: See, for example, Hylton and Thomson, 2007. For my own take on these issues see various articles in *Monthly Review, Historical Materialism, Against the Current* and *New Socialist* since 2005.
15: Crabtree and Whitehead, 2008, p113.

consequently required. "The contention here", Barrios Suvelza writes, "is that the current process of change in Bolivia involves a tendency...to reshape the style of the state in the direction of an unbounded and unconstrained democracy, one lacking restraint on the passions—what we might call in stoic terms a pathetic state". "Pathetic" in this sense refers to "a style of state where democratic and politicised forces have come to permeate the state".[16] One can almost see Suvelza recoiling in horror as he writes of "the way in which democracy has overflowed into the decision-making sphere" during the Morales government "to the detriment of a-democratic and apolitical state functions".[17] This is the sort of political philosophy marshalled recently in Honduras by Roberto Micheletti and his cronies as they sought to justify to the world their military coup d'etat in late June 2009 against the democratically elected Manuel Zelaya.

Constitutional reform

Part four of the book, on constitutional reform, navigates the same terrain as the preceding section on state-society relations. It is unsurprising that Eduardo Rodríguez Veltzé, author of the longest chapter on the topic, takes as the acceptable parameters of debate the liberal-conservative divide over the appropriate strategies for the sustenance of the basic tenets of the political order and maintenance of the existing class structure. His biography, after all, includes an education in law at the Kennedy School at Harvard University, a period as president of the Bolivian Supreme Court and a brief stint as President of the Republic between Carlos Mesa's overthrow in June 2005 and the elections that brought Morales to office in December of that year.

A brief reprieve from ruling class intellectuals' anxieties over social order will reward the reader who manages to make it to chapter 9—where one of the most important radical political theorists in contemporary Bolivia weighs in on questions of "constituent" and "constituted" power. Luis Tapia is, alongside Álvaro García Linera and others, a founding member of the radical intellectual forum *La Comuna*, named after the Paris Commune of 1871.[18] His theoretical and political writings are essentially split in focus between interpretations of the opus of René Zavaleta Mercado (arguably the country's most important 20th century Marxist intellectual) and incisive interventions seeking to understand and influence the trajectory of left-indigenous insurrectionary movements in recent years. While this contribution

---

16: Crabtree and Whitehead, 2008, p125.
17: Crabtree and Whitehead, 2008, p133.
18: For some background, see Hylton, 2006, pp69-72.

is far from being Tapia's best work, it does constitute the most theoretically sophisticated and historically grounded piece in this collection.

The terms "constituent" and "constituted" power are drawn from the Italian autonomist Marxist Antonio Negri but Tapia gives them an original spin in the context of Bolivian state formation and social struggle over the last two centuries. "Constituted power", Tapia explains, "tends to be identified with the constitution and with the various institutions that operate as a state at a particular place in time".[19] Constituent power, on the other hand, is formed "when projects or forces emerge that seek to change the relationship between the state and civil society, the arenas within them, the subjects involved, the relationships between them, and consequently the political form that society adopts. In this sense, a constituent power is something that emerges at points of crisis, or provokes a political crisis that, among other things, can lead to the reconstitution of a country".[20]

Unlike many of the other contributors to this book, Tapia is sensitive to historical and material processes and structures. "All constituted power has a history," he writes. Rather than emerging from the ether, "it is a political, social, and historical accumulation that brings with it learning and experience, as well as conflicts and contradictions, leading (on occasions) to development in particular aspects or (at others) toward exhaustion and decay".[21]

Tapia thus reminds us that the first constitution of the Bolivian Republic that flowed out of its independence in 1825 almost entirely ignored the majority indigenous population of the new country. The political situation changed with independence from the Spanish *conquistadores* but there was no accompanying social revolution. The 1938 Constituent Assembly introduced a labour code and other social reforms as peasants and workers were increasingly able to project their social power through militant social movements. In 1952 the national revolution carried things further, ushering in new changes out of the context of profound crisis in the social order. Perhaps more than any of these other historical periods, however, the terrain of class struggle and politics of indigenous resistance within the Constituent Assembly process of 2006-7 showed the most promise for change because the assembly was taking place in the wake of dramatic social and political upsurges from below between 2000 and 2005.

Ultimately, however, Tapia demonstrates how the assembly fell well short of its promise, partially as a result of the MAS's attempt to monopolise

---

19: Crabtree and Whitehead, 2008, p161.
20: Crabtree and Whitehead, 2008, p162.
21: Crabtree and Whitehead, 2008, p161.

the representation of the popular classes. Despite Tapia's debateable belief that the MAS is a workers' party that has captured state power, he fully recognises the compromised outcome of the assembly process:

> The assembly became closely linked to the presence of political parties, both those of the opposition (which were against it in principle) as well as that of the ruling party, which, as leader of the executive, tended to subordinate constituent power to constituted power. In so doing, it limited the scope for change which had previously emerged from the waves of protest and which might well come about if the new political order included the full diversity of social organisation in the design of new political institutions of government.[22]

Economic development and globalisation

The last sections of the book, parts five and six, cover "strategies of economic development" and Bolivia's relationship to "globalisation". Carlos Miranda, an energy consultant and former hydrocarbons superintendent under one of the previous neoliberal regimes, writes on "Gas and Its Importance to the Bolivian Economy". Fernanda Wanderley's accompanying article is a basic neo-structuralist article on the need for Bolivia's political economy to move beyond the "narrow-base" of gas to a "broad-based" economy, including a host of non-traditional commodities in its export profile.[23] Following this is a piece authored by Juan Antonio Morales, president of the central bank of Bolivia between 1995 and 2006, and perhaps the only intellectual in the country who still fundamentally believes in the orthodox neoliberal model that was first introduced in Bolivia in 1985.

Fortunately, a chapter by Carlos Arze Vargas, a Marxist economist and director of the extraordinarily important Centro de Estudios para el Desarrollo Laboral y Agrario in La Paz,[24] returns us to the real world of Bolivia in the 1980s and 1990s, at least insofar as that world was experienced by the vast majority of the working class and peasantry.

Arze starts off by pointing out at a general level that there is nothing inevitable about neoliberal globalisation, whatever the "suppositions of

---

22: Crabtree and Whitehead, 2008, p171.
23: Neostructuralist arguments of this variety have been the principal counter to orthodox neoliberalism in Latin America since the mid-1990s. They find their deepest articulation theoretically and empirically in the work of the United Nations Economic Commission for Latin America and the Caribbean. For a trenchant critique of neostructuralism from a radical perspective that draws from Marxism see Leiva, 2008.
24: See www.cedla.org

sociological and economic theories that see development as a historical process leading to the unchallenged rule of market forces".[25] Nor has it been merely a natural unfolding of enhanced cultural and economic interdependence driven by technological progress. Instead, Arze correctly argues, neoliberal globalisation since the 1980s has been "an intentional process, driven by certain dominant capitalist sectors and geared toward restoring conditions propitious for accumulation".[26] Moreover, the state did not disappear as neoliberal ideology would have it; rather, "the state continued to fulfill its basic function of guaranteeing the reproduction of capital accumulation within a specific geographical unit".[27]

In the world of work, neoliberal restructuring had a tremendous impact in Bolivia. "The working day became longer over the period of adjustment," Arze shows, "enabling employers to produce more surplus value. Average working hours increased by a couple of hours per day, with blue collar workers most affected. The average hours worked per week were...rising to 50 in 2000. The working day was also affected by the use of double shifts or by other secondary jobs which workers undertook to make ends meet".[28]

While Arze's chapter offers a welcome relief, it is unfortunate that the editors were unable to include some of his more recent material. His piece in this volume covers the neoliberal period of the 1980s and 1990s lucidly but offers nothing on the period since the Morales administration assumed office. It therefore offers no effective counter to the various liberal and conservative commentaries on these matters which dominate the bulk of the volume.

Conclusion

While marketing *Unresolved Tensions* as a simple presentation of the range of views that exist in contemporary Bolivian politics, Crabtree and Whitehead have in fact subtly shifted the centre of that debate significantly to the right. Drowned out of the discussion—with the exceptions of Tapia and Arze—are voices from the left wing of the MAS government and its sympathisers, as well as those intellectuals (not insignificant in number), who position themselves to the left of the MAS altogether. The actual polarisation on the ground during the first years of the MAS government has spawned, in my opinion, a debate that is polarising both to the left and the right. Steering the middle, liberal course has become an increasingly tenuous position as the

25: Crabtree and Whitehead, 2008, p238.
26: Crabtree and Whitehead, 2008, p239.
27: Crabtree and Whitehead, 2008, p240.
28: Crabtree and Whitehead, 2008, p249.

real socio-political divisions and contradictions at work below the surface reveal themselves more nakedly.

In reading this book, however, one is helpfully guided, by the "uncommitted" outsiders, to the conclusion that social harmony without a profound transformation of existing class relations and racist colonial relations is possible, so long as modest reforms are incorporated into the status quo.

This orientation is on display in the closing paragraphs of editor Laurence Whitehead's conclusion to the volume. "Major improvements are possible," he writes:

> The outcome could be called a refoundation of the republic, and it might rally sufficient support to sustain itself against some inevitable resistance and backlash. But the secret of success is not indiscriminately to discard or disregard all previous accomplishments... Constrained originality could truly provide the foundation for a more consensual future, whereas a utopian dogma of unconstrained refoundation is more likely to recreate the vicious cycles of the past. [29]

A consensual path towards a more egalitarian liberal capitalist democracy in Bolivia is possible, one in which social improvements can be achieved in all areas without vicious cycles of conflict and dispute... Who is being utopian?

References

Fuentes, Frederico, 2005, "Bolivia: The Real Divide", *Green Left Weekly*, 23 February 2005, www.greenleft.org.au/2005/616/35332

Hylton, Forrest, 2006, "The Landslide in Bolivia", *New Left Review 37*, January-February 2006.

Hylton, Forrest, and Sinclair Thomson, 2007, *Revolutionary Horizons: Past and Present in Bolivian Politics* (Verso).

Leiva, Fernando Ignacio, 2008, *Latin American Neostructuralism: The Contradictions of Post-Neoliberal Development* (University of Minnesota).

Webber, Jeffery R, forthcoming 2010, *Red October: Left-Indigenous Struggles in Modern Bolivia* (Brill).

Weisbrot, Mark, and Luis Sandoval, 2008, "The Distribution of Bolivia's Most Important Natural Resources and the Autonomy Conflicts", Center for Economic and Policy Research, Washington, July 2008, www.cepr.net/documents/publications/bolivia_land_2008_07.pdf

---

29: Crabtree and Whitehead, 2008, p269.

Book reviews

The public enemy
Mike Wayne

Dennis Broe, **Film Noir, American Workers and Postwar Hollywood**
(University Press of Florida, 2009),
£62.95

Film noir is a sub-genre that has attracted
a lot of popular attention and commentary in the mainstream media. Although
its classic black and white Hollywood
period was in the 1940s and 1950s, its
style and thematics live on in many examples of contemporary cinema. Popular
criticism duly notes its aesthetic characteristics (the canted camera angles and
lighting set-ups that swamped the image
in darkness except for a few shards of light
that cast unsettling shadows) and con-
nects its themes of doomed anti-heroes
and betrayal to the rise of fascism (many
writers, directors and technicians entered
Hollywood from Europe in the 1930s).
Additional "contextualisation" includes
references to historical generalities such as
the Second World War, the subsequent
Cold War, and a vague existential sense of
unease about society and its institutions.
Academic studies often distinguish themselves from such a general and superficial
social analysis of this interesting cinematic
form only by reaching for Freud and the
Oedipus complex.

Admittedly sexual desire plays a very
significant role in film noir. The femme
fatale (the dangerous seductive women
who entraps the male protagonist) is
one of noir's most recognisable features

and a major contribution to film culture
in general. However, there are precise
social and historical reasons for the emergence of the femme fatale figure. After
the Second World War women were
being pushed back into the role of the
homemaker in the US, when a very different role for them (as workers) had been
briefly opened up in the war years. Some
academic feminist critics have explored
these social roots behind the frustration
with restricted opportunities and conditions that the femme fatale is brimming
with in this period. It is a frustration
that produces a very dangerous dynamic
vis-à-vis the male protagonist on whom
she depends, but who she also destroys,
or tries to. However, while gender has
loomed large in academic studies, the
relationship between film noir and the
class struggle has been, if not entirely
neglected, rather marginal.

For this reason Denis Broe's book,
which seeks to reconnect noir with a
largely repressed history of class conflict (repressed or sublimated in the
films and in the commentary on the
films) is welcome. Students of noir
might be surprised to learn that its emergence is coterminous with the biggest
wave of strikes in American history.
This period of workers' militancy also
affected the Hollywood studios which
found themselves having to deal with
a revived unionised labour force challenging their total control of the film
industry. The strikes inevitably brought
working people hard up against the law
and the state, which used sections of the
Taft-Hartley Act to outlaw their actions.

In the late 1940s and 1950s the House Un-American Activities Committee (HUAC) investigations began a period of political witch-hunts against anyone with left leaning sympathies. This period is often decried in liberal histories as a moment of paranoia and persecution. Yet it rested on a rational fear among the business class of workers' militancy and an understanding that such challenges to their control of industry had to be crushed. In this context, HUAC provided the political cover to weed out leaders and suppress dissent.

This history returns in film noir in the form of the working class protagonist who is forced by the circumstances engendered by inequality to become a fugitive from the law. Broe identifies the key period for noir's orientation towards a left paradigm as 1945-50. In many of the films of this period the key figures are outside and against the law, and the films work to align audience sympathies with the predicament of these outsiders. Such was the impact of the broader historical struggle against corporate America in this period that it sees the emergence of narratives that feature middle class protagonists kicking against their integration into the post-war business society.

The classic example of this type of film is *Double Indemnity* whose doomed male protagonist Walter Neff is a respectable insurance salesman. However, in the 1950s a new paradigm emerges which Broe identifies as "a cultural counterrevolution" where the central protagonists are once more law enforcement officials of one type or another. These "police procedural" films involved narratives of infiltration, surveillance and information gathering. This paradigm, where audience sympathies are aligned to the forces of "law and order" as they police working class locales, clearly aligns itself

with the "red-baiting" years of HUAC which resulted in taming the unions and integrating them as junior partners into US corporate imperatives. Broe tells this parallel history of labour's battle against the bosses and the state in some detail and provides compelling evidence that it makes sense to read these films in relation to this history.

That the emergence and shifts in noir so closely parallel broader historical realities is, of course, no coincidence. It is evidence of the links between culture and society that justify and require an analysis that reconnects what the films can only obliquely articulate and what the broader dominant culture often represses completely. Broe's work here finds a parallel with studies of British cinema of the immediate post Second World War years. Again, in a brief moment between the end of the war and the consolidation of post-war capitalism, a space opened up for alternative visions, social roles and values in film that would be subsequently closed down as the 1950s advanced. This moment, with its embryonic resistance to the dominant order, is registered in film culture.

Broe makes use of Raymond Williams's suggestive notion of a "structure of feeling" to mediate between the films and their historical context. A structure of feeling for Williams refers to those emerging qualities of practical experience which have not and perhaps cannot be given official expression because dominant society cannot recognise or value them. Yet in culture such "feelings" as class antagonism towards figures of authority can acquire a presence and form (a structure) in those cultural products that for whatever reason are attuned to them.

Broe goes further and suggests that in film noir in the 1945-50 period, there was something like a working class/middle class alliance (or Gramscian bloc) that was hegemonic in terms of this anti-corporate "structure of feeling".

In a useful appendix Broe breaks down this group of films into various categories according to the social and narrative position of the leading protagonist. For example, there are the social problem film, the working class fugitive film, the Depression-era drifter, the war veteran, the middle class fugitive and the detective figure who is outside the law. Broe notes how these films opened up a space for working class protagonists and even a kind of affirmation of working class language, experience and values, in contrast to upper class or business figures or agents of the law who are represented as self-interested or corrupt.

In a process of cultural struggle, this countercultural hegemony was broken down and dispersed in the films of the 1950s. The predominant form this took was to shift the centre of narrative gravity back towards police officials involved in the nitty gritty of surveillance, information gathering and manhunts. Here the state apparatus and its control over working class districts are normalised. Other films deployed a different strategy, by focusing on the fugitive, but making him psychotic and thus turning the audience against the type of outsider character who they would have identified and sympathised with in the earlier films. Broe illustrates this process very well with the 1953 film *Niagara*, a rare early colour noir. Here the psychotic figure, George Loomis, is initially presented in at least quasi-sympathetic terms, but gradually becomes more threatening towards the bourgeois couple on their honeymoon at Niagara Falls. As Broe puts it:

"The narrative works initially to introduce Loomis (Joseph Cotton) as the typical protagonist of the noir film, replete with subjective voice-over narration, but then slowly to pull back from him, refocusing instead through the bourgeois wife, Polly, who understands George but whom he also menaces, and ultimately to distance him to the point where his death is seen as necessary to return bourgeois life to normal."

Yet despite the closure on noir radicalism in the 1950s, the cultural struggle between the fugitive outsider and the state enforcer, once created, can be mobilised and revised in new contexts that reprise the earlier duel between contending visions of America. Here Broe's analysis shifts focus towards television. He charts this dynamic in the contest between two popular US television serials in the 1960s. *The Fugitive* clearly recalled the themes and working class locales of the radical noirs of the 1945-50 period, while the police procedural show *Dragnet* clearly modelled itself on the status quo orientated films of the 1950s.

Finally Broe explores the trajectory of neo-noir into the Ronald Reagan and George Bush Senior years and, beyond that, noir after 9/11. After 9/11, George Bush Junior launched his "war on terror". This served, as the red baiting years had in the 1950s, to silence dissent and shore up support behind an administration that had been widely seen as illegitimate following the disputed presidential elections of 2000. The Fox channel's popular series *24* was hastily rewritten while being broadcast, shifting from critical paranoia about right wing extremists in the state apparatus apparently planning the assassination of a black politician with presidential ambitions to blaming foreign terrorists. The series' hero, Jack Bauer, meanwhile was rapidly converted into an enthusiastic practitioner of torture. The conservative and status quo orientation of the police procedurals had now reached a new level.

Broe's analysis of television programmes after the classic period of film noir does raise questions as to how one defines film noir. It was always an unstable blend of quite disparate materials: a social realism that sought out urban locations and working class experiences; an expressionistic and paranoid style evoking a general social alienation; an intricate thematic of sexual desire and social power struggles; and an ambiguous and shifting relationship to agencies of the law and the state more generally, with the position of the key protagonists (outside the law, private detective, or salaried employee of the state) often being decisive in shaping the ideological orientation of the text.

Beyond noir's classic period, different parts of noir get adapted and combined with other generic materials in different ways leading to a widespread influence of noir on the general culture but also at times a dilution of that original nexus of elements that made up the classic noir film. Broe's analysis thus loses something of its focus after the discussion of the classic period and the subsequent focus on television, which perhaps cannot sustain a full-bloodied noir aesthetic.

Nevertheless Broe's book very usefully reminds us of the necessity to ground films in a rich historical understanding and boldly sets out what has often been only hinted at in much of the literature and commentary on noir: namely that it is an aesthetic forged by class, class struggle and class consciousness.

Matches made in hell
Andrew Stone

*Louise Raw, **Striking a Light: The Bryant and May Matchwomen and their Place in Labour History** (Continuum, 2009), £70*

In 1888 roughly 1,400 mainly young women match workers went on strike at the Bryant and May factories in east London. The conventional explanation goes something like this: middle class socialist Annie Besant wrote an article in the *Link* newspaper, denouncing what she described as "White Slavery in London", the "slaves" being the matchgirls. They were suffering from poverty pay, unjust fines, and toxic conditions that led to the debilitating "phossy jaw" (disfiguring and sometimes fatal phosphorous poisoning). The management at Bryant and May then began to bully the workers to deny Besant's account, so the match workers came to her for help and she organised a strike, which was ultimately successful. However, this was a relatively isolated dispute over very specific "bread and butter" issues with little of the wider significance of the organisation of the gas workers or the Great Dock Strike in the advent of New Unionism.

In this well-conceived and researched re-evaluation of the match workers' strike Louise Raw contends that the above account is flawed and misleading; that the historical image of the workers is clouded by gendered class preconceptions, and that their action helped to inspire the upsurge of 1889, which provided a radical challenge to the insular "craft unionism" that had held sway since the defeat of Chartism. She places them in the context of their East End community and tries to rediscover their authentic voice.

This is no small task. Annie Besant has

value—would be contested by contributors to this journal. Nonetheless, their thought-provoking article is well worth engaging with.

The November issue of *Monthly Review* contains an article by Stephen Eisenman entitled "The Resistable Rise and Predictable Fall of the US Supermax".* The growth of the US prison population over the past three decades has been astonishing, and with it has come a resurgence in solitary confinement, dubbed the "supermax" system.

Eisenman's article charts the history of this form of torture from its 19th century origins through to its revival in prisons such as Tamms C-Max, in Southern Illinois, where "men are locked in their concrete cells for 23 hours per day, seven days a week, with an hour each day available for solitary exercise in another cell fitted with a mesh roof open to the sky. Meals are served through a slot in the cell door, and prisoners are allowed one shower per week. There are no communal activities, religious services, jobs, counseling, or rehabilitation, and no phone calls are allowed... Many men at Tamms have been subjected to this regime for years."

Issue five of the *International Journal of Scottish Literature* carries an interesting article by Dougall McNeill on the politics of Irvine Welsh's most famous work, *Trainspotting*. McNeill builds upon the incongrous appearance of a parody of Trotsky's "Testament" in one section of the novel to argue that *Trainspotting* represents an example of "literary anti-Trotskyism" and an attack on the Socialist Workers Party in particular.†

Finally, the Marxist Internet Archi continues its superb work. For the inspired by our special collection on Ch Harman's legacy, there is now a section the archive devoted to his writings. T contains pamphlets, out of print articl transcripts of speeches and book revie from the 1960s written under his pse donym Colin Humphreys.‡

JC and *JJ*

---

* www.monthlyreview.org/091116eisenman.php
† www.ijsl.stir.ac.uk/issue5/mcneill.htm

‡ www.marxists.org/archive/harman/

Pick of the quarter

There were several good articles in the November/December issue of *New Left Review*.* Ho-fung Hung's piece, "America's Head Servant?", contests glib claims that China will emerge out of the economic crisis as a serious challenger to US hegemony. The article traces in detail the emergence of a relationship in which China and other East Asian economies are heavily dependent on markets in the most highly developed countries.

A piece by Mary Callahan explores the resilience of Burma's military dictatorship, which, she argues, flows from the divisions fostered by British colonial rule. An interview with A Sivanandan, writer and founding editor of the journal *Race & Class*, discusses his background in Sri Lanka and the roots of the recent assault on the Tamil population by the Sinhalese dominated government. There was nothing inevitable about these divisions. As Sivanandan says of his youth, "I had no sense at all of being a Tamil."

The highlight of the most recent issue of *Historical Materialism* to reach us (volume 17, issue 3), is an archive collection of two pieces by Paul Levi introduced by David Fernbach. Levi was one of the most able leaders of the German Communists in the revolutionary period following the First World War. He was sidelined, and eventually expelled, in favour of a group of ultra-leftists within the leadership, a shift supported by the Comintern leadership. The "March Action" of 1921 followed.

This disastrous and unprepared assault on power saw the Communist Party hemorrhage members.

The documents reproduced here are Levi's comment on the March Action. They will give readers the opportunity to assess Lenin's comment on the leadership of the Germany party and Levi after his expulsion, that though he "lost his head entirely...he, at least, had something to lose. One can't even say that about the others."

The current crisis has sparked a renewed interest in the relationship between finance and the broader capitalist economy. The fall 2009 issue of *Review of Radical Political Economics* contained a series of articles on "financialisation". By far the most interesting is a contribution by Dick Bryan and Mike Rafferty, coauthors of an important Marxist analysis of derivatives,[†] along with Randy Martin.

They challenge the notion that financialisation is simply financial speculation grafted onto a non-financialised "true capitalism". For them, financialisation is best understood as a process of capitalist development, accelerated since the 1980s, that has important implications for our analysis of the system. Some of their conclusions—notably that "the reproduction of labour power is itself a source of surplus value, in the form of interest payments", rather than this representing a redistribution of surplus

* Available from www.newleftreview.org

† *Capitalism with Derivatives* (Palgrave Macmillan, 2006).

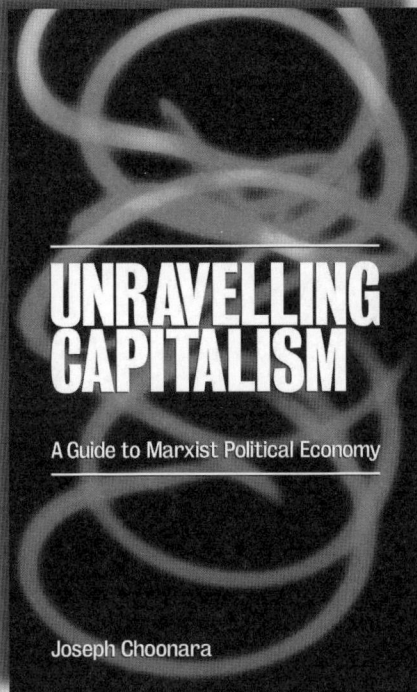

Unravelling Capitalism:

A Guide to Marxist Political Economy

Joseph Choonara

Capitalism is facing its most severe crisis since the 1930s.

The neoliberal orthodoxy of the past 30 years has been discredited almost overnight. State intervention and the ideas of the economist John Maynard Keynes are back in vogue as world leaders desperately seek to save capitalism from itself.

But capitalism's greatest critic, Karl Marx, offers a far more radical understanding of the dynamics of the system.

Joseph Choonara provides a concise guide to Marx's method, his concepts and how they can be applied to capitalism as it has developed since Marx's time.

Available from Bookmarks, £7.99

Bookmarks—the socialist bookshop

1 Bloomsbury Street
London
WC1B 3QE

020 7637 1848

mailorder@bookmarks.uk.com

www.bookmarks.uk.com

mostly barred. Although there are fewer workers in the state sector than before, those who are left are arguably more powerful, as the Tonghua protest showed.

A recent report from the Hong Kong based *China Labour Bulletin* entitled "Going it Alone—the Workers' Movement in China 2007-2008"* analysed 100 strikes and workers' protests over the previous two years. A total of 21 of these were in state-owned enterprises around issues such as redundancy payments and official corruption, though the report doesn't give the outcome of any of the disputes. Hurst's book is a sobering account of how a key section of China's working class have lost important battles over the past 20 years, but the fight is far from over.

 Available from www.clb.org.hk/en/ node/100507 See also www.socialistworker.co.uk/ rt.php?id=18501